BOMBER SQUADRON AT WAR

Preface

It is an interesting observation on modern society that as the years of peace increase from 1945, so popular interest in the happenings of World War 2 grows rather than diminishes. Perhaps this is due to the increasing number of young people who know nothing of war and want to learn, or perhaps it is an indictment of future prospects that people need to seek inspiration in the great deeds of the past, but there is no denying that histories of war grow ever more numerous and popular with each passing year. This is particularly true of the history of wartime aircraft, and the Ian Allan series on 'Aircraft at War' is foremost in this field, but we all know that the finest technology can be as nothing if the right men and women are not available to put it to good use. The heart of an aeroplane is undoubtedly its engine, but the people who maintain and fly it are its soul.

This book therefore is not so much a history of machinery as an attempt to round off the Ian Allan 'at War' series by underlining the human dimension of World War 2. 'I had meant to go on to a Squadron', wrote T. E. Lawrence in *The Mint*, 'and write about the real Air Force', and in similar vein, I have tried to show what it was like to serve on an RAF bomber squadron up to 1945, having performed a similar task in *Fighter Squadron at War* (Ian Allan Ltd, 1980).

The unit I have chosen had a varied and exciting combat history, but I have made no attempt to put together a complete 'official' history of one particular unit — rather this is more of a kaleidoscope of life in wartime as seen through the medium of the official reports, letters, diaries and mementoes that the members of one squadron left behind. This is how they saw themselves, and how others saw them; the words are theirs, the pictures are theirs, the emphasis is theirs, and if this book reinforces some points and neglects others it is only a measure of what the Squadron personnel regarded as important and, by implication, what they deemed of less consequence.

In selecting my bomber squadron at war, I have deliberately not chosen one of the more glamorous squadrons such as 'The Dambusters' because, for all their bravery and achievement, they were not typical of Bomber Command. This is the story of a very good squadron, but one whose personnel were at pains to impress upon me that they were only one of the best and that they were never the be all and end all of Bomber Command. In their opinion, the bomber war was a combined Command effort, and to do justice to that effort I have chosen a squadron that served within Bomber Command throughout World War 2 and which was to typify the rest if for no other reason than that it lost more men on operations than any other squadron in the Command.

Bomber Squadron at War should therefore be regarded as a scrapbook of an age, for it attempts to portray how men and women in RAF uniform worked and played, fought and died. This is the story of a perfectly ordinary generation which was plucked from its studies and civilian jobs to take part in a conflict which was not of its making, which was often beyond its understanding, and which promised not ripe old age but rather death on the morrow. This story therefore is dedicated to everyone everywhere who served in the RAF, and in particular to those who fought for a peace they did not live to see.

Acknowledgements

Most of the material in this book comes from members of the 101 Squadron Association and their families, and I must say how grateful I am for all their generous and unstinting help. I also wish to record my gratitude to the many authors from whose works I have taken quotations and inspiration, and a full bibliography appears at the front of this book. The H. E. Bates quote on p116 is produced by permission of Lawrence Pollinger Ltd and the author's estate. Finally I must pay tribute to the help and assistance I have received from the staff of the Imperial War Museum and the Public Record Office, Kew, and I gratefully acknowledge permission to reproduce Crown Copyright material.

In the Beginning

The Royal Flying Corps came into existence as a form of airborne cavalry which sent out aeroplanes to reconnoitre on behalf of the army below, but by 1916 each side had become so tired of being spied on by the other that fighting in the air had become a regular adjunct to reconnaisance work. Yet once fighting machines arrived, it became obvious that their use would not be restricted to attacks on enemy aircraft — bombing raids on enemy positions also became a regular duty of the Flying Corps.

However, a machine laden with bombs in 1917 was clumsy and slow to manoeuvre — it stood little chance of outflying the attacks mounted upon it by light enemy scouts, and as such became, in the words of the time, 'cold meat in the air'. Hence it was decided that heavy bombing raids could only stand a chance of success if they were carried out at night.

No 101 Squadron was therefore formed at South Farnborough on 12 July 1917 as the Royal Flying Corps' second specialised night bomber unit. Lt C. H. Wallis was one of the first to report to the Squadron headquarters which were temporarily housed in a bell tent, but as 101 at the time comprised little more than the Adjutant, Capt Errington, there was not much for the new arrivals initially. The Squadron remained at Farnborough for all of a fortnight, whereupon its presence was demanded in France so 101 moved across the Channel to the RFC headquarters at St André-aux-Bois.

The first Squadron Commanding Officer was Maj the Hon L. J. E. Twistleton-Wykeham-Fiennes, and his first priority on arriving in France was to find his 18 crews something to fly. Their pleas were answered in the shape of the Fighting Experimental (FE) 2b, a somewhat elderly aircraft by 1917 and one which the Squadron was probably given because its low ceiling made it unsuitable for Zeppelin interception work back home. No 101 Squadron's FE 2bs, with their top speeds of 81mph at 6,500ft, came from No 22 Squadron and were fitted with 'luminous instruments comprising compasses, rev counters, aneroids, air speed

1
FE 2b night bomber floodlit on the Western Front. The cost of an FE 2b 'pusher' fresh from the factory but minus engine, instruments, and guns was £1,521 13s 4d — the 160hp Beardmore engine fitted to each 101 aircraft cost an extra £1,045. *IWM*

2

3

2
Crew positions in the FE 2b. The pilot sat in the rear cockpit by the main fuel tank while the observer/gunner sat in an exposed and unprotected plywood-skinned semi-circular nacelle at the front.

3
Mechanics attach a 230lb bomb in preparation for a night raid. *IWM*

Squadron, 'and a weird-looking contraption it was. The whole thing had an appearance of insecurity. Painted black, those old night bombers certainly presented a terrifying sight. It made me shudder every time I looked at mine.'

Perhaps his fear was compounded by the fact that night flying was then a somewhat novel and imprecise art. As W. G. McMinnies said in *Practical Flying by a Flight Commander* (Temple Press, 1918): 'A prospective night pilot is seldom given any dual control for night flying. His instructor can tell by his daylight flying if he is likely to make a successful night pilot, although it does not follow that because a pupil is only a fair daylight pilot he will be no use for night flying. He is generally considered fit for night flying, under moderate conditions, if he can make six or ten successful landings and attain a height of 6,000 feet in the dark. He must familiarise himself by daylight with the aerodromes equipped for night flying where he may have to land. He must possess a good knowledge of the country and be familiar with those parts of it which are open, and those which are wooded or otherwise dangerous. He can acquire this knowledge by moonlight nights as well as by day.' Not that the Squadron had much time to practice because it was soon moved closer to the front line and the action. 101 was assigned to the Ninth Wing of the RFC at a time when the August rains had halted the Battle of Ypres, but as the ground began to dry preparations went ahead to resume the offensive. So 101 was moved north to Clairmarais to take part in the Battle of the Menin Road Ridge which was planned to start on 20 September. Such was the stalemate on the Western Front that the average depth of objectives at that time was 1,000yd, and 101's first contribution to this war of attrition was to attack Hooglede, Rumbeke, Ledegham and Menin before dawn on 20th as these were rest billets which housed German reserve troops behind the immediate battle area.

The Squadron bombed Menin and other detraining centres on the night of 20/21 September, but the following evening air reconnaissances reported that German reinforcements were 'still pouring into Menin by rail, whereupon they were transported by motor-buses to the front'. The Germans were trying to sneak reinforcements through under cover of darkness so 101 was ordered to attack the town as well as the roads along which the troop transports were reportedly moving. By the light of parachute flares dropped from time to time, it was possible to see that the Menin-Ypres road was crowded with troops and vehicles: 101 Squadron crews began their attacks as soon as it was dark, and that night they dropped two 230lb

indicators and watches' plus navigation lights.

Bombing raids in those days were of the short distance variety, aimed at the aerodromes, munition stores and communications of the German forces on the Western Front. Racks were therefore fitted to the Squadron FE 2bs to allow them to carry one 112lb bomb or eight 25lb bombs on either side of the fuselage, and another rack underneath just behind the axle to carry one huge (for the day and for the aircraft) 230lb bomb. Finally, the aircraft top planes were painted brown with standard red, white and blue roundels, but to prevent detection from the ground the rest of the machine was finished in dull black with dark grey nacelles and the usual underwing roundels were replaced by white circles.

'I was now allotted an FE 2b,' wrote a brand new pilot when he arrived on the

8

bombs on Menin, and five 230lb and 12 112lb bombs on Rouliers station to the north. Such bomb loads seem relatively inconsequential by later standards, but it took a long time for an FE 2b to get anywhere and return to re-arm. Notwithstanding, on the night of 26 September, 101 and its sister night bombing squadron, No 100 Squadron, dropped a total of nearly five tons of bombs on enemy billeting and railway centres, interspersed with salvos of pom-pom shells. RFC Operation Orders instructed 101 Squadron to pay 'special attention to the attack of troops' and such night forays, which supplemented concentrated attacks by day, must have had an effect on tired enemy nerves if not property. Then the fog came down.

The Battle of Ypres dragged on throughout the autumn of 1917 and on the typical night of 20/21 October, 101 dropped three 230lb, eight 112lb, and four 25lb bombs on Ingelmunster station and aerodrome. The following night, a bomb dropped on Ingelmunster was seen to explode among aeroplanes lined up to leave the ground, so it was a contented crew that returned to base. The Squadron was now running up to speed and on the night of 27/28 October they dropped the following loads:

'Aerodromes: Gontrode (one 230lb), Rumbeke (six 112lb, four 25lb), Moorseele (four 112lb), Abeele (two 112lb), and Bissengham (two 112lb). Also Ingelmunster station (12 112lb, two 230lb), Isegham station (four 25lb) and various trains (one 230lb and 12 112lb).'

The method of attacking trains at night was to glide down with the engine cut and then open up for a slow run along the track. Bombs were then dropped in sticks along the

Life during the day on 101 Squadron at Clairmarais.

4–5
'Swinging' the compass of an FE 2b.

6
Lieutenant Basker indulging in a little gun firing practice.

7
Captain Vickers' aircraft comes to grief after colliding with a plough. The airfield at Clairmarais was an expanse of grass approximately ¾ml long and 300 yards wide alongside a forest. Being so narrow, it forced aircraft to take off either due East or due West, which eventually produced ruts in the soft earth. The wheels of an FE 2b were only held on by a collar and split pin, and under the strains imposed by a cross wind take off these wheels sometimes fell off, causing two crashes and the death of one pilot.

8
Captain Vickers after his contretemps with the plough; he was eventually to be awarded the Military Cross for later gallantry.

9

9
The sort of target Squadron crews had to find and bomb at night — a railway station by a field in France in 1918.

10
Officers of 101 Squadron at Catigny in March 1918. Notice the differing uniforms — officers were only attached to the RFC from their respective regiments. The Bessoneaux hangar in the background housed the Squadron aircraft. It was protected by an armed guard but the rest of the aerodrome was left unguarded — sabotage was unknown in those days.

such features as railway junctions, woods of various shapes, bends in rivers and so on which would be sure to stand out at night. As new crews came to us, they were flown in daylight to the southern outskirts of Ypres town and had all the landmarks pointed out to them.'

The aircraft were housed in Bessoneaux hangars — huge, wooden-framed buildings covered with camouflaged canvas — and during the day the riggers, fitters and armourers cleaned the guns, loaded the ammunition drums and generally prepared the FE 2bs so that they were ready for operations. Another officer wrote in his diary:

'Just before dark the machines would be got out of their hangars and loaded up with bombs in accordance with the armament laid down in the daily operation orders. Then they would be got into line of flights, and ready to be taxied out to the flare path. Flares were out and ready for lighting at the appointed time. Pilots and observers would arrive, climb into their machines, and await the order to start. Presently an orderly is seen doubling down to the flight ordered to start first. Directly afterwards the roar of an engine was heard, and machine number one was on its way to the flare path. A hurried shout to the Flares Officer, conveying to him the names of the pilot and observer, together with the number of the machine and time away, and in less than a minute machine number one was on the flare path, engine all out, and fast disappearing in the failing light, until its navigation lights fast dwindling into twin stars were all that could be seen. Hardly had this machine left the ground, when the second was after it, soaring into the night, its twin lights following the first, and so on until all the machines were in the air, which seemed full of the drone of engines, getting fainter and fainter until the silence of a summer's evening once more reigned supreme. The mechanics who had been engaged in the dispatch of the machines are seen strolling back to pass the time in what manner they cared until the return of the machines. The average time taken on a raid was about two hours, according to the distance away of the targets. Quickly the time slips by, and all are beginning to cast their eyes around the sky to try and pick up the lights of a returning machine. Soon the drone of an engine could be heard, the pilot could be seen blinking his lights, intimating that he was going to land, and required the flares on to give him his position. These were put on and sometimes a searchlight beam was displayed on the ground. One last turn to get into the wind, and the machine is gliding towards the flare path, the roar of the engine gradually lessens and dies away, and in a few moments the slight shock of the machine landing is heard.

trucks or carriages and a flare released afterwards to observe the results.

By the time of the Battle of Cambrai at the end of November, when the main targets were again the railway stations that supplied the battle area, the Squadron had settled into a distinctive pattern of operations. 'Being nocturnal,' said Lt Wallis, 'pilots and observers were not required to put in an appearance until lunch time. Having acquainted themselves with the orders of the day, they went at the specified time to the Operations Room to get their orders for the target of the night. On receipt of these, each pilot and observer studied maps to acquaint themselves with the best way of reaching their objectives — they had to memorise

Immediately the engine roars out again and the pilot taxies the machine towards the hangars. He shouts his name to the Flare Officer who notes the time of arrival of the machine, and then hands his machine over to the mechanics, who either overhaul it and load it up for another raid, or put it away in its hangar. The pilot then makes his way to the CO's office to hand in his report, and then retires to the mess for a little well-earned refreshment.'

On 16 February 1918 the Squadron moved south to Catigny in the Fifth Army area primarily in order to attack those airfields such as Etreux which housed German night bomber squadrons that were active against the Third and Fifth Armies as well as Paris. However, the Squadron was actually given a wide choice of objectives depending on weather conditions, and it was also briefed that attacks were to be 'concentrated, ie attacks on a particular target, once begun, were to be continued for several nights'. Thus 101 hit the aerodrome at Vivaise on the night they arrived at Catigny, but although they were ordered to bomb Etreux between 20 February and 4 March, such was the effect of bad weather on flying in those days that a raid on Etreux was only possible on 21 February. At 17.20hr, 15 FE 2bs set out, not in formation but individually, and all crews found the German airfield without difficulty, reporting that it was well protected by anti-aircraft guns. Thirteen hits were claimed on aerodrome buildings, mostly with 25lb bombs, and the same crews returned to attack again at 22.35hr. By this time the visibility had worsened considerably but direct hits were reported again and a total of two 112lb and 300 25lb bombs were dropped. Some 4,400 rounds of machine gun ammunition were also expended against hangars and searchlights.

The weather having lowered its protective shield over Etreux, the Squadron attacked alternative short-distance targets at Montbrehain on 24 February and rest barracks in the woods east of Fontaine-Merte the following night. This latter raid involved all pilots making two or more trips, and the men of the German 352nd Regiment at Fontaine-Merte had their rest disturbed that night by a total of 378 25lb bombs and 12 40lb devices.

One man who flew on that occasion was Lt Edgar Hall. Born in Batley, Yorkshire, on 3 April 1889, he was apprenticed as an electrical engineer before joining the Northumberland Fusiliers in February 1915. He transferred to the RFC in October 1916 and completed flying training with No 76 Home Defence Squadron, Ripon, on 12 May 1917. By this time the flying training syllabus for pilots had been standardised by the Central Flying School, a good description of which

11
An FE 2b night bomber pilot examines a 25lb bomb before it is attached to his aircraft. *IWM*

was given in The War in the Air (Raleigh and Jones; Oxford UP, 1922): '... lectures on engines, aeroplanes, wireless telegraphy, meteorology, tactics, and organisation. Flying was taught in four flights of service machines, two of them being made up of various types of BE machines, while the other two consisted of Henri Farmans and Avros. The pupil was first taken up as a passenger, and the method of using the controls was demonstrated to him. He was then allowed to attempt flight for himself, either on a machine fitted with dual controls, or with a watchful instructor on the pounce to save him from dangerous mistakes. If he prospered well, the great day soon came, which, however carefully it may have been prepared for, is always a thrilling experience and a searching test of self-reliance, the day of the first solo flight... The training was almost wholly directed to producing airworthiness in the pupil. The various activities which had developed at the front, such as... bombing, had no counterpart as yet in the training establishment.'

By the time he graduated in May 1917, Lt Hall had amassed 80hr solo flying on Maurice Farmans, Avros, BE 2cs and 2es, RE 7s and FE 2bs. However his 'Report on Posting to Expeditionary Force' records that his 'Total Hours on most advanced type of machine flown' was '25 minutes on FE 2bs'; moreover, his 'Total Time Night Flying' was '4hr 50min'.

Lt Hall had gained more flying experience by the time he joined 101 Squadron in October 1917, and such was to be his proficiency in night bombing that the French eventually awarded him the Croix de Guerre.

'CITATION
BY ORDER OF THE ARMY

'Lieutenant Edgar Dean Hall, 5th Battalion Northumberland Fusiliers (Territorials) and 101 Squadron Royal Flying Corps.

'For his part in 34 squadron night bombing raids, notably on 21 February 1918 on Etreux airfield, and on 25 February at Fontaine-Merte barracks, displaying the greatest courage in spite of extremely adverse weather.

'A most fine example to all.

Grand General HQ
6 January 1919
Commander-in-Chief
Pétain'

Night navigation was always something of a hit and miss affair. 'But for the excellent system of lighthouses used on our side of the line, it was quite an easy matter to get lost. These lighthouses were placed at intervals of roughly 15 miles apart, some running toward the line and others parallel. They each flashed a letter in morse, so that any pilot, once he picked up a lighthouse, knew his position. Unfortunately, the enemy was not so considerate towards us. He put nothing out to guide us, and once over the line it was a matter of "by guess" plus a very erratic compass, which often acted in such a way as to make us doubt its accuracy.'

Thus on 22/23 March 1918, when 101 made many raids against German positions that were being strengthened opposite the Fifth Army front between St Gobain Wood and Bellicort, crews had roving commissions and 'were to judge their targets by lights displayed by the enemy'. In all, 484 25lb and six 40lb (phosphorous) bombs were dropped that night, and dumps near Travecy and Castres were set on fire. For part of the time operations had to be stopped when German aircraft bombed 101 Squadron's airfield in retaliation, but in spite of poor visibility, Squadron pilots and observers brought back a fair amount of useful information, notably that there was a great deal of westward troop and transport movement on the Mont d'Origny — St Quentin road. The last great Battle of the Somme was under way.

Such was the pace of the initial German onslaught that 101 could do no bombing on the night of 23/24 March because the Squadron had to pull out of Catigny before it was overrun and withdrew to No 2 Aeroplane Supply Depot at Fienvillers. From here the FE 2bs struck out the following night and dropped 284 25lb bombs on the Somme bridges and roads to the east, claiming four hits on the bridge at Béthencourt.

The next day saw the Squadron move again to Haute Visee where it was ordered by RFC HQ to attack Ham as heavily and con-

12
Sunday at Fienvillers being celebrated from the best available 'pulpit'.

tinuously as possible, paying particular attention to the roads through the town and bridges over the Somme. But after the attacks on Ham had begun, the Squadron received new instructions to direct all further efforts against Cambrai instead. Between 25 and 27 March, nine new divisions reinforced the German Second Army on the Cambrai front: 'It is hoped,' declared an RFC HQ message, 'that a record number of bombs will be dropped. It is of the utmost importance to delay enemy reinforcements coming up at this crisis, and to inflict casualties on him.'

Bombing by the Squadron was continuous for seven hours and 502 25lb bombs were dropped on Cambrai 'where great activity was seen'. Cambrai station was hit twice, a bomb fell on a canal bridge in the town, five hits were recorded on a transport column, two bombs struck a train, and another blew up an ammunition dump. In addition, 4,270 rounds of machine gun ammunition were fired at moving lights, into streets at Ham and Cambrai, and at trains. Ironically, 101's operations were hindered to some extent by the frequent passage over Haute Visse of enemy bombers on their way to inflict the same sort of damage on British lines of communication as the FE 2bs were handing out to the Germans. 'One machine, with Lieutenant Dunkerley and Lieutenant James (observer) met an enemy aircraft east of Arras with its lights on — one red and one white. They immediately proceeded to engage it. On observing that he was being attacked, the enemy LVG at once endeavoured to get well across the line, but after some manoeuvring Lieutenant Dunkerley succeeded in getting within 25yd, whereupon Lieutenant James opened fire. This lasted some minutes, Lieutenant James firing 100 rounds in all. The enemy aircraft was seen to make a vertical nose dive and appeared to crash finally apparently out of control.'

The orders for 101 Squadron on 27/28 March were as follows: 'The enemy have been attacking all day between the river Somme and Rosières, and will without doubt send up reinforcements in personnel and material during the night through Péronne and along the main Péronne-Amiens road. As it is most important to hamper this as much as possible, you will bomb Péronne and the bridge over the river Somme at Brie throughout the night.' Subsequently 101 crews found great activity at Péronne and claimed many direct hits on transport columns. A large tent encampment near the town, foolishly showing lights, was hit and partly set on fire, and a dump east of Brie also received a direct hit and blazed throughout the night.

The independent Royal Air Force came into being on 1 April 1918 but 101 Squadron personnel probably slept through most of that momentous day because there had been considerable bombing of enemy communications the night before. The Squadron had been given objectives on the Amiens-Roye road where German troop concentrations, estimated at two divisions, had been reported from the air. The FE 2bs operated for 10hr and their crews claimed many direct hits on billeting villages with 78 112lb and 150 25lb bombs. At 0530hr on 1 April, just as the last aeroplane was landing, German bombers hit 101's airfield after apparently following the final FE 2b back from the lines. The Germans obtained their revenge by killing one officer and two men, wounding two others, and wrecking four aeroplanes. It was not an auspicious beginning for the new RAF so far as 101 was concerned, but it did not prevent the Squadron from launching 14 aircraft the following night to bomb enemy billets and roads south of the Somme.

This was a very hectic period in 101's history as the fledgling RAF tried to stem the German advance without being overrun. On their way to attack the railway station at Chaulnes on 19/20 April, Lt S. A. Hustwitt and his observer, Lt N. A. Smith, saw a train near Rosières and attacked it with three 112lb bombs which hit the train and started a series of explosions that continued for most of the night. On the same night, 2-Lt Day crossed the line and bombed his objective in spite of a failing engine. 'On the return journey his engine stopped twice, but by skilful piloting he succeeded in reaching the aerodrome despite the fact that he was losing height all the way.'

Four nights later, 2-Lts Brooke and Chantrill obtained three direct hits with 112lb bombs on the railway junction at Chaulnes, while at 2250hr, 2-Lts Preston and McConville made a direct hit on an ammunition dump on the south side of the railway near Rosières. 'A great explosion took place immediately, followed by a tremendous blaze and further explosions. The fire and explosion were seen by several other pilots, who reported the matter on their return. When the second raid took place the fire was again observed by all pilots, who reported that it had increased enormously and was rapidly spreading; at one place it had crossed the railway line and was burning on the north side as well as on the south, and explosions were still taking place.' The fire served as a useful landmark as it could be easily distinguished from Amiens, and it guided crews as they went on their way to and from Chaulnes throughout the night.

FE 2b observers such as Smith, Chantrill

and McConville were worth their weight in gold; to quote again from *War in the Air*: 'The observer's duties were usually undertaken by officers or non-commissioned officers who volunteered for the business ... It has always been the tendency of our air forces to make more of the pilot than of the observer. When battles in the air became frequent, this tendency was strengthened. The pilot is the captain of the craft. If he is killed, the craft cannot keep the air. But if more depends on the pilot, it is equally true to say that a higher degree of cold-drawn courage is demanded from the observer. He suffers with the pilot for all the pilot's mistakes. For hours together he has nothing to do but sit still and keep his eyes open. He has not the relief that activity and the sense of control give to strained nerves. He is often an older man than the pilot, and better able to recognise danger. There is no more splendid record of service in the war than the record of the best observers.'

Eventually Ludendorff's last throw ground to a halt and it was time for the Allies to regroup and prepare for their final telling blow. For instance, a minor operation which began in the early hours of 4 July was preceded by the Squadron's FE 2bs flying up and down the front line to mask the noise of tanks while they were assembling. But this was small fry, and on 8 August 1918 the 17 aircraft and crews of 101 Squadron were thrown in to the Amiens Offensive which marked the beginning of the end.

The Squadron was then at Famechon where its role was to make life as difficult as possible for the troops, transport, and billeting villages facing the British Fourth Army which was detailed to lead the assault. Field Marshal Haig had selected 101 for 'independent action' and they acted under the direct orders of the Army Commander, Gen Sir Henry Rawlinson, with a brief to bomb selected targets at night. By the afternoon of 8 August, the enemy was retreating in no little confusion and reports indicated that German troops were converging on various bridges spanning the Somme. If these could be cut, the enemy would be trapped, so the FE 2bs carried on where the day bombers left off and attacked the bridges throughout the night. Although this intense activity was probably the first example of 'round the clock' bombing, it had to be acknowledged as a failure because of the lack of concentrated accuracy and the limited bomb loads involved. Nevertheless, there was no denying the commitment of the 101 Squadron crews to the offensive. They attacked stations at Péronne and Velu when the targets were invisible and the bombing was therefore of little practical value, but 'these attempts may be looked upon as an expression of the will of

the pilots and observers to take an outside chance to help the attacking infantry'.

September saw 101 attacking defended villages opposite the Fourth Army in preparation for the assault on the Hindenburg Line, and it was here that Captain Stockdale earned the DFC. Stockdale had joined the Squadron at the end of July after lengthy military service which included command of a company during the Boer War, and he took part in 24 raids and reconnaissances during his first two months on 101. However his most famous exploit came on the night of 17/18 September, his CO's description of which could have come straight out of the *'Boy's Own Paper'*:

'*CONFIDENTIAL* 2/Lt (Hon Capt) HENRY WALTER STOCKDALE
'Sir,

'I have the honour to lay before you the name of the above-mentioned Officer for immediate award of a decoration for gallantry and devotion to duty.

'While bombing Bohain from a height of about 2,000ft, he was caught by at least 10 searchlights. His efforts to evade them by clever manoeuvring of his machine were useless and accordingly he dived steeply, but in doing so received a direct hit by an anti-aircraft shell in his engine. As there was considerable moonlight at the time he succeeded in landing without using his parachute or flares thereby escaping notice. He was at this time about 15 miles behind enemy lines and as his machine could be of no further use to the enemy, he took a rough direction West and commenced to walk home. He succeeded fairly well in avoiding enemy traffic and movement along the roads by laying in a

13
Lt S. Golding with his gas-operated Lewis gun on its tube mounting. The Lewis gun was fed from an ammunition drum which revolved as the gun fired and the canvas bag hanging down caught ejected cartidges before they went back through the propeller. A 101 Squadron observer also carried a second Lewis gun placed on a pillar mounting to fire backwards over the top plane. It was a hazardous business for the observer had to undo his solitary lap strap, climb on to the ammunition lockers situated between him and the pilot, and stand precariously with his legs astride so that the pilot could see where he was going. The observer's only means of security while his pilot was manoeuvring violently was to cling to the pillar mounting with one hand and fire his gun with the other, and the RFC did not issue parachutes to its crews in those days!

ditch and then, when it had passed, running still further west.

'He and his observer, Second Lieutenant Shergold, were almost overcome with thirst and they attempted to drink water from ditches and shell holes but found it unfit for drinking and had, therefore, to carry on without it. At this point the observer was overcome by fatigue and Captain Stockdale had to half drag and half carry him further. By this time they had reached the St Quentin Canal about Bantouzelle and it was necessary to ford this. The observer was the first to get in and the immersion in cold water caused him almost to faint. Thereupon, Captain Stockdale jumped in and succeeded by his own sheer physical strength, which was by this time practically exhausted, in reaching the opposite bank with the observer. They then walked along a road towards Gouzeaucourt and while walking down the main street of this village, had the greatest difficulty in avoiding German soldiers.

'After passing through the village they came to a sunken road. At this point they were challenged by a German but they attempted to walk straight past without heeding him. He kept shouting and to avoid attracting attention, Captain Stockdale and his observer went back. The German, seeing that they were British officers, shouted something in German and struck Captain Stockdale in the mouth. Immediately they attacked the German and succeeded in knocking him down, rolling him in the mud, thereby dazing him for a few moments. They then took to their heels and bolted for the British trenches which they found by the Very Lights which were being sent up. They had considerable difficulty in crossing the barbed wire but after searching for a short while, they found a gap and reached the lines in safety.

'The time taken by them to reach their own lines was about eight hours during which they were running or walking the whole time. The fatigue must have been very great. I cannot speak too highly of the brave way in which Captain Stockdale succeeded in escaping and getting his observer back with him.

E. L. M. L. Gower
Major
In the Field   Officer Commanding
21.9.18   No 101 Squadron, RAF'

As the Allied advance grew in momentum, other Squadron personnel were congratulated by the General Officer Commanding, RAF France, for their sterling work on night bombing raids. Capt Halford for example, who completed 90 bombing missions in all and who three months earlier had made three trips to Bray in one night and dropped 52 bombs in the process, took off from Famechon to bomb Busigny junction. When he got there, he found the searchlights and anti-aircraft guns to be very active so he flew in as low as possible to escape the hail of fire. Unfortunately the bomb release gear was faulty so, rather than take the weapons back, the observer, Lt Anderson, crawled along the bottom mainplane to drop his bombs by hand. He scored direct hits.

A few nights later the weather was so bad along the British front that only 101 Squadron got airborne. Capt Beeston took off in heavy rain to carry out a low patrol over an area where tanks were assembling; after this 'most demanding and arduous patrol' he set course to bomb Levergies, finally landing back at Famechon after having been up in the drenched and cold night air for three hours.

Not that the bad weather was unwelcome to some. The Squadron also possessed a Special Duty Flight of BE 2cs, though no one talked about them much because they were set apart from the FE 2bs and were out of bounds to most personnel. The role of the Special Duty Flight was to drop spies by parachute behind enemy lines, a task that was accomplished by fixing a special type of sidecar to the fuselage side behind the mainplane trailing edge. The sidecar had a trap-door bottom which was operated by the pilot and the parachute was enclosed in a tubular container which was fixed to the side of the sidecar. The parachute cords came out through stout paper and led through a hole in the trap door to a harness worn by the spy. As the pilot sent him on his way, the falling agent dragged the parachute from the container and hopefully landed in one piece, to be picked up later at a prearranged time and place by a pilot who landed secretly behind enemy lines.

The Squadron was at Hancourt when the Armistice was signed, whereupon it moved into Belgium to unwind. In 16 months of active service the Squadron had earned four MCs, eight DFCs and four DSMs among its awards for gallantry; on the debit side, 101 recorded the loss of seven men killed in action or died of wounds, 13 killed and seven injured in accidents, and 23 taken prisoner of war. These figures are small beer by World War 2 standards but the mental and physical demands made on men who had to fly exposed to the elements as well as to the enemy night after night must have been as great. For example, on the night of 1 October only one of the Squadron's aircraft managed to get through the bad weather and bomb the target. The pilot, exhausted with the strain of it all, fainted when the aircraft was 10 miles behind enemy lines. His observer, Capt

Harold Smith, could not fly but he leant over his pilot, took hold of the controls, and after turning the FE 2b round in a series of flat turns, headed towards base. He 'landed safely on our side of the lines' even though the engine started to give trouble.

Not only pilots succumbed to cold and exhaustion. On 7 September Lts Stockman and Cock claimed a direct hit on a train at Vermand which caused a fire, but shortly afterwards Lt Cock fainted. Nothing daunted, Lt Stockman pushed him to the bottom of the nacelle and went on to complete the reconnaissance, staying in the air for over three hours. Thus, although 'our number of casualties was extremely light', World War 1 was just as much a battle of nerves as World War 2 because 'most of our losses were caused by forced landings, the pilot's worst enemy at night'.

Not that the old FE 2b let many people down. 'It can truthfully be stated,' wrote an officer in August 1918, 'that there was no machine that served its country so well as did the FE 2b. It was undoubtedly a most excellent machine for night bombing, all Squadron personnel made the best of the machine and it did them more than credit.'

Maj W. J. Tempest DSO MC took over the Squadron on 28 January 1919, but he soon found himself in command of a unit that was disappearing into thin air. In March the Squadron returned to an England where the prewar £1 was worth 9s 6d, where wartime service expenditure of £1 million per day had dropped to £1 million per week, and where there was little demand for night bomber squadrons.* Consequently, 101 was initially reduced to cadre status at Filton, Bristol, and eventually, on 31 December 1919, it was disbanded, its faithful FE 2bs sold for scrap, and its pilots and observers mostly demobilised. So it came about that Capt Edgar Hall received another letter to add to his Croix de Guerre citation:

'Telephone No.   AIR MINISTRY
Regent 8000   KINGSWAY
                LONDON WC2
            9th January 1920

'Sir,
'I am commanded by the Air Council to inform you that you have been placed on the Unemployed List of the Royal Air Force with effect from 8-5-1920 and you will cease to draw pay from the Air Force funds from that date.

*The RAF had to cut its personnel from 22,000 officers on 31 March 1919 to 3,280 during 1920, and suffer a reduction in other ranks from 160,000 to 25,000.

'I am to say that, on demobilisation, you will retain the rank of Captain but this does not confer the right to wear uniform, except when employed in a military capacity or on special occasions when attending ceremonials and entertainments of a military nature.

                I am,
                Sir,
Your obedient Servant,
        H. McAnally.'

14
101 Squadron bases and principal bombing objectives during the First World War.

15
Squadron aircrew wrapped up against the night elements and noise of open cockpits. Standard flying kit at the time was a lined, leather jacket and thigh-length, sheepskin-lined boots plus thick gloves. The pilots here are wearing goggles.

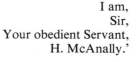

14

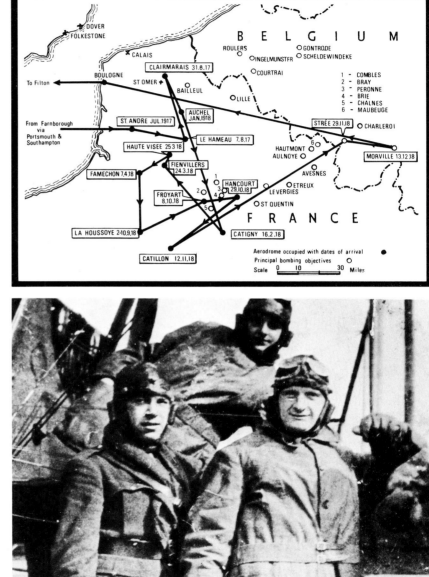

15

17

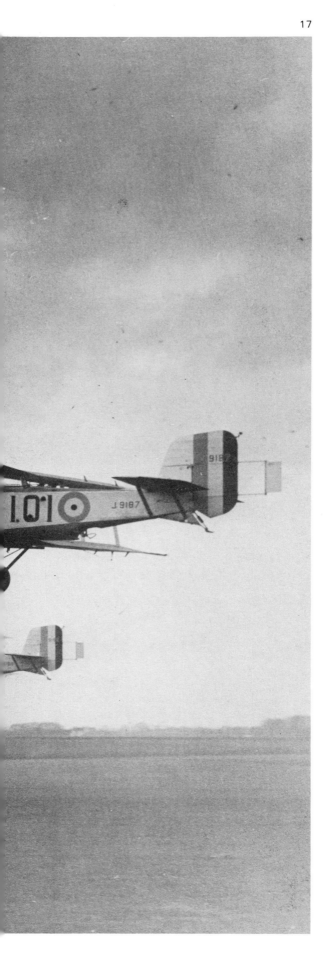

The Lean Years

In the years immediately following 1919, neither the Navy nor the Army looked with much favour on the fledgling RAF. At a time when funds were scarce, the two elder Services fought to regain control of aerial forces operating within their own spheres of influence; consequently Sir Hugh Trenchard, now Chief of Air Staff and chief sustainer of the RAF, laid special emphasis on aerial bombing over and beyond the armies and battlefleets as the prime raison d'etre of his independent air arm.

It was not until the Interim Report of the Salisbury Committee was published in June 1923 that the issue was finally settled and the RAF could look forward to a secure future. By that time the Government had realised that the postwar run-down of the RAF had gone too far and the Salisbury Committee enunciated a new principle in its Report — 'British air power must include a Home Defence Force of sufficient strength adequately to protect us against air attacks by the strongest Air Force within striking distance of this country.' But in Trenchard's view this did not mean mere reliance on a defence force of fighters — it meant being in a position to go on the offensive and strike at the very aircraft factories and airfields that sustained the enemy's bombing might. Here lay the foundations of total war and the main justification for a separate air arm — as Trenchard told his staff in 1923, 'The Army policy was to defeat the enemy Army — ours to defeat the enemy nation'.

Thus Trenchard insisted that the ratio of bombers to fighters should be increased in the force to be raised, which was christened the Air Defence of Great Britain Command (ADGB) in 1925, and the intention was to have 52 squadrons (ie 35 bomber and 17 fighter squadrons) operational by 1928. Yet the only possible enemy at this time was France, and as it soon became apparent that she posed little threat the RAF's ambitious expansion programme was slowed down to save money. Consequently, although 25 of the 52 planned home squadrons were in being by the autumn of 1925, the growth rate was reduced to two regular squadrons a year

16
A Boulton Paul Sidestrand with the Squadron number boldly emblazoned on its side. The Sidestrand's bomb racks are just visible underneath — they did not impose a drag penalty as they were hidden within the contour of the fuselage.

17
101 Squadrons Sidestrands in formation. Although the Squadron practised formation flying, the standard day bomber operating procedure in the early Thirties was that 'a single Sidestrand should go out by itself on a bombing raid'. *Aeroplane*

by 1927. Another four units were added the following year, one of which was 101 Squadron which re-formed on the authority of H.D./730 dated 21 March 1928 just in time to greet the RAF's 10th birthday.

Not that there were many Squadron members to celebrate anything in the beginning. 101 came back into being at Bircham Newton, Norfolk, as an ADGB unit within the Wessex Bombing Area, but when Sqn Ldr J. C. P. Wood was posted in from RAF Uxbridge on 28 March 'to command on formation' he found that the Squadron had only 23 airmen to its name. On 2 April, 'Flying Officer J. W. Duggan and Flying Officer J. G. Elton were posted in from No 100(B) Squadron and No 11(B) Squadron respectively. Both officers then proceeded to Martlesham Heath [the home of the Aeroplane and Armament Experimental Establishment] for a short course of instruction on the Sidestrand'.*

This Sidestrand aircraft at Martlesham was the first to be constructed and it ushered in a new era. Sir Hugh Trenchard was insistent that his precious aerial resources should not be frittered away on long-range fighters to protect his bombers: in his view, fighter squadrons should only consist of short-range interceptors for home defence to placate civilian susceptibilities. As it was generally agreed that the RAF could only strike to maximum effect if it bombed by day

*This, and many subsequent quotations, are taken from the *Squadron Operations Record Book* (RAF Form 540). 'The Object of the Operations Record Book,' declared *King's Regulations for the RAF*, 'is to furnish a complete historical record of the unit from the time of its formation ... During major operations, or when a unit is placed on a war footing, the Operations Record Book is to be compiled from day to day'.

18
A magnificent view from the pilot's cockpit of the Sidestrand looking over the front gunner into sun.

18

and night, the day bomber squadrons would lack the protective cover of darkness and would therefore have to fight their way through to their targets unescorted.

No 101(B) Squadron was to be a day bomber squadron, and as this role demanded more speed and manoeuvrability as well as armament if it was to be credible, the Squadron was to receive the Boulton and Paul Sidestrand. Named after a village near Cromer in Norfolk, for Boulton Paul's factory was then located at Norwich, the Sidestrand was to mark the return of the twin-engined, high performance bomber to the RAF inventory after a gap since the retirement of the DH10.

The first year of 101's new life was taken up with ironing out such snags on the new aeroplane as the replacement of balanced ailerons with Frise ailerons and the fitment of a servo rudder for better control. By 25 January 1929 the Squadron complement had grown to 13 officers and 117 airmen, but it still had only one Sidestrand so continuation training had to be carried out on a couple of elderley Avro 504s and some DH9As donated by 39 Squadron when they left Bircham for India at the end of 1928.

The first production Sidestrand appeared on 101 in March 1929 and the Squadron establishment of an HQ and two Flights only materialised as more aircraft rolled out from Boulton Paul.

Having gained considerable twin-engined bomber experience through the Bourges and Bugle, Boulton Paul's Chief Designer, John North, was in a good position to produce a Sidestrand bomber that was very shapely and efficient aerodynamically for its time. It displayed remarkable manoeuvrability for a twin-engined aircraft and not only could it fly on one engine but it could also be looped, spun and rolled without difficulty. Once in Squadron service it soon became known as a superb pilots' aeroplane and, although the controls demanded considerable muscle, the Sidestrand was a pleasure to fly.

Unfortunately, some became too exhilarated for their own good:

'17 September 1929. Flying Officer X tried by General Court Martial for low flying at Hunstanton, Norfolk on 17 July 1929. Sentenced to be severely reprimanded and to have his seniority to date from 17 September 1929.'

The Sidestrand carried a crew of four — pilot, observer and two gunners — and its offensive load consisted of two 230lb or 250lb bombs plus a single 520lb or 550lb bomb, two more 230lb or 250lb bombs, or four 112lb bombs. 'Recently the position of the man who releases the bombs has been changed. He used to lie prone on his chest in

The whole of No 101 (B) Squadron at No 1 Armament Training School, Catfoss (near Hornsea, Yorks) in 1931. At Catfoss a year later, 'secret experiments have been carried out by this Squadron. The object is to climb to an altitude of 10,000ft, glide down at a speed of 135mph for 2,000ft, and whilst gliding down drop bombs. Then we flattened out and flew straight for a certain period, before repeating bombing by gliding down another 2,000ft. The effect of this is more accurate bombing and it defeats the ground defences. Experiments are being continued.'

a very uncomfortable position but now he sits in a very comfortable seat in the nose of the machine in front of the pilot. Panels of glass have been inserted in the nose in front of him, through which he can see his target as the machine approaches the position from which the bombs are to be released. This is a great improvement and leads to much greater accuracy of aim.' Thus endowed, and being a very stable aiming platform, the Sidestrands of 101 and their crews soon set new records for accurate delivery:

'1 September-27 September 1930. RAF Practice Camp, Catfoss. Combined results of A and B Flights are as follows:

'Bombing 84 yards, Gunnery 33%.

These results place the unit on top of all the other day bomber squadrons.'

'29 September 1930. Flt Lt Collins (pilot) and Cpl Thrussell (bomb-aimer), bombing from 6,000 ft, broke the record for Catfoss. Their error from 6,000ft was 21 yards.'

By now the Squadron was at Andover, Hants, where, as the only day bomber unit in the Wessex Bombing Area, it could be closer to any continental conflict. Andover was then commanded by Wg Cdr W. B. Hargrave, a 101 Squadron CO back in 1917, and from here his old unit settled down to formalising such serious business as the design of the Squadron tie — 'diagonal lines coloured dark blue, light blue, red and black.' More importantly, 101 also set about demonstrating the Sidestrand's ability to strike and survive far and wide.

'28 July-4 August 1930. Affiliation with No 111(F) Squadron. Results of Affiliation Exercises carried out with fighter squadron proved that the Sidestrand was a difficult proposition to tackle and that fighters at present had no attack to meet them.'

'12 August-14 August 1930. Air Exercises. These took the form of Redland against Blueland. This unit was allocated to Blueland and operated from Andover. Long distance bombing raids were carried out chiefly against Cranwell and Hucknall. The raid against Cranwell was most successful. On one raid to Catfoss the aircraft reached their objective and returned in a 60mph gale to land after a flight lasting $5\frac{3}{4}$ hours.'

Informed observers were very impressed by all this. Maj F. A. de V. Robertson in *Flight* of 24 April 1931 wrote: 'During the Air Exercises of last summer a formation of Sidestrands made an effective raid on the HQ of Air Vice-Marshal Dowding at Cranwell. But generally speaking the idea is that a single Sidestrand should go out by itself on a bombing raid. There is more than one reason for this. Naturally a single machine is not such a conspicuous object in the sky as a formation, and therefore it has a better chance of winning through to its objective than a Flight or a complete Squadron would have. A Sidestrand can carry a bomb load of 1,000lb and so even one is a formidable weapon of offence. Finally, the fighting powers of the Sidestrand are such that it is considered very well able to take care of

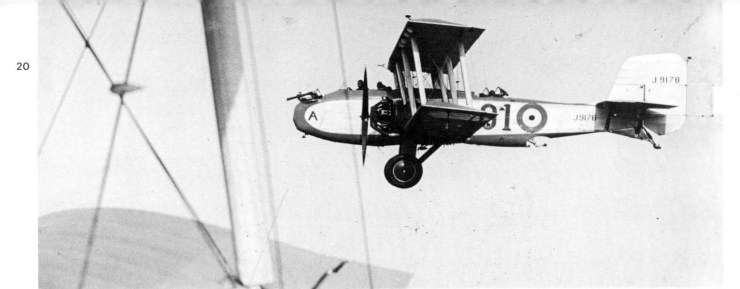

20
A good view of the Sidestrand's defensive weaponry of one forward gun, one rear upper gun amidships, and a third in a ventral turret pointing downwards towards the tail. All three Lewis guns were moveable and their very extensive field of fire left few blindspots.
Because of its manoeuvrability, excellent rate of climb and top speed of 140mph, the Sidestrand was the best light bomber of the decade. The Sidestrand's crew of four could talk to each other through a revolutionary new 'electrical inter-communication system'.
Aeroplane

21
Squadron dispersal at Andover.
Aeroplane

22
On Air Defence of Great Britain air exercises during May 1931. The Squadron was part of 'Blueland' forces and here its ranks are supported by Hawker Harts. Not that such fighter protection was necessary — 'Blue' forces were attacked en route by Siskins of 29 and 111 (F) Squadrons from the 'Redland' Air Defence Brigade and 'afterwards the fighter pilots admitted they had no definite form of attack which they could bring off safely against Sidestrands'.

23
A Sidestrand on a visit to Waddington, Lincs, in 1931. The Sidestrand was equipped with W/T radio, and when the trailing aerial was wound out crews could listen to broadcast morse messages 'as well as the ordinary wireless programmes which makes for brighter flying'.

itself. It has three machine guns, all of them moveable . . . This gives a very extensive field of fire and leaves very few blind spots on the machine. The gun mountings, too, are made simpler and therefore easier to work. Important details such as these often make all the difference between a hit and a miss, and a single-seater fighter runs a particular risk when he attacks a Sidestrand . . . It is reported that two fighter squadrons have been very puzzled to arrive at a plan of attack on Sidestrands which would not involve risk of heavy casualties to themselves. The guns of a fighter are fixed, and the whole machine must be aimed at the target. The fighter is only dangerous when flying towards his target. When turning off after an attack, usually in a zoom with speed diminishing, he presents a more or less helpless target to the gunners on board the bomber.'

By the end of the year, therefore, the Squadron had cause to be pleased with itself, and no one more so than the latest CO, Sqn Ldr F. H. Coleman, DSO, who was something of a perfectionist:

'20 November 1930. The Air Officer Commanding's Inspection by Air Vice-Marshal Sir John Steel KBE CB CMG was held in No 12(B) Squadron's hangar owing to bad weather. The AOC congratulated No 101(B) Squadron on its excellent results at the Practice Camp, and also the Squadron spirit and teamwork. He further congratulated the Squadron on being the best turned out and efficient Squadron on parade. During the inspection of aircraft, the AOC had a level half-crown bet with Squadron Leader Coleman that he (the Squadron Leader) had not read and understood properly an Engineering Servicing Instruction on a mechanical tail trolley. It is sufficient to say that the AOC lost and paid the half-crown.'

1931 was the first year in which no wooden aircraft were ordered for RAF squadrons, and this gradual modernisation of the Service had its impact on the front line.

'8 April 1931. The Squadron was selected to carry out Bombing Trials against HMS *Centurion* in September 1931, and in this connection was supplied with Gyro-rectors, Tail drift-sights, Mk VIIA Vector bombsights, electrical inter-communication sets and an electrical bomb release. In addition, new Jupiter VIII engines with 4-bladed propellers were supplied along with Mk II starters. All this modification work was completed at the unit in three weeks with the help of Messrs Boulton and Paul Ltd. The Squadron is now the most up-to-date equipped Unit in the Royal Air Force.'

This growing prowess was justified to the British public in the following manner in *Flight* of 24 April 1931.

'Bombing is becoming more and more of an accurate art — one might almost say, an exact science. The civilian who dreads outbreaks of "frightfulness" in the next war takes comfort in the thought that a pin-point target can still only be hit by good luck rather than skill. But the most useful targets, namely aerodromes, railway junctions, factories and such like can be seriously damaged and thrown out of gear even though the bomber and the bomb sights do not possess quite the accuracy of a King's Prize-man at Bisley. Moreover, the British citizen, who perhaps has lost more than any other national through the coming of air power, should find his chief comfort in the thought that the aim of British bombers is more accurate than the aim of any possible enemies. In that lies his best hope of security.'

No 101 (B) Squadron continued to impress throughout the early 1930s, be it among the hierarchy at ADGB Headquarters or in front of the crowds at the annual Hendon Display who delighted to watch the Sidestrand looping in mock combat with Bulldog fighters:

'25 June 1932. To OC No 101(B) Squadron. On behalf of the Flying Com-

24
The officers and men of 'A' Flight in 1932.

25
The Prince of Wales approaches the officers and men of 101 Squadron during a visit to Mousehold Heath aerodrome at Norwich. Notice the Boulton Paul hangar in the background. Sqn Ldr Coleman and his two flight commanders are in the front row. Notice the other ranks' uniforms in 1933. Lord Swinton, the Secretary of State for Air from 1935 to 1938, hated the tight cloth collar which he considered both uncomfortable and unhygienic. To improve comfort and efficiency, and thereby recruiting during the RAF's expansion programme in the late 1930s, Lord Swinton and the Air Council decided to make some radical changes — 'We substituted the open collar on the tunic and a shirt, collar and tie. We also got rid of the useless puttees.'

26
Sidestrands, together with their crews and groundcrews, prepare for flight.

mittee of the Royal Air Force Display, I shall be obliged if you will convey our thanks to Sergeant Pilot Methven who flew the bomber in this event. Whether the event was a success or failure depended more upon him than any other individual.

Hendon Display
Air Vice-Marshal F. W. Bowhill CMG, DSO'

Nevertheless, officialdom never felt the need to equip any other squadrons with the Sidestrand though it did allow development of the big biplane to continue. One particular problem associated with the relatively high speed of the Sidestrand was that its front gunner had difficulty aiming his Lewis gun satisfactorily in the increased pressure of the slipstream. John North concluded that the only solution was to enclose the gunner in a protective, power operated turret. This was a revolutionary feature for the time, and together with an enclosed pilot's cockpit, warm-air cabin heating, and an autopilot, altered the Sidestrand to such an extent that the modified airframe was rechristened Overstrand after another Norfolk village. The RAF ordered 24 Overstrands in all, but once again only 101 Squadron took operational possession of the type, its first aircraft arriving on 24 January 1935. (In fact this was a converted Sidestrand; the first production Overstrand 1 did not arrive until early 1936).

By now 101 was at Bicester in Oxfordshire to whence it had moved in December 1934 to replace 33 Squadron within the Central Region of ADGB. Having achieved the distinction of being the first RAF squadron to operate an aircraft with a power-operated gun turret, 101 then set about commemorating the fact in its Squadron crest.

Back in 1929, the unofficial crest had centred on the figures '101' with an eagle emerging from the 'O' carrying a bomb in its talons. Underneath were the words *Mens Agitat Molem* (Mind Over Matter); this was taken from the motto of Rossall School and it was doubtless adopted (with the Headmaster's approval) because the CO of the time was an old boy who wished to instil a few good old fashioned virtues into his men.

This motto stuck, if not the bomb-toting eagle, for in February 1938 King George VI gave approval for the new Squadron crest which was officially described as 'Issuant from the battlements of a tower, a demi-lion rampant guardant'. Symbolism was everywhere — the lower battlements signified the power-operated turret and the lion, being a fierce fighter, represented the Squadron's fighting spirit. *Mens Agitat Molem* remained, interpreted by the irreverent as 'They don't mind and I don't matter': on a more serious note, some argued that the words should have been transposed because there was very little that the mind could do against the small 'matter' of a high explosive bomb.

The Overstrand was an advance over the Sidestrand in that it was regarded as the prototype modern medium bomber, and so 101 found itself reclassified as a medium bomber squadron with a brief to pave the operational way for the introduction of the Blenheim by investigating new techniques such as intensive night flying. In fact the Squadron had started night flying in a cursory fashion back in March 1932, but most of the old tactics of the Sidestrand age were hardly adequate for a modern European war in the late 1930s.

'21 May-23 May 1935. The Squadron took part in a demonstration given at Porton

27

Sqn Ldr E. B. C. Betts DSC, DFC, Officer Commanding No 101 (B) Squadron from 21 December 1933 to 12 January 1936, in full dress uniform. Sqn Ldr Betts was a crack shot who represented Ireland at Bisley, but he did not have to suffer the discomfort of the full dress uniform for much longer — it soon went the way of puttees.

28

The official 101 Squadron crest which was approved by King George VI in February 1938. The badge is described as 'Issuant from the battlements of a tower, a demi-lion rampant guardant.' Officially these Squadron crests 'stand for tradition and foster an *esprit de corps* and this promotes the very necessary efforts of the individual.'

29

The unofficial 101 Squadron badge in the early 1930s.

28

No. 101 SQDN

29

30
An Overstrand (foreground) stands next to one of the Sidestrands it was to replace on the Squadron flight line at Bicester. Note the enclosed pilot's cockpit and front turret on the newcomer — on the Overstand service trials, gunners enjoying the protection of the powered front turret achieved an average success rate as high as 85%, whereas the average on the Sidestrand had only been 15%

31
In 1933 the Under Secretary of State for Air, Sir Philip Sassoon, presented a trophy for competition between the night bomber squadrons of the Wessex Bombing Area of ADGB. This trophy was subsequently awarded for prowess in aerial photography, for all bomber squadrons carried plate or film cameras for reconnaissance work when required. In between bombing and gunnery therefore, Pilot Officer Williams (pilot), AC 1 Goad (observer) and LAC Gregory (camera) won the Sassoon Trophy in 1935 for 101 Squadron with a score of 89.5%, which was the best result in the competition to date.

This photograph, taken after the Trophy presentation, shows (L-R): Sqn Ldr Betts, Sir Philip Sassoon MP, Air Cdre H. R. Nicholl (AOC Central Region, ADGB), and Wg Cdr M. L. Taylor (School of Photography). Another reform later initiated by Lord Swinton was the abolition of field boots for officers. 'They were the last things that anyone would rush to fly in, and we had no horses.'

32
The first Squadron Overstrand on parade for a royal inspection by King George V, the Prince of Wales and the Duke of York at the Mildenhall Jubilee Review on 6 July 1935. 'The King inspected the turret of the Overstrand and Sgt J. L. Thrussell was presented to His Majesty as the best bomb-aimer of the year on day bomber squadrons.'

and Andover to students of the Imperial Defence College. The task was distributed salvo bombing against a target representing a bridge 200yd long by 30yd wide over which three salvos were dropped, all hitting the target.'

It was great stuff for the uninitiated, but hitting undefended, immobile, short-range targets in friendly airspace and in fair weather proved little. Certainly the Squadron tried to fly more realistically with its Over-strands, as during the ADGB Air Exercises of 1936 when the aircraft raided in flight formation at dawn and dusk, but at least one leg and the bombing had to be undertaken during daylight because Squadron crews had no means of finding a target at night. 101 won the Armament Officers' Trophy for the second year running because they completed the Long Distance Bombing Exercises with an average bombing error of 53.7yd, but the Overstrand could not get to Germany and back even from the south coast and such bombing scores were unlikely to be repeated in the blitzkrieg war around the corner.

The Squadron soon had two flights of Overstrands with four aircraft held in reserve, and each flight normally had around six aeroplanes for use at any one time. The Overstrand could carry 1,500lb of bombs and had a top speed of 153mph, but its normal operating altitude was only around 7,000ft and this restriction, like many others, only highlighted the deficiencies of the RAF in the mid-1930s. The daily flying programme was displayed on a blackboard in the flight office showing aircraft number, type of exercise, crew, time of take off and approximate duration, but there was not much more organisation. For a start there was no real air traffic control as such. The duty pilot sent off a signal to the destination airfield informing them that an aircraft was on its way; if he felt that the Overstrand might arrive before the telegram he might try to telephone, but as likely as not he kept silent on the matter.

Neither was there a station meteorological office, so the Squadron crews had to rely on weather forecasts which were transmitted several times a day in morse code from the Air Ministry in London. Not that there was a specialist navigator on board to use up-to-date 'met' if it had been available. The Overstrand crew numbered five — pilot, bombardier, nose and two rear gunners, who also operated the wireless — and not only was there no professional navigator but also four of the crew were only part-timers. Such navigational duties as there were on the relatively short-range and slow Overstrand were left to the pilot, the only full-time aircrew member on board, who map-read from ground feature to ground feature backed up by wind speed and drift calculations derived from an elementary computer disc strapped to his knee.

Aircrew members of the RAF in the 1920s fell into just two categories — pilots and observers — and the bulk of the 'back seat' jobs were left to volunteer ground tradesmen who were eager to fly. T. Stanhope Sprigg wrote in *The Royal Air Force* (Pitman,

33
Squadron Overstrands over Oxfordshire in June 1936. Apart from the powered turret, the chief differences between the Overstand and its predecessor were an increase in top speed of 153mph, an enclosed pilot's cockpit, warm air heating for the pilot's and rear gunner's cockpits, a wind shield for the rear gunner's cockpit, a tail wheel, larger main wheels with wheel brakes and servo operated elevators. 'Essentially though,' recorded the Squadron, 'the aircraft were identical.'
Charles E. Brown

34
The Overstrand's famous powered turret, the front of which was closed by a zip fastener when not in use. The 'power' came from a compressed air bottle though the cylindrical cupola turret could only be fully rotated when its Lewis gun was elevated by 70°. One RAF staff officer, who expressed a wish to try it for himself on the ground, commenced rotation only to become so overwhelmed by the turret's speed that he remained transfixed, whirling like a top, until both he and the air system were exhausted.

34

33

35
An Overstrand in its natural
element.
Chaz Bowyer Collection

1935): 'It is the Air Ministry's intention to draw from airmen entered as boys the bulk of observers required by the Service. Ex-boy entrants recommended for these posts will usually be selected during their seventh year of service, provided they are willing to re-engage to complete 24 years total service. They will be given a short course of training, promoted to Corporal, and thereafter employed on such observer duties as aerial gunnery, signalling, navigation, photography and look-out, until they have completed 18 years' service or have been promoted to Flight Sergeant. Whilst serving as observers they draw additional pay at the rate of 1s 6d a day.'

It all sounded good in theory, but in practice, gunners and bomb aimers were just as often chosen from amongst the keenest Squadron groundcrew who were then taught the rudiments of the job. These men did not even receive automatic advancement to the giddy heights of Corporal, but despite the 'second-class' nature of rear-crew duties there was never any lack of volunteers from among the other ranks. They might attain AC1 (Aircraftman First Class) or LAC (Leading Aircraftman), and they might have to service the machine they had just flown as soon as they landed, but merely to fly was sufficient reward in itself and therein lay the chance of advancement to 'real' aircrew status as a pilot.

Once a year, 101 Squadron crews were given a chance to drop real bombs and fire live ammunition at Armament Training ranges such as Catfoss or North Coates Fitties. Small smoke bombs were deposited with enthusiasm from high or low level, in steep or shallow dives, while the air gunners blazed away at ground targets or banners

towed behind apprehensive aircraft. Back at Bicester, the crews could only refine their bombing skills by using a rudimentary 'camera obscura' device in a small room. Thus, in spite of new drift sights and electronic release mechanisms, precision in bombing only came by dint of experience, and the Squadron crews had no means of finding and accurately identifying targets which were masked by bad weather or night.

That the RAF was still largely geared to bomber techniques that were not far removed from those of World War 1 was due almost entirely to the many intervening years of retrenchment and neglect. The deteriorating international situation after 1933 put a stop to this and provided sufficient impetus for the RAF to embark on its first expansion scheme in July 1934, but the fact that Scheme A was to be superseded by no fewer than 10 other such schemes during the next four years gave some indication of the uncertainty of the time. Parity with the emerging Luftwaffe was to be the aim of the game as the Government strove to deter possible German aggression by sheer weight of numbers. Consequently, as aircraft rolled off the production lines the metropolitan air force became too large and unwieldy to be effectively controlled from a single ADGB Headquarters. Moreover, the work of its various branches was becoming increasingly specialised, so in July 1936 ADGB was separated into four independent Commands. One of these was Bomber Command, and its first Group was to be No 2 (Bomber Group) commanded by 101's first CO, Laurence Twistleton-Wykeham-Fiennes, who was now a Group Captain.

Having been forced in the name of 'parity' to go for quantity in the short term rather than quality, the RAF had to accept a pre-

36
An Overstrand in its unnatural
element, having come to grief
outside a Bicester hangar at the
hands of an embarrassed flight
commander!

ponderance of light and medium bombers which were cheaper and easier to build, needed fewer crew members, and demanded smaller airfields and support facilities to keep airborne. Not that this was necessarily a bad thing because the Service needed time to absorb the implications of the rapid advances in airframe and engine technology that were then taking place. For example, when the Bristol Aeroplane Company designed a high-speed, twin-engined, personal transport monoplane for Lord Rothermere, its sleek, low-winged design together with retractable undercarriage, variable pitch propellers, and advanced engines gave it a top speed some 50mph in excess of the RAF's latest production fighter. Lord Rothermere generously presented his aircraft to the nation for further tests, and Bristol redesigned it as a medium bomber to be known as the Blenheim.

No 101's Overstrands graced the Hendon Display for the last time in 1937 because events had rapidly overtaken this stalwart of the biplane age. The Squadron began to re-equip with the Blenheim I on 27 August 1938, though conversion on to type was pretty rudimentary. 'One or two pilots did a quick circuit at Bristol's airfield, Filton, in the company of the firm's test pilot, but not in a dual control aircraft. Then we took off in the Blenheims allocated to the Squadron and we flew in formation back to base. That was the conversion course in its entirety.'

No 101 was 're-allocated from a training to a mobilisation Squadron' on 16 September, just in time for the Munich crisis which the Squadron Adjutant discreetly referred to in the following manner:

'26 September 1938. As a result of events in Central Europe, an International Situation occurred which necessitated the Squadron immediately preparing for a major war. Intensive training was done in an attempt to make as many crews as possible fit to perform long distance bombing raids by day and night. These preparations were somewhat hampered by the shortage of air observers and wireless operator air gunners, and the non-availability of certain essential items of equipment.'

Although the Squadron continued training after Munich was over 'so as to achieve complete operational fitness as soon as possible', there was no immediate solution to the manpower problem. RAF personnel, who numbered 31,000 officers and men in 1934, totalled approximately 118,000 by 1 September 1939; thus in these few years the aggregate intake amounted to some 4,500 pilots and 40,000 airmen and boys compared with the annual pre-expansion entry of 300 pilots and 1,600 airmen. The implications of this rapid expansion rate were considerable. Blenheims for instance were readily forthcoming — the Squadron was up to its established strength of 16 IE (Initial Equipment) plus 5 IR (Immediate Reserve) by 5 October 1938 — but skilled groundcrews to service them and proficient aircrews to fly them took longer to arrive.

Back in 1919 Trenchard had laid the foundations of his officer corps by pushing through the unprecedented proposal that permanent commissions should only be offered to one-third of his future officers, and that the remainder should be recruited on a short-term basis 'in order to give a good curve of promotion to those officers who were permanent'. The principal method of obtaining a permanent commission was either through a university or via the RAF College, Cranwell. Entry through either of these doors was theoretically open to all, but although there were scholarships available to those of limited means there were no university grants in those days and the fees for the two years' training course at Cranwell were £300 in 1934. To enter Cranwell a boy had to be between $17\frac{1}{2}$ and $19\frac{1}{2}$ years of age, of proven academic ability, and impress a board of officers as to his 'Interview and Record' which gave information as to 'mentality, character and athletic prowess'. Yet the fact that a member of the 'officer class' in the prewar RAF had to maintain a social standard alongside brother officers who might keep a private horse in the Mess stables or even a private aeroplane in the hangar makes it clear that the ranks of the permanently commissioned were more likely to be filled by boys who went to public schools such as Rossall rather than to grammar schools. This is not to say that the average prewar RAF officer on a permanent commission was a chinless blockhead — in fact much of the Service's success in World War 2 was undoubtedly due to the standard of leadership and example set by men taken into Cranwell during the 1930s. Rather, it was more a question of glamour and challenge. Neither the Army nor Navy had come out of World War 1 with overmuch glory, and to sons of men who had suffered at the hands of uninspiring admirals and generals, the RAF in the thirties often promised a brighter and less conservative prospect than the other two services. As a result the RAF was able to select the elite of the

elite because it could afford to pick and choose from the best youth in the land.

The Cranwell men were the 'career' stream who would eventually fill such prime executive posts on the squadron as CO and flight commanders. 101 Squadron was divided into two operational Flights: OC 'A' Flight and OC 'B' Flight were then flight lieutenants each responsible for eight crews, their aircraft and their groundcrews. Only pilots on the Squadron held the King's Commission before the war and, excluding the executives, these were either young Cranwell men or officers who could not gain, or did not aspire to, a permanent commission. The latter served on short-service commissions which were available to 'those between 18 and 22, unmarried, and of pure European descent' and which allowed a man to serve for four years followed by six in the Reserve. A £100 gratuity was paid for each year served, though those of proven worth were allowed to transfer to a permanent commission if they so desired.*

Yet there were only 10 officers on 101 at this time, and as each Squadron Blenheim carried a crew of three — pilot, navigator/observer, and gunner — some of the pilot posts and all the rear-crew positions were

*The rank of flight lieutenant could be reached by a Cranwell graduate in $3\frac{1}{2}$ years, but could not be reached by other officers for $4\frac{1}{2}$ years, by which time a short service officer would have transferred to the Reserve.

37
Line-up of Squadron Blenheim Is. As the threat of war increased, bomber squadrons painted out all their unit markings and replaced them with code letters. Thus 'LU' identified 101, though after August 1939 this was changed to 'SR' for the remainder of the war. Eventually a third letter was added after the unit code to identify individual aircraft.

37

filled by lesser mortals. The non-commissioned pilots were drawn from men who had worked their way up from direct entry into the ranks or from apprenticeships. A newly commissioned (and unmarried) pilot officer fresh out of Cranwell earned £381 14s 7d a year in 1938, which was more than an experienced sergeant pilot, but few SNCOs complained because they were flying as well as earning 3s a day more than when they had been on the ground.

The status of an SNCO pilot was certainly much higher than that of the remainder of his crew. Now that the modern Blenheim had arrived, the old unsatisfactory state of navigation affairs was improved somewhat by the decision to put selected rear-crew men through a 16 weeks' course in navigation and bombing, on successful completion of which they would receive the acting rank of sergeant. After six months duty as 'Acting Observer' they would be confirmed in rank and crew category, and allowed to wear the winged 'O' flying badge of an air observer above their left tunic pockets.

This advance placed non-commissioned observers on a par with non-commissioned pilots, but even so there was always a shortage of trained navigators during the expansion period. At a time when the Air Ministry was producing no fewer than 13 grandiose Western Air Plans for use in a forthcoming war, all of which presupposed pinpoint accuracy to strike at German military, industrial and transportation targets, the facilities available to RAF bomber navigators were totally inadequate. Too much flying was done in the local vicinity of aerodromes, and anything farther afield relied on a hit-and-miss method known in the Service as 'by guess and by God'. On 17 May 1939 a report to Bomber Command declared that dead reckoning navigation by day when above cloud could be expected to bring an aircraft only to within about 50 miles of a long-range target. Thus it was only gradually being realised that accurate navigation was a full-time job and one moreover that, if it was to prove successful over reasonable distances and unfamiliar terrain, not to mention in bad weather and at night, required special training and facilities. This in turn would necessitate such an education as would often make commissioned rank as desirable for the navigator as for the pilot.

The third man in the Blenheim was the gunner who sat in a power-operated semi-retractable dorsal turret containing a single Vickers K or Lewis gun. Although the advent of the 'new' generation of RAF bombers had seen the first regular inclusion of straight air gunners into each Blenheim crew, the role of 'Air Gunner' as a specific aircrew 'trade' was not formally recognised by the Service until 19 January 1939. Air Ministry Order A.17/1939 finally gave full-time employment to air gunners, but then only in the category of wireless operators. Existing air gunners were expected to take the wireless operators' course but henceforward all new recruits had to train first as W/Ops at RAF Yatesbury before undertaking a course of gunnery instruction at Jurby on the Isle of Man. The men who succeeded at all this became WOp/AGs but they could still remain aircraftmen first class or leading aircraftmen until well into the war at a maximum pay of 5s 6d a day plus 1s 6d a day flying pay. Prospects of further advancement in status were restricted by the Air Ministry Order to the possible selection, after some three years' crew service, for training as an air observer.

Yet it was impossible to train hordes of new RAF aircrew overnight. As Viscount Swinton, the then Secretary of State for Air, wrote in *British Air Policy Between the Wars 1918-1939* (H. Montgomery Hyde; Heinemann, 1976). 'We had to mobilise and improvise by every means in our power. For the training of pilots we proceeded on the basis of separate initial training and advanced training. For the initial training we used and expanded all the existing Civil Training Schools, and the men who had pioneered and persisted without much encouragement in these schools played a notable part in the expansion; most, if not all of them, old Air Force officers. The advanced training schools were entirely run by the RAF. For the intructional staff in both initial and the advanced schools we drew largely upon the Reserve of Officers. Then we had to expand the specialist schools, and build new ones for navigation, gunnery and the like.'

So manning levels on 101 remained a headache and cockpit seats had to be left empty, 'resulting in monthly flying hours being often well below the required number'. The situation was not helped when the Squadron lost a considerable proportion of its skilled manpower in the first three months of 1937 to form the nuclei of 90 and 144 Bomber Squadrons. Thus, although 101 was 'mobilised' in response to Munich, this was largely a cosmetic exercise because, in the words of the Air Ministry, 'Less than 50% of the crews in the mobilisation squadrons were fit for operations as judged by Bomber Command's peacetime standards.' But the quest for the right sort of manpower went on:

'The new bombers require not only extra pilots but crews, wireless operators, observers and gunners,' wrote Viscount Swinton to the Prime Minister. 'These we cannot improvise . . . These men are vital to sustain a war effort.'

The remainder of the 114 non-commissioned members of 101 Squadron who were the maintainers and sustainers were equally vital. In *The Mint*, T. E. Lawrence praised the aircraft mechanics as more important in their way than the pilots themselves since, but for their conscientious work, the pilots could not carry out their tasks. This was a very sound attitude and one that was certainly reflected in the aircrews' approach to the groundcrews of 101.

Direct entrants to the ranks swelled in number with the RAF Expansion Scheme and they were initially paid between 2s and 3s 6d a day depending on their trade group. At the end of the training course, say for a flight rigger at No 2 School of Technical Training, Henlow, there came the great day of the Control Test Board. 'A senior NCO took each trainee on the oral part of the subject. There were practical jobs to be done, a built-up riveting and a splicing exercise. There was also a written paper to complete. The results were collated from each part and the average of all was the final result. Below 40% was a fail, 40-60% made one an aircraftman 2nd class, with 60-80% one became 1st class, and 80% and over elevated one to the dizzy heights of leading aircraftman. It was a good man indeed who passed out LAC with the high standard demanded.'

The longest serving engagements in those trades most directly associated with aircraft maintenance was reserved for those who undertook an RAF apprenticeship. Introduced by Lord Trenchard, the apprentice scheme was designed to provide the service with a nucleus of highly skilled technicians at the end of an intensive three-year course, and from this cadre were to come the engineering officers and NCOs of the future. Boys between the ages of 15 and $17\frac{1}{4}$ could sign on for 12 years from their 18th birthday if they were accepted for apprenticeships, but like the permanent commission, an apprenticeship was a coveted prize only awarded to the elite.

Having said that, there was still much that was anachronistic about the attitude of the RAF before the war. E. C. Shepherd could write in *The Air Force of Today, 1939* (Blackie and Sons Ltd): 'The maintenance of aircraft, like the care of horses, is a specialist job ... The apprenticeship ideas was one of Trenchard's best, for it combined an engineering training with an education in the ways and traditions of the Service. In effect it permeated the units with a mechanical aristocracy who ... were familiar with the way the Service tackles its work and with the reasons why certain things are important ... The boys arrive at the squadrons *full of the spirit of the game ...*'

Unfortunately, if airborne warfare was ever a game, the Germans were then in the process of unilaterally re-writing the rules.

A skilled LAC on 101 Squadron in 1938 earned 35s a week less 7s for food and accommodation. Good conduct badges were worth an extra 3d a day, these being awarded after 5, 8 and 13 years. 'There was a tremendous esprit de corps, and comradeship was the operative word.' Life revolved around the barrack block for 'very few personnel lived, or had their homes within, easy reach of the camp and weekends were invariable spent at Bicester. Fewer still could afford the luxury of a car or even a motorcycle although I remember a few "souped-up" bangers usually with two or three or even four bods in part ownership, and their antics were not altogether in favour with the station warrant officer. ... Booking IN and OUT was compulsory at the Main Guardroom where each individual would come under the scrutiny of the duty service policeman and, unless you were dressed to the required standard, you would be refused permission to leave camp.

'There were no exceptions when administrative duties were promulgated in daily routine orders — duty crew, fire picket and station guards come quickly to mind. The duty crew consisted of a corporal and six airmen (mixed flying and ground personnel) and the duty lasted for one week. The duty crew were responsible for opening and closing the hangar doors daily. They remained at the flight line until all the aircraft had returned, manually moving each aircraft into its allotted position; if outside the hangar, they ensured that each aircraft was pegged down into wind, chocks positioned, and aircraft searched for 'left overs' etc. Working parades were held daily when both flights would assemble outside their respective barrack blocks and, after inspection, would be marched to the hangars and be dismissed. The reverse would take place at the cessation of work.'*

Nevertheless, despite numerical deficiencies, the quality of the manpower from the top to the bottom of 101 Squadron was excellent. The man largely responsible for this, Lord Trenchard, certainly found cause for satisfaction in September 1940: 'I have also been round nearly every squadron. The spirit they are all imbued with is wonderful ... They are what I had not thought possible, — better than in the last war. On the RAF I feel will fall the heavy burden of fighting all through the winter in very hard conditions, but I know their spirit will pull through whatever happens.'

*Aircraftmen First Class V. Noble, 1936 — via *Special Operations*; R. Alexander, 1979.

Trial and Error

Although 101 was always short of aircrew right up to the war, the RAF was right not to lower its standards in order to make up numbers. This policy was to create a pool of superb manpower which was to stand the Service in very good stead in the long term, but in 1939 it only added to the problems facing Bomber Command. New Blenheim air gunners might be better motivated, but they had such little opportunity to perfect their skills on the armament practice ranges 'that their results were not very satisfactory'. In addition, although the gunners were now encased in power turrets, the weapons they fired were little different from those their fathers had used in World War 1. Consequently the C-in-C Bomber Command, Air Chief Marshal Sir Edgar Ludlow-Hewitt, felt moved to write in the following manner to the Air Ministry on 17 July 1939:

'As things are at present, the gunners have no real confidence in their ability to use this equipment efficiently in war, and captains and crews have, I fear, little confidence in the ability of the gunners to defend them against destruction by enemy aircraft. Under these conditions it is unreasonable to expect these crews to press forward to their objectives in the face of heavy attack by enemy fighters.'

Even more crucial were the failings of the aircraft themselves. Back in 1935 the Blenheim had been a fleet-footed beast, but by the end of the decade, the Blenheim I was some 70mph slower than the Me109. In April 1939 the post of Officer Commanding No 101 Squadron was elevated to wing commander status, reflecting the growing number of personnel on 101; and just as Wg Cdr J. H. Hargroves was settling into the post his Squadron started to equip with the Blenheim IV. This aircraft sported a longer nose to improve the navigator's position, but it was no faster than its predecessor, and as soon as the RAF's eight-gun fighters became the mock adversary it became clear that the Blenheim had neither the speed, manoeuvrability nor armament to take on the Luftwaffe in daylight.

Operations under cover of darkness were the only alternative, but the problems of training bomber crews in night operations were never really faced in the prewar period. It was impossible for instance to simulate blackout conditions with no lights visible from the ground, and blind flying aids were in short supply. 'Consequently group commanders hardly dared to send up their crews on flights of any length at night or if the weather was not set fair. While all squadrons were required to do some night flying, only a small proportion of it was done in the dark, though it was generally recognised that in war time it would probably often have to be done.'*

Observations such as these only added weight to the view put forward by an air marshal at the time of Munich that, 'We have during the past few years been building up a front line Air Force which is nothing but a facade'. In an even more damning indictment of his 'shop window' force, Air Chief Marshal Ludlow-Hewitt reported that if a determined attack was made on Germany his

*From *The Strategic Air Offensive Against Germany* (Webster and Frankland; HMSO, 1961).

38
Squadron Blenheim IV over Orleans on the long-range flight over France on 11 July 1939. Note the longer nose of the Blenheim IV.

38

medium bomber force would be eliminated in only $3\frac{1}{2}$ weeks. In the end, the only Western Air Plan which was endorsed with any degree of enthusiasm involved the dropping of propaganda leaflets by night; it might have bored the Germans into surrender but would have achieved little else.

Not that nothing was done to try to improve matters in the last months of peace. Some 50 new air stations were authorised during the expansion period, many of which were built in eastern England to get as close as possible to northern Germany. Thus between 6 and 9 May 1939, '101 moved from Bicester to West Raynham, Norfolk, and transferred from No 1 Group to No 2 Group'.

As befitted part of a 'shop window' force, 101 also set about displaying its wares for the benefit of all potential customers. 'Massed formation practices' with 90 Squadron were in vogue in February, and then on 21 March the Squadron took part in a 'flypast' over Dover during the state visit of the French President, M. Lebrun. This Anglo-French entente progressed into a series of sorties over France to prove that Bomber Command was capable of operating into Europe.

'11 July 1939. On this occasion, No 101 Squadron led a formation of 18 aircraft (9 from 101 Squadron and 9 from 110 Squadron). The route followed was: Tangmere-Le Treport-Orleans-Le Mans-Barfleur-St Catherine's Point-Tangmere. The flight was without incident. The formation of 18 aircraft covered 615 miles in 3hr 20min.'

Finally in August 'the Squadron took part in major air exercises as part of the "enemy force". High and low level attacks were carried out on distant targets. The weather was consistently bad with rain and low cloud. All attacks were successful'.

On 12 August the Squadron detached to No 5 Armament Training School, Penrhos with nine aircraft and crews for their last peacetime live bombing and gunnery practice. Training proceeded satisfactorily but the international situation deteriorated to such an extent that at 0915hrs on 24 August, Readiness State C came into force. This involved the delivery of official green envelopes bearing the word 'MOBILISA-TION' — hastily overstamped as a security afterthought — to the main body of the RAF Reserve and Volunteer Reserve. The signing of the Anglo-Polish Treaty of mutual assistance the following day eased the situation slightly but, although 'Mobilisation' was cancelled, 'the Squadron was recalled to West Raynham in view of the National Emergency'. Flying training was to continue but personnel were briefed to hold themselves ready for recall from leave at six hours' notice.

Readiness State D came into force on 26 August whereby aircraft were to be dispersed around the perimeter of the airfield to minimise the destructive effects of possible air attack. Only essential air test flying was now permitted, and although bombs were not yet to be fused all personnel were recalled from leave and all aircraft made serviceable. Mobilisation began in earnest on 1 September as 'E' class Reservists (the reserve of all airmen in all trades with and without previous service in the RAF) started to arrive, and on 2 September 'the peacetime Squadron

records were closed in concurrence with Mobilisation Instructions'. The following day the Squadron heard that they were at war with Germany.

'3/9/39. No 101 Squadron on the declaration of war was stationed at West Raynham as part of No 81 Wing within No 2 Group. The Squadron Commander was Wing Commander J. H. Hargroves. Establishment — 22 officers and 207 airmen. Equipment — 21 Bristol Blenheim Mk IVs. Squadron Adjutant — Flying Officer D. S. Dawson. OC "A" Flight — Squadron Leader W. R. Hartwright; OC "B" Flight — Squadron Leader T. E. Morton, Today is the third day of mobilisation which is proceeding satisfactorily.'

As Blenheims from Wyton had attacked the German fleet in the morning, retaliation was feared likely and, in order to give potential Luftwaffe bombers less to aim at, at 1415hr eight of the Squadron aircraft and crews were hastily ordered to deploy to West Raynham's scatter aerodrome at Brize Norton.

Mobilisation was completed on 5 September 'except for certain items of equipment such as oxygen bottles, rubber dinghies, anti-gas clothing, field dressings etc'. Like all 2 Group squadrons, 101 had been ordered to stand by for 'ops' against German naval units off Wilhelmshaven and electricity and oil plants in the Ruhr, but after a few days a feeling of anticlimax set in. On 9 September after six days of sitting around the Squadron record still had 'nothing of importance to report'; two days later, the eight dispersed aircraft and crews were recalled from an uneventful sojourn at Brize Norton on the amusing grounds that 'the enemy might discover the Scatter Plan'. Whatever hopes there were of action always came to nought.

'12/9/39. Squadron standing by from 0700hr at 45min notice to operate against fleeting targets on North Sea. Squadron stood down at 2000hr without operating owing to bad weather conditions over North Sea.'

Higher authority soon saw the need to reduce this feverish pitch of inactivity:

'HQ 2 Groups 17/9/39. 1714 hr. The following message was received from Bomber Command: "In order to allow Groups to proceed with training with the minimum amount of interruptions, the Air Officer Commanding-in-Chief is willing for one squadron only to be regarded as at four hours' readiness for operations. Remaining squadrons may be regarded as free for training at 24 to 36 hours notice for operations."

'2008hr. Wings informed of the preceding message. The Squadron standing by at four hours' notice is to be known as the Duty Squadron. Thanks to this arrangement, satisfactory training programmes can be made.'

101 took their turn as 2 Group's Duty Squadron, not that it got them any nearer to the action.

'HQ 2 Group, 21/9/39, 2020hr. Orders issued to West Raynham to the effect that NINE aircraft from 101 Squadron are to attack German surface warships during daylight hours on 22 September. Aircraft to standby at 60 minutes' readiness from 0930hr.

'22/9/39. Nine aircraft of 101 Squadron stood by at 60 minutes' notice from 0930hr to attack fleeting targets at sea, but at 0940hr the Squadron was instructed to stand down and revert to four hours' readiness.'

Bomber Command's greatest problem at this time was that it lacked the strength to undertake any far-reaching bomber offensive. Of the 33 front-line squadrons available on the outbreak of war, 10 had gone to France with the British Expeditionary Force and the remainder were wholly equipped with aircraft that could do no more than pin-prick the outer fringes of German territory. Thus it was of paramount importance to conserve Bomber Command's limited manpower resources and not to fritter them away on all-out bombing of the enemy until the Command was fully equipped with four-engined 'heavy' bombers backed by adequate reserves. For this reason Bomber Command was initially authorised to do little beyond reconnoitring, dropping a few token bombs on enemy ships at sea, and depositing propaganda leaflets.

In the first year of the war, Bomber Command dropped some 74 million leaflets.

40
Blenheim IV merging with the fields below where hay making is in progress.

Known as 'bumphleteering', it was not a very popular pastime on 101 because crews felt that they were being exposed to a great deal of danger for not much purpose. So one day, while they dropped leaflets proclaiming in German that 'This might have been a bomb', one Squadron wag took along a huge brick, wrote on it in German, 'This might have been a leaflet', and heaved that out.

Unfortunately 101 Squadron's chances of glory were now to be reduced even further. One of the main problems with the Blenheim I had been its range — it could manage no more than 900 miles when bombed-up* and so it was decided that the Blenheim IV should have additional fuel tankage in the outer wings. However, this modification was only incorporated on the Bristol production line with the 81st Blenheim IV, and so the previous 80 had to be modified at station level. By 27 September, 101 was one of only two squadrons left with unmodified aircraft, bringing them down to what was known as Range State 1; it was a bad time to be so underendowed.

World War 2 transformed the whole social fabric of the Royal Air Force. Before 1939 it had consisted of a small, regular élite of officers and men, but now the gates were open to a growing influx of volunteers to swell the aircrew ranks. 'By the end of 1937,' wrote a young Scotsman by the name of Scrymageour Wedderburn, 'it was obvious to me that war was coming as sure as fate, so I decided that I would rather fight *my* war in the RAF, if they would have me, rather than in either of the other Services. I therefore applied for a Short Service Commission, was accepted for training, and set off in my £100 car (a Ford 8) for the Civil Flying School at Ansty.'

The Air Ministry decreed in *Air Ministry Pamphlet 101*, 5th edition of July 1940, that 'direct appointment commissions for flying duties are only made in exceptional circumstances. Entry into the General Duties (Flying) Branch is normally through the ranks... As vacancies occur for commissions, they are filled by promotion from the ranks, either on completion of flying training or subsequently.'

Having learned the basics of flying at Ansty and Little Rissington, Scrym Wedderburn was then sent down to the RAF depot, Uxbridge, 'where we were taught how to become officers and gentlemen in the space of two weeks. I always remember one senior

*From East Anglia, the approximate distance to Berlin and back was 1,100 miles; to Hamburg and back 900 miles; to Hamm and back 800 miles, and to the Ruhr and Cologne and back 700 miles. More distant targets such as Turin, Danzig, and Prague were way beyond the range of the 'medium' Blenheim.

officer summing it all up when he said, "Gentlemen, officers do not frequent pubs, they visit hotels!" '.

A newly commissioned officer received an outfit allowance of £40 in 1940 and if he was suitable for immediate posting to a service unit he was paid 14s 6d a day as a pilot officer. He was provided with free accommodation and rations and if he was separated from his family 'by the exigencies of the service', he received an extra 4s 6d per day to put a roof over their head. He also knew that if he was 'invalided in consequence of wound, injury or disease directly attributable to the conditions of service, he may be granted disability retired pay or other award calculated according to his rank and the degree of disablement. Disability retired pay will not be granted or continued if the degree of disablement is assessed at less than 20%.'

Having completed advanced flying training, Pilot Officer Wedderburn found himself posted to 101 at the beginning of 1940 to join other prospective bomber pilot, observers and WOp/AGs. Whereas Training Command had taught them the basic skills, it was left to Bomber Command to weld individuals into fighting crews and to familiarise them with the type of aircraft in which they would have to operate. Before the war such conversion training had been left to the front-line squadrons, but now they were unable to cope with both training and wartime operations so in September 1939 13 squadrons were 'rolled up' and made into advanced training centres. These Group Pool Squadrons (rechristened Operational Training Units (OTUs) in April 1940) did sterling work but the operational squadrons could only absorb a limited number of replacement crews at any one time; something had to be done with the remainder, and on 21 September 1939 Air Chief Marshal Ludlow-Hewitt made the following poposals to the Under Secretary of State for Air:

'There is a further requirement which has become apparent, namely the provision of reserve operational squadrons to absorb the output of Group Pool Stations in excess of requirements. It is most necessary to avoid cluttering up the training units with surplus crews. The syllabus of a Group Pool Station is the very minimum necessary to put crews into an elementary state of operational efficiency. It is most desirable that they should get more operational practice and experience if time is available, before going to operational squadrons.

'Hence it is necessary to provide a unit into which crews from Group Training Stations can go pending absorption by operational units. These intermediate units will be called Reserve Squadrons, and ... in each Reserve Squadron, a minimum of three of the most efficient and experienced crews in each flight will be retrained for training purposes . . .

'I propose to use the balance of the non-mobilising squadrons for this purpose. In the case of the Blenheims, I have had to put one squadron down from the operational first line for use as a second line reserve. This will bring the Blenheim organisation into line with the other Groups, namely six operational squadrons, one reserve squadron and three group pool squadrons.

'Any reduction in the strength of our Striking Force is, of course, undesirable, but it must be accepted if it is the only means of conserving our strength. Under existing circumstances it is necessary to take the long view.'

Thus, although all 2 Group's Blenheims would receive their long-range fuel tankage by October, someone had to be Reserve Squadron and it might as well be one of the Range State 1 units. 'HQ 2 Group, 25/9/39, 1255 hours. Duty Squadron is 101 Squadron which, with effect from today, is the Reserve Squadron for this Group and was ordered to stand down.'

101 eventually became a very large unit with 27 aircraft compared to the usual Blenheim squadron complement of 16 aircraft plus five reserves. Its size reflected the scale of the task foreseen in supporting the other six Blenheim squadrons in 2 Group, and for the next six months the Squadron spent its time converting new crews to operational flying and ferrying them around for all the other Blenheim units. 'On 101 pilots converted from the Blenheim I to the Blenheim IV and learned what it was really like to work operationally with navigators and WOp/AGs.' Not that life for the fledgling aircrew was without incident:

'2/11/39. A Blenheim IV piloted by Plt Off C. H. Keedwell crashed on landing after carrying out air firing exercises. The aircraft was written off.'

'14/11/39. The port engine of a Blenheim piloted by Plt Off T. R. Goodbody, with Sgt Eden and AC Jeffries as crew, failed in cloud on descending from a height test up to 20,000ft. Pilot ordered crew to abandon aircraft when at 2,000ft. Sgt Eden made a successful landing in a field at Sohan near Mildenhall with a torn parachute. The canopy was probably torn on the light series bomb carriers beneath the fuselage through pulling the rip cord too soon. The aircraft broke cloud and pilot ordered AC Jeffries not to jump. The pilot then landed successfully at Mildenhall aerodrome. Engine failure was probably due to hot air intake shutters being buckled due to backfire.'

Then at last something came along to really make the adrenalin flow. Back in August Germany had signed a non-aggression pact with the USSR which left Hitler free to make war in the west while the Soviet Union could absorb its Baltic neighbours. Once 'pacts' were imposed on Estonia, Latvia, and Lithuania, it was Finland's turn, but the Finns, with great courage, refused to accept Soviet demands on their sovereignty and at the end of November war broke out. Given the respective might of the two nations, the Soviets should have wrought a swift and crushing defeat, but initially the Finns not only held out but also inflicted humiliating losses on their aggressors. This David and Goliath struggle aroused considerable British sympathy for the gallant Finns, and though they were both at war with Germany, Britain and France were prepared to send an expeditionary force if Finland asked for it. In the event this joint initiative floundered over transit arrangements, but in February 1940 the Finnish defences finally cracked and the French government unilaterally decided to send 50,000 volunteers and 100 bombers to Finland. 'We could certainly not act on this scale . . . ,' wrote Winston Churchill in *The Second World War* (Cassell & Co, 1950); 'however, it was agreed to send 50 British bombers.'

As the Finns had acquired 18 Blenheim bombers after 1937, it made sense to supplement their air arm with similar aircraft. Unfortunately the Bristol Aeroplane Company did not have any aircraft immediately available for dispatch, so it was decided to use aircraft from the RAF's second line reserve.

On 16 February 1940, Bomber Command signalled HQ 2 Group that '12 short-nosed Blenheims are to be flown to Finland. Aircraft are to be flown by volunteer crews'. As 101 was non-operational, five Squadron crews — captained by Sqn Ldr J. F. Stephens, Sqn Ldr P. E. Meagher, Flt Lt E. J. Little and Sgt Hill (with Flg Off E. J. Palmer's crew in reserve) — had no hesitation in volunteering for some action. 'It was all cloak and dagger stuff,' recalled one Squadron member. 'The Blenheim did not have the range to fly direct, so the route was to be Bicester-Dyce-Stavanger-Basteras — finishing up at a Finnish aerodrome to be named later.' But Norway was then neutral, 'so we were all to go as civilians'. They were told to wear 'plain clothes' and they were to be 'relegated to the reserve without loss of pay'. The crews had to be given passports describing them as 'Bristol Engineers', but 'at the outbreak of war, our civilian clothes had been sent home, so all our passport photographs were taken with everyone wearing the only civilian jacket that anyone could find on the station'.

A formation of Squadron
Blenheims in 1940.

Subsequently it was announced publicly that '36 British volunteers have been engaged by the Finnish Government to ferry aircraft to Finland'. 'In time our civilian outfits were assembled, and our forged passports stowed in the Intelligence Officer's safe. We were due to take off in two days, taking our bomb loads with us, when a signal came direct from the Air Ministry telling us to hold everything. The whole exercise was called off a few days later when Finland capitulated.'

So it was back to the old routine of bombing practice and formation training, for it was felt that the unescorted Blenheims could only survive if they massed together for mutual protection.

However, once France fell and the Germans started massing across the Straits of Dover, the RAF could no longer afford the luxury of reserve squadrons. Too many good men had been lost over France and so, on 4 July 1940, 101 went to war at last when three aircraft and crews were sent to attack oil targets in northern Germany.

'First crew Flg Off Messervy, Sgt Forgeard and Sgt Whiteman carried out first run over target but bombs failed to release, so in spite of heavy fire pilot made second run up at 1725hrs to drop 4×250lb bombs in salvo from 2,000ft. Bombs burst large pipeline at Ostermoor between fuel tanks and Kiel Canal, and obliterated scene.

'Second crew returned owing to lack of cloud cover. Third crew, captained by CO, Wg Cdr Hargroves, failed to return.'

Official recognition of the Squadron's new status came through the following day.

AIR MINISTRY
'SECRET   LONDON SW1
S.5457/DCAS   5 July 1940
To: Air Officer Commanding-in-Chief
    Bomber Command.
'Sir,
    'I am directed to say that, in view of the present critical state of the war, you are requested to convert all Reserve squadrons in your Command to first line operational squadrons.
2. The functions heretofore carried out by the Reserve squadrons will have to be shared between the operational training units and the first-line squadrons.

I am, Sir,
Your obedient Servant

Douglas
Air Vice-Marshal
Deputy Chief of Air Staff'

However, the Squadron's experiences the day before served to illustrate the problems facing Blenheim units in the summer of 1940. For a start, the loss of an experienced crew such as the Wing Commander's underlined the question of Blenheim vulnerability in daylight. Lacking either speed, manoeuvrability, or ceiling, the Blenheim's only hope of avoiding destruction lay in its armament, yet initially the turret was only endowed with a single machine gun which stood little chance against modern wing cannons. Not that the workman could always blame his tools:

'19/9/40. One aircraft took off at 0600hrs to attack Dunkirk. This aircraft returned

owing to lack of cloud cover. Two aircraft took off at 0640 hours and 0730 hours respectively to shoot down drifting balloons in Norfolk area. Balloons were located but shooting was not successful.'

Where possible Blenheims still sought sanctuary in darkness, but as the situation in Western Europe became desperate, the AOC 2 Group deemed it 'essential that the destructive efforts of our night bombing operations over Germany should be continued throughout daylight by sporadic attacks on the same objectives. *The intention is to make attacks only when cloud cover gives adequate security.*'

As a result the second 101 crew to visit Kiel on 4 July was probably wise to return when their main means of defence failed to materialise, whereas Wing Commander Hargroves probably pressed on for too long and paid the penalty.

As German preparations for the Battle of Britain got under way, Bomber Command's attentions moved nearer home, to quote from Operational Instruction No 38 dated 3 July 1940: 'The enemy are using airfields and landing grounds in France, Belgium and Holland ... The intention is to destroy as many aircraft as possible on the ground thus forcing the enemy to withdraw. Airfields are to be attacked by sections escorted by fighters, or sections of individual aircraft using cloud cover when definite information is received from fighter reconnaissance.' The latter was something of a let-out clause because Fighter Command has its own duties to perform in 1940 — thus there were no fighter

43

42
'Bomb train' of 250lb GP bombs and incendiaries on its way out to the Blenheim dispersal for loading. *IWM*

43
Observer at his position in the Blenheim nose. *IWM*

escorts available when 101 flew off to attack airfields in northern France and Belgium, and Squadron Blenheims had to run the gauntlet of the German air defences alone by day when their crews were sent to bomb the long-range guns on the Pas de Calais or invasion barges in the Channel ports. It was the price that had to be paid in a crisis. 'You must bear in mind,' signalled the AOC, 'that your forces may have to play a most important part in repelling an invasion of this country, and you should be prepared at short notice to divert your squadrons to the attack of the invading enemy force at ports of departure and subsequently at sea, and points of landing in this country. To meet the threat of invasion, twelve aircraft (at each station) are to stand by every morning at 20 minutes notice from twilight to sunrise.' These daily stand bys in Squadron rotation did nothing to ease the Blenheim crews off the horns of their dilemma. If the skies were clear enough to see the target properly, they were probably clear enough for the enemy to detect the intrusion. On the other hand, if the skies were cloudy enough to prevent detection or destruction, they probably restricted visibility sufficiently to thwart accurate navigation and bomb delivery. After all the recommended minimum safe weapon delivery height to avoid bomb blast was 1,000ft for 250lb bombs and 700ft for 40lb weapons, and as attacks from great heights reduced accuracy, this kept the Blenheim crews right in the optimum firing bracket for the anti-aircraft guns which ringed the invasion ports. Despite the gravity of the national situation therefore, Blenheim vulnerability was such that on 14 August 1940 'the Squadron ceased to operate by day and commenced night operations'.

Yet even with inadequate aircraft, 101 Squadron crews still gave of their all. 'On the night of 9 September 1940, Plt Off Bicknell and crew were ordered to carry out an attack on Antwerp aerodrome. Whilst flying across the North Sea, their port engine gave trouble and finally stopped completely just before reaching the Dutch coast.

'The Captain decided to abandon the original target and bomb Haamstad aerodrome instead — this was located by his observer and bombed from 5,000ft.

'On return journey, the aircraft commenced to lose height and continued to do so despite every precaution taken by crew. Before reaching English coast and flying just above the water, the aircraft started to lose speed and captain decided that a landing on the sea was necessary. He warned crew and landed in every rough sea near a trawler. Pilot and observer forced a way through broken perspex and then went to assistance of air gunner. He was unconscious and trapped in cockpit but in spite of heavy sea, pilot and observer struggled to try and release him until aircraft sank five minutes later.

'Pilot and observer picked up by trawler some 30 minutes later. Pilot was cut about head and observer unconscious. The crew had already carried out a number of successful raids over enemy country and have always shown greatest determination, skill and coolness in reaching and attaining their objectives.'

On 29 September, 'Plt Off N. Bicknell and Sgt W. B. Gingell were awarded the DFC and DFM respectively for their courage and devotion to duty in operations against the enemy on the night of 9 September'.

There was no let-up in the tempo of night operations against the invasion ports and the lines of communication that supported them; 101 launched six aircraft on the night of 31 August/1 September alone, but such concentrated effort only resurrected the old problem of finding precise targets in darkness after a lengthy flight with very limited navigational aids.

'4/9/40. Operations — Night. Four aircraft took off to attack Hamm marshalling yards and one to attack Berck-sur-Mer aerodrome. Owing to searchlight activity and poor visibility, no aircraft succeeded in locating Hamm.* Alternative targets attacked were — a ship by one aircraft, an unidentified aerodrome by one aircraft, a cluster of lights by another aircraft, and Berck-sur-Mer by two aircraft.'

'8/9/40. Operations — Night. Ten aircraft took off to attack Boulogne Harbour and shipping in harbour. Five aircraft did not reach target area owing to bad weather conditions and returned to base. Three aircraft succeeded in reaching target, bombs released but results unobserved. Two aircraft and crews did not return; one was captained by Flt Lt Palmer who had been with this Squadron since May 1937.'

Nevertheless, there were successes to sustain morale:

'18/9/40'. Twelve aircraft were ordered to attack Dunkirk barge concentrations and to complete two raids during the hours of darkness. The first series of raids commenced at 1930hr and were completed at 2300hr. The aircraft proceeded in the second series of raids commencing at 2359hr and ending at 0340hr on 19 September. All aircraft attacked target under ideal weather conditions with satisfactory results.

'19/9/40. Following telegram of congratulations received:

'To OC West Raynham. From AOC-in-C Bomber Command. I have noticed with much pleasure the extreme keenness and efficiency behind your recent night operations which reflect great credit on all concerned with flying, arming and maintenance.' The AOC 2 Group also sent his congratulations to 'the CO and crews of 101 Squadron for their efforts last night and to the ground personnel who effected the rapid turn round'.

As winter approached though, the crews had to face another foe besides the Luftwaffe, and that was the weather.

---

*Hamm was a natural target in that it possessed the largest and best equipped railway marshalling yards in Europe. It was of crucial importance to the German war effort because it not only maintained and reinforced the invasion forces in France and the Low Countries but it was also the focal point for the supply of raw materials to and armaments from Germany's great industrial centre, the Ruhr. The main consideration here though was its sheer size - Clapham Junction would have been swallowed several times over in the Hamm yards and its connections which covered an area four miles long by about $\frac{1}{4}$ mile wide — yet the Blenheim crews could not even find it.

'2/3 October 1940. One crew (Plt Off Brown, Sgt Collis and Sgt Loughlin) took off at 2331hr. They did not succeed in locating target owing to 10/10 cloud extending from 1,000ft to 15,000ft. Severe icing conditions encountered with this aircraft causing pilot to abandon task and return to base with bombs.'

'20/10/40. Five aircraft dispatched to one target and four aircraft to another target with 4 × 250lb bombs. Three crews managed to bomb first target at heights between 7,000 and 11,000ft. One aircraft returned to base owing to illness of pilot and one aircraft unable to locate target after search lasting 20min, so crew released bombs "safe" in sea and returned to base. A ground mist covered aerodrome during this night's ops, causing some considerable difficulty to pilots locating aerodrome. All flares were finally illuminated ie Money flares, gooseneck flares, hooded gooseneck flares and glim lamps.* All aircraft finally landed safely on aerodrome. Some anxiety was felt for last two aircraft until they both arrived over aerodrome boundary on their approach to flare path in line astern with an interval of approximately 50 yards. They did land successfully in formation however.'

But the most insidious enemy of all was the cold. Time and time again aircraft returned because a crew member was ill, and usually it was because he was sick with cold. 'It is cold of a different kind to that experienced on the ground. It seems to bite into you and attacks your will-power making you physically and mentally incapable of doing anything except going to sleep. The half-open turret in which the gunner sat was the coldest place in the aircraft and after a time I found it difficult just to reel out the trailing aerial to pass the relevant code to the ground station to prevent us being shot down.'

Later, electrically heated suits would be provided, but in the winter of 1940 crews had to make do as best they could. 'Having put on as much clothing as possible and still able to walk, I now added inner and outer flying suits and three pairs of gloves — silk, woollen and leather. I collected my gas-operated Vickers machine gun, plodded out to the waiting lorry and was driven to our faithful Blenheim.'

At the dispersal the crews were met by groundcrew who were often frozen

*Although 101 had been operating at night as far back as 1917, such was the unpreparedness of the RAF for night wartime operations that, apart from these flares, almost every other airfield lighting aid had to be improvised. Thus, on many occasions, two motor cars were positioned 100 yards either side of the up-wind end of the runway to act as touch-down markers whilst an early attempt at providing an approach funnel consisted of four goosenecks taken out by a lorry.

FORTUNA II (RIGHT) AN

44
Although this photograph was taken from an aircraft belonging to 18 Squadron, 101's one-time stablemate at West Raynham, it gives an interesting view from the gunner's position of a Blenheim. The blur in the foreground is the single gun barrel of a Vickers gas-operated machine gun with drum feed. Squadron aircraft sported yellow stripes on their trail planes for a time to catch the gunner's eye because, despite the fitment of an interrupter gear, it was still possible to shoot off the Blenheim's tail.

themselves after hours spent preparing the aircraft on the open airfield. Everyone stood patiently by as the swaddled air gunner struggled to fix his machine gun on to its mounting, and then the crew taxied out to await a 'green' for take-off. 'We were away. A watery haze spread over the countryside ... Like a great strip of silver paper the North Sea hove into view. It looked cold, unfriendly, and I always had the feeling that once you started to fly over it you cut your last link with everything that meant safety and warmth.' (Quoted from *2 Group RAF* by M. J. F. Bowyer (Faber, 1974).

Now that they were airborne, the freezing conditions became even more intense.

'The clouds congeal with ice and snow as the aircraft passes through them; this collects, often to a thickness of six inches, on the surfaces of the planes and windscreens, cutting off the crew still further from the outside world. In the form of fine rime it penetrates through the interstices of the aircraft, covering the crew with white powder and freezing on clothes and equipment.' Sometimes thick ice formed inside the cockpit — instruments froze, oxygen bottles were known to freeze to crew fingers, and on occasions the oxygen system failed too. 'Worst of all, ice accumulates on the controls, jamming them and rendering the aircraft temporarily uncontrollable. Despite the fact that the majority of these aircraft are equipped with de-icing gear it has proved often ineffective in conditions of this kind. Neither will heating equipment stand up against temperatures of −20° to −30° Centigrade.' (Quoted from *The RAF in Action*, Adam & Charles Black, 1940).

Given all this, it is remarkable that there was never any lack of men to fly the Blenheim on 101. 'When I finished my WOps course at Yatesbury,' recalled Jim Marshall, 'you stayed on the ground if you remained just a WOp. Men who wanted to fly had to do the air gunners' course, and I remember an air commodore who visited Yatesbury saying that the operational life of Blenheim aircrew was five hours. But there was never any shortage of volunteers — men cried if they weren't accepted as aircrew.'

On 25/26 October the Squadron hit German targets in the Cap Gris Nez area. 'All aircraft located the gun positions and dropped their bombs. This attack was carried out for its nuisance value and Squadron aircraft were over the target area for 30 minutes and released their bombs singly, to be followed over the target by another squadron.' If the object was to arouse the enemy, it succeeded admirably:

'27/10/40. West Raynham. 1815hr. Six enemy aircraft made two attacks dropping 50 bombs (50 kilos and 250 kilos). Aircraft believed to be Ju88s; six Blenheims, one Battle and one Tutor damaged, all aircraft capable of repair by unit. One hangar hit, one bay blown in, offices and crew room destroyed. Ground defences opened fire immediately at low flying enemy aircraft but were themselves machine-gunned by raiders. Aerodrome rendered U/S (unserviceable) by bomb craters.'

The Luftwaffe also sought revenge on West Raynham's satellite airfield at Massingham just up the road.

'27/10/40. Massingham Satellite, 1800hr. Three enemy aircraft, (believed Ju88s) made three attacks. Ten bombs dropped. One Blenheim destroyed and 11 Blenheims damaged — capable of repair by unit. One hut destroyed and one hut damaged. Landing ground rendered U/S by craters. Casualties — four killed, three seriously injured, four minor injuries. All aircraft attacked below 300ft — one aircraft known to have been brought down by ground defences. Operational ability of Squadron not affected.'

These raids immediately led to a decision to disperse the aircrews away from the airfield for their own safety, and on 9 November, 'Weasenham Hall was taken over by this Squadron to accommodate flying personnel. A provisional "house warming" was held during the evening'.

But such light relief could not disguise the fact that the winter of 1940/41 was no picnic for Blenheim bomber crews.

'24/11/40. Target — Wanne Eickel oil refinery in the Ruhr. Owing to 8/10 to 10/10 cloud cover over target, it was only with considerable difficulty that five crews were able to bomb target area. Results could not be observed although bomb flashes were seen under cloud. One aircraft crashed near West Raynham village. The lock nut on the spider

in the reduction gear of starboard engine of this aircraft became loose, causing reduction gear casing to be churned away. Airscrew shaft and airscrew left engine on return over North Sea and pilot (Sgt Redmond) returned on one engine. He located aerodrome but crashed during circuit of airfield, pilot and gunner (Sgt Woodruff) received minor head injuries but air observer (Sgt Green) received fractured skull and is dangerously ill.

'Two other aircraft abandoned task — bombs brought back — one owing to ice accretion and one because fixed aerial broke away from mast and wrapped around tail plane. One aircraft overdue and presumed lost. The crew took off at 1703hr, were heard on R/T at 1905hr, and then no further communication was received.'

'26/11/40. Sgt Observer Green died today as a result of injuries received.'

'16/12/40. Target — Mannheim. Seven aircraft detailed and three aircraft attacked primary target, bombs seen to burst in target area. One aircraft unable to locate target and bombed small town with railway at 2310hr from 12,000ft. Bomb bursts observed in town but railway missed by 100yd. One aircraft abandoned task owing to sickness of WOp/AG.

'Two crews were lost — Sgt Plt Clarke's aircraft was heard sending SOS from St Quentin, France. W/T fix passed to aircraft but no further communication received.

'Sgt Plt Skipworth had broadcast SOS, and a W/T fix and courses to steer were given to crew. Aircraft crashed at Fairlight Place Farm, just east of Hastings, at 0235hr on 17/12/40, and burnt out. All crew were killed.

'Three more aircraft got lost on return flight. Plt Off Brown and crew landed wheels-up in a field at Cornwood near Plymton, Devon. Plt Off Hill and crew ran out of petrol off Plympton and abandoned aircraft — all crew landed safely. Flt Lt Graham and crew landed at Christchurch aerodrome without a flare path. Aircraft landed without sustaining any damage. Wing Commander Singer was only pilot to land at base after proceeding to target.'

In fact, Wg Cdr N. C. Singer continued to command 101 right through to the end of his tour on 31 March 1941 when he was posted to HQ 2 Group. Perhaps survivors like him survived because they lived long enough to learn when to press on and when not to push their luck too far. Fortune certainly smiled on the favoured at times:

'13/12/40. Primary target not attacked as cloud cover proved insufficient, so crew (captained by Sqn Ldr Cree, OC B Flight) turned for Flushing. When flying at 500ft, pilot saw ship of between 800 and 1,000 tons in entrance to Flushing in vicinity of Jouteland. Beam attack made from about 400ft with two 250lb bombs and 13 40lb bombs. A steep turn was made and it was seen that the stick had straddled the ship. The ship was down at the stern and listing to port with steam escaping. Ship did not open fire as it appears they were taken by surprise as aircraft came out of broken cloud at 500ft.'

But Lady Luck could also be a fickle mistress, and she was at her cruellest when crews, mentally and physically exhausted as well as frozen stiff, had to land back at base in cloud and darkness after a five-hour raid into Germany.

'24/9/40. Aircraft crashed one mile south of Swaffham at 0530hr. This aircraft exploded and caught fire on impact with the ground. Sgts Lorimer, Booth and Simms killed.'

'27/9/40. One aircraft (Sgt Turner — pilot) crashed on landing, 350yd to right of landing lights. Two aircraft on ground damaged.'

'30/31 October 1940. One aircraft crashed at Coleby, Lincs, and all crew were killed.' Squadron morale was not helped by the fact that the Blenheim had a reputation as a bad aircraft to evacuate in the event of a crash.

By the end of 1940, 101 Squadron had lost 27 officers and NCOs killed in action, but for those who came back there was a welcome breakfast of eggs and bacon and a thorough intelligence debriefing before drifting off into the fitful sleep of exhaustion. For the fortunate few though, there were also the honours and awards.

'23/10/40. Plt Off C. R. Brown awarded DFC. Sgt (now Plt Off) Collis awarded DFM. Sgt Loughlin awarded DFM. This crew has shown great skill and determination in locating their targets and pressing home their attacks in spite of encountering heavy AA fire on nearly every occasion. A telegram of congratulations received from AOC 2 Group.'

But for the unlucky ones, like Sgt Skipworth's crew who died on 16 December, it was left to the Recovery Inspector to pick up the pieces.

'No 49 Maintenance Unit, Faygate.
AIRCRAFT COLLECTION ORDER.
Date 18/12/40
To. Messrs NICHOLLS & CO (BRIGHTON) LTD
100 NORTH ROAD, BRIGHTON.
Please arrange to collect immediately and dispose of aircraft as follows:-
TYPE & DESCRIPTION. BLENHEIM.
P.6953   M.U's SERIAL NO. B/10
LOCATION.   FAIRLIGHT.
HASTINGS.   CATEGORY. E.
DISPOSAL INSTRUCTIONS: To Faygate
Confirmation of phone message.
Ref CSO/FAY/10125.

(Driver's copy of this order to be delivered to the Receiving Depot with aircraft).
Superintendent, CSO
No 49 Maintenance Unit, RAF
at Faygate, Horsham, Sussex'

But even bravery was not enough in the long run — '31/3/41. Plt Off Brown DFC, Plt Off Collis DFM and Sgt Loughlin DFM reported missing after raid on Wilhelmshaven.'

Nor did the experience that usually went with senior rank necessarily mean much in the lottery of Blenheim operations, as Wg Cdr Singer's successor found out within four days of taking over command of 101.

'3/4/41. Eleven aircraft detailed to attack Brest, taking off at 1915hr from West Raynham and landing back at Boscombe Down. Three aircraft reached target and landed without difficulty at Boscombe. Four aircraft returned to West Raynham on considering weather conditions hazardous. One aircraft landed South Cerney owing to weather and poor visibility. One aircraft landed at Shrewton owing to adverse weather. One aircraft crashed at Warmwell on return from target — all crew killed. The remaining aircraft was missing and the crew — Wg Cdr Addenbrooke, air observer Plt Off Fenton and WOp Sgt Blomely — presumed lost. No results of bombing were observed by the three aircraft which attacked target owing to cloud cover and ground haze.'

If the Blenheim crews were chancing their arm in September 1939, they were certainly pushing their luck over occupied Europe in the spring of 1941. Protection was the answer, and now that the threat of invasion had receded it was decided to send fighter-escorted bombers on daylight raids against 'fringe' targets in France. Any bombing results they achieved would be a bonus — the main aim was to entice German fighters to battle in the hope that this would prevent the Luftwaffe from either renewing daylight attacks on Britain or deploying aircraft to the impending assault on Greece. These forays were known as 'Circuses' and 101 led one on 17 April.

'17/4/41. Weather — light haze, cloud 4/10 at 3,000ft. Visibility — 3-4 miles. Two boxes of six 101 aircraft, together with six aircraft from 18 Squadron, carried out formation attack on Cherbourg with fighter cover. Course was set at 1600hr from Tangmere — formation in three boxes of six aircraft led by OC 101 Sqn, Wg Cdr McDougall.* First six aircraft attacked

*Wg Cdr J. McDougall took command of 101 following the death of Wg Cdr Addenbrooke. He remained on the Squadron until 5 May 1941 when he was posted to 90 Squadron.

45
101 Squadron Blenheim dives for the sea. *IWM*

46
Blenheim runs in at 50ft to attack enemy shipping. *IWM*

target at 1633hr, followed by other two formations at two-minute intervals. Good view of target obtained by all bombing leaders, and majority of bombs were seen to burst in target area. All aircraft returned safely to base.' As was customary the bombs were released on their leader's signal and, although this was the first time that as many as three boxes were employed on a Circus, the enemy fighters still did not react to the increased bait.

With the conclusion of the Battle of Britain and the dispersal of the invasion barges, at the beginning of March 1941 Prime Minister Churchill directed that the Battle of the Atlantic was now to have full priority with Bomber Command concentrating on naval targets. Coupled with this was the tightening of the sea blockade around Germany, and orders were given to halt the movement of all coastal shipping between the Brittany peninsula and Germany. Any Axis vessel that was sighted in these waters was to be sunk, and the AOC 2 Group, Air Vice-Marshal Stevenson, was ordered to see that this was done irrespective of cost.

On 24 April Sqn Ldr R. O. M. Graham led a detachment of nine Squadron aircraft down to Manston in Fighter Command's No 11 Group. Now assured of immediate escort, the Flight set about implementing 'Channel Stop', an exercise designed to close the Straits of Dover to enemy shipping by daylight while MTBs continued the task by night.

The trouble with the enemy ships which plied these coastal waters was that they were generally small, so the maximum number of available aircraft had to be launched to make a concentrated attack. Moreover, the enemy protected his merchantmen with flak ships, each of which had tremendous fire power, so surprise was essential and this could only be achieved by flying very low over the sea. This was no picnic for the Blenheim crews because the visibility at low level could be very poor and a momentary lapse of concentration could lead to a watery grave, but as wise Axis merchantmen clung to the European coast, low flying was the only way to avoid radar detection and the adjacent fighter and anti-aircraft battery protection that the early warning stations could summon up. To lessen the odds against them therefore, Squadron crews were briefed to remain in their allocated areas for only a few minutes, even though fighter escorts were supposed to keep the enemy off the backs of the Blenheim crews while they concentrated on their destructive errand. The laid down instructions were for the Blenheim formation to fly extremely low in line abreast — 50ft was the maximum suggested altitude though many flew lower — at the start of the 'beat'. On arrival at the allotted start line, usually some 30 miles from the coast, the Blenheims would fly towards the coast until the leader was approximately three miles from the shoreline, whereupon he led the formation parallel to the coast for three minutes before turning home. Any ship that saw them would surely report them, so the order was to sink the first vessel sighted, and indeed any ship in the beat area, with the minimum delay. With these tactics in mind, the Manston detachment set about its business.

'27/4/41. Weather fine and clear with good visibility. Three aircraft from 101 Squadron detachment at Manston carried out attack on enemy shipping off Calais at 1100hr. These aircraft encountered nine trawlers and attacked them in trail from 50ft with 12 250lb bombs fused for 11sec delay. Much opposition from shore batteries and machine-gun fire from ships encountered, as a result of which one of Blenheims shot down — crew posted as missing. Other two aircraft claimed to have sunk one trawler and damaged another. One of these aircraft was engaged by Me109 but not hit. Fighter escort of six Spitfires from 74 Squadron, Manston, was provided.'

'29/4/41. Weather cloudy with bright periods. Visibility moderate. Squadron detachment at Manston sent out three aircraft to attack four merchant vessels — one large and three small — reported in Zuydcoote Pass steaming towards Dunkirk. An interception made three miles off Nieuport at 0908hr and large merchant vessel and one small ship (of 2,000 tons and 500 tons respectively) were attacked from 50ft with four 250lb bombs. No results observed by bombers owing to low level of attack and violent evasive action which had to be taken to avoid flak, but it is believed that the large ship was hit and damaged. A gun crew on one ship put out of action by rear gunner. High fighter cover provided by 12 Hurricanes of 609 Squadron, Biggin Hill, and close fighter escort by six Spitfires of 74 Squadron, Manston, who beat off three Me 109s. However, one Blenheim (Captain — Sgt Pilot Deane) was badly damaged on both wings, fuselage and rudder, and port engine also damaged. Observer (Sgt Jordan) was wounded in the elbow but in spite of all this, aircraft made a safe landing at base.'

There was nothing easy about shipping strikes even with fighter protection.

'3/5/41. Weather fine and clear, visibility good. Six aircraft from Squadron detachment at Manston, with close support of 12 Spitfires from 74 Squadron, took off at 1330 hours to intercept steamer of 2,000 tons heavily escorted by four trawler-type vessels and five E-boats. Leader of first section of three aircraft returned to base at 1340hr owing to U/S rear guns*; his No 2 and 3 aircraft turned off track near ETA (estimated time of arrival) to attack what they thought to be target but proved to be two wrecks off La Panne. These two aircraft returned to base with their bombs.

'Second section sighted and intercepted target, a motor vessel (MV) of 2,500 tons, heavily escorted and positioned two miles west of Ostend. The Section leader (Pilot Officer Brown) scored three hits on large vessel and claimed it sunk whilst other two aircraft hit two escort vessels and claimed them as sunk. All ships heavily machine-gunned. Height of attack was 50ft, dropping four 250 pounders with 11-second delay.

'Again at 1930hr, six aircraft in two sections of three made rendezvous with 12 Spitfires of 74 Squadron at Dungeness and set course to intercept convoy estimated to be eight miles SSW of Boulogne. Convoy, consisting of large motor vessel (5-6,000 tons), smaller MV of 2,000 tons and two flak ships found 1½ miles south of DR (dead reckoning) position and formation, led by Sqn Ldr Graham, went in to attack each ship by sections at 1956hr. Attack pressed home in face of concentrated and accurate fire from ships, their escort vessels, and from French coast. Larger ship hit just above the beam with four 250lb bombs and was observed later to emit a violent explosion and catch fire. This vessel claimed as sunk by formation leader, No 2 and No 3 of whose section also scored near misses.

'The second section attacked smaller MV and although thought she was probably hit,

*By now, Squadron Blenheims carried twin Browning guns with higher rates of fire and continuous belt feed, but survival aids such as these together with armour plating and self-sealing tanks also increased aircraft all-up-weight which in turn reduced performance still further.

this was not confirmed. The Section leader (Plt Off Brown) was hit by fire from ship and last seen heading for French coast on fire. No 2 of this section (Sgt Deane) also hit and was observed by one of fighter escort to go down in sea bearing 110° Dungeness at 10 miles. Pilot and navigator seen to get out of aircraft but although Air Sea Rescue service carried out search very soon afterwards, no trace of them was found. No 3 of this section also hit in fuselage and port engine, but made safe return to base.'

The Manston detachment returned to West Raynham on 9 May. For their outstanding efforts in making 'Channel Stop' as good as its name, Sqn Ldr Graham, Flt Lt McLaren and Plt Off Redmond, were awarded the DFC, and Flt Sgt Cooke received the DFM. Life in their absence had not been dull. 'I did three daylight low level shipping strikes,' recalled Sgt H. L. Mackay, a Wop/AG, 'and although we flew in formation on all of them for protection, they were still very grim. My first mission was not only terrifying but also we were the only aircraft out of three to return. In my fearfully paralysed state, I sent a request back to base in *very* shaky morse for an ambulance and doctor to meet us. On landing, I was met by an angry and abusive Squadron signals officer who asked what the hell I was doing sending it all in "long" and thereby wasting signal time. The fact that five of us were sent direct to West Raynham from gunnery school without an OTU so that I didn't know many of the operational procedures didn't bother him at all. I did notice that in his outburst he had a very chronic "twitch" — a bad case of ops fatigue.

'Incidentally, of the five of us who joined 101 together, four were lost on ops within three weeks. Perhaps I was destined for a charmed life!'

To lighten the load Squadron crews periodically participated in high level 'Circus' operations which all agreed were 'a piece of cake compared with those low level strikes'. One particularly appealing idea to emanate from the planning staffs was the blocking of the Kiel Canal, and on 8/9 May five 101 Squadron crews were ordered to attack Holtenau at the Baltic end of the Canal. 'Four of these aircraft, although carrying out correct identification procedures when returning to base, were fired on by a large convoy on crossing the English coast near Cromer. All managed to return to base. The remaining aircraft did not attack primary target owing to intense searchlight activity.' Like many that had gone before, it was not a particularly war-winning raid, and so there were few tears shed when it was announced that this was to be the last mission that 101 would ever mount with the Blenheim.

The Wellington Era

In the middle of April 1941, while one flight commander was leading 'Channel Stop' from Manston, the other, Sqn Ldr Cree, was somewhat more comfortably employed on detachment at No 14 OTU Benson, gleaning 'information on conversion to Wellington aircraft'. By the end of the month, Wellington flying was taking place at West Raynham and on 11 June 1941, Sqn Ldr Jones and Sgt Caunt captained the first two 101 Squadron Wellingtons to be sent on an operational mission. Both crews successfully attacked the docks at Rotterdam, dropping a total of 6,000lb of high explosive (HE) bombs, before returning safely. 'It is worthy of mention,' recorded the Adjutant proudly, 'that 101 Squadron carried out their last operational sortie on Blenheim aircraft on 9 May 1941 and their first operation on Wellington aircraft on 11 June 1941 after only one month in conversion, during which period only one aircraft was very slightly damaged while night flying'.

Squadron Wellingtons hit Germany, or Cologne to be more precise, for the first time on 21 June 1941, and thereafter 101 settled down to employing their new aircraft operationally.

'27/6/41. NFTS carried out during day. (Night Flying Tests — during the day before each night raid, all aircraft designated for duty would be flown around the aerodrome for about half an hour to test all the systems.) Operations — of the nine aircraft that took off tonight, four crews successfully attacked Bremen. (Captains — Plt Off Todd, Sgt Caunt, Plt Off Redmond and Plt Off Rickinson.) Of the rest, Sqn Ldr Jones located primary target but bombs failed to release — he subsequently successfully attacked Den Helder. Sgt Fooks abandoned primary target owing to adverse weather conditions and attacked Oldenburg. Sqn Ldr Colenso and Sgt Taylor abandoned primary task owing to adverse weather conditions and each attacked Den Helder instead. One crew set out to attack Dunkirk (Captain — Plt Off Hardie) but they abandoned task owing to technical failure. They returned to base, changed aircraft and took off again within 45min of landing but were recalled by Group. Sgt Plts Taylor, Hart, Cook, Caunt and Allen granted commissions in the rank of pilot officer on probation.'

The Squadron mounted seven operations (or 55 sorties) with its new aircraft from

47
Wg Cdr D. R. Biggs — OC 101 Squadron from 16 May 1941 to 14 January 1942 — with his officers outside Weasenham Hall in the early summer of 1941. The lady seated in the middle was the owner of the Hall, and she was known somewhat cryptically to the Squadron as 'The Pheasant'.

47

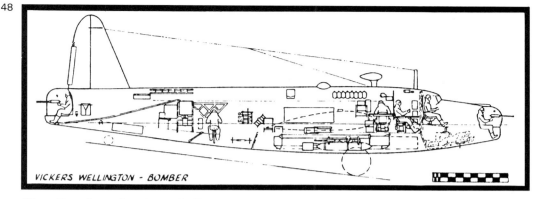

VICKERS WELLINGTON - BOMBER

West Raynham, but it made little sense to keep a solitary Wellington unit in 2 Group, so on 6 July 101 moved to Oakington near Cambridge and transferred to 3 Group the following day. Two nights later 101 was back in business when it detailed 11 aircraft for operations.

The Wellington I was certainly a welcome improvement over the Blenheim in that it could carry twice the bomb load over nearly twice the range, ie 2,000lb to Danzig or northern Italy. The Wellington was also superior in terms of defensive armament — 101 Squadron was equipped with Wellington ICs and these carried a pair of .303in Browning machine guns in the hydraulically-powered nose and tail turrets, plus beam guns in the midship position. Barnes Wallis' famous geodetic construction also endowed the Wellington with a considerable reserve of strength, enabling some aircraft to return home with appalling battle damage.

Nevertheless, despite its strengths in comparison with what had gone before, the Wimpy (in view of its rotund, 'well fed' appearance, the Wellington was soon likened by its air and groundcrews to Popeye's stout, Hamburger-eating friend, 'J. Wellington Wimpy') was still too lumbering and under-powered for comfort, and its drawbacks were underlined when it came to attacking those targets that were either so precise or so important that they could only be profitably

bombed in daylight. Two of these were the battlecruisers *Scharnhorst* and *Gneisenau* which had wrought havoc in the North Atlantic between January and March 1941, and in order to curtail their future activities it was decided to bomb them in a surprise daylight raid on 24 July. Even so, in order to stand a reasonable chance of hitting such relatively small and well-defended targets, it was considered necessary to dispatch between 140 and 150 heavy and medium bombers against them (the Wellington was classed as a medium bomber).

The plan was to open the attack with unescorted Fortresses operating at high altitude, followed 15 minutes later by 18 Hampdens closely escorted by long-range Spitfires. It was hoped that these would draw off the German fighter cover, leaving the main force of Wellingtons and heavy bombers free to attack, without escort, in the shortest possible time. But the best laid plans often seem to go astray — at the last minute the *Scharnhorst* moved to La Pallice and so the heavy bombers were redirected there.

The Fortresses and escorted Hampdens went in as arranged, but unfortunately they did not exhaust the defences by the time the main force arrived. 'Sqn Ldr Colenso led the 101 Wellington element, supported by crews captained by Sgt Fisher, Flt Lt Craig and Plt Off Rickinson.' This section had to keep station to enjoy the protection of mutual fire-

No. 101 Squadron.   BATTLE ORDER.   24th July, 1941.
SECRET.

A/C Letter.

  B. O   S/Ldr. Colenso . P/O. Ashton, P/O. Street, P/O. Osbon, Sgt. Rainbeck, Sgt. Cormack, Sgt. Hytton.

  F.   F/Lt. Craig. Sgts. Sainsbury, Love, Hesmondhalgh, Price, Smith,

  V.   P/O Rickinson. Sgts. Watson, Bridgett, Jinkinson, Litton, Thompson.

  D. D   R E S E R V E   A I R C R A F T.

BOMB LOAD - 5 x 500 lbs. S.A.P.,   fused .12 seconds delay.

FUEL   - 692 galls.   BRIEFING - 0845 hours.

DISTRIBUTION:
Officer Commanding.   Met. Officer,   Armoury.   O.C. "B" Flight, 101 Sqdn.
Operations.   Officer's Mess.   Signals.   Regional Control.
W/Cdr. Biggs.   Sergeants' Mess.   O.C."A" Flt, 101 Sqdn.   Instrument Section.

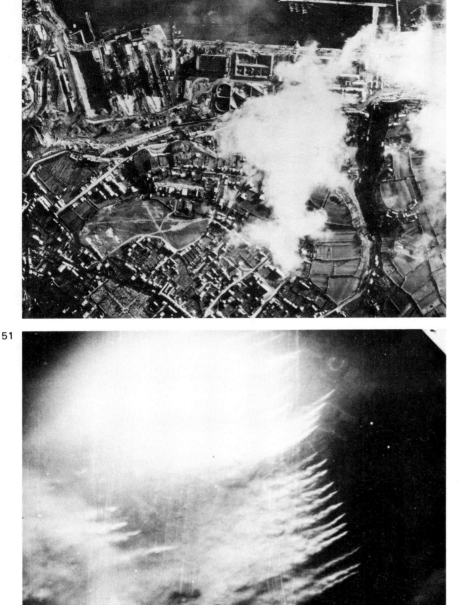

50
The *Scharnhorst* and *Gneisenau* berthed in Brest (upper left). On such a clear day they looked an easy target.

51
Spot the battlecruisers — Brest obscured by a German smoke-screen.

Wellington, 'which lacks armament, speed and handiness, and especially rate of climb, is a most unsuitable type of aircraft for daylight operations . . .'. This view was endorsed by a signal from Bomber Command declaring that henceforward, 'No 101 Squadron will be used for night bombing only, undertaking tasks similar to those of the heavy bomber Groups'. Not that concentrating on raids under cover of darkness was necessarily easier, and the Squadron lost 19 aircrew killed in action during August alone.

What of those aircrews on 101? The Squadron manning establishment increased as more Wellingtons arrived because not only did the larger aircraft, with their new hydraulic and electrical systems, need more groundcrew support to keep them in the air, but also they required more aircrew to operate them once they got up there. Squadron Wellingtons carried a crew of six — pilot, co-pilot, navigator (after April 1942, the title of 'observer' was officially changed to 'navigator'), WOp/AG and nose and tail gunners. Gone therefore were the days when most of the responsibility fell on the pilot; bigger teams demanded closer crew co-operation and operational training revolved around the motto, 'United we fly, divided we fall'.

A typical description of a bomber crew at this time was provided by an Air Ministry publication entitled *Bomber Command*, which was issued by the Ministry of Aviation in 1941. 'The men of Bomber Command are appointed to fulfil a special mission. Their life is not that of other men — not that even of those in the other branches of the service. Its very physical conditions are different. For them nowadays much of the night is the day, much of the day a time for sleep and repose. Discipline is constant yet flexible . . . Triumph and disaster are met and vanquished together.

'The captain and his second pilot do the actual flying, the observer navigates and drops the bombs; the wireless operator helps the navigator and with the air gunners does the fighting. The same spirit and practice of co-ordination is required of a bomber crew as of a crew of a racing eight or the members of a football eleven . . .

'The bomber pilot differs in training and environment from his colleague flying a Spitfire or Hurricane. A pilot of the Royal Air Force is subjected at an early stage to a process of selection by which it is determined whether he is better fitted to fly a fighter or a bomber. Both will have to fly aircraft; both will wear pilot's wings; but here their ways diverge. The fighter pilot is in action for an hour and a half to two hours at most, often far less. He is usually led into the fight by his squadron leader.

power, 'but they lost the main formation south of Point de St Mathieu while waiting for Flt Lt Craig to catch up. His aircraft was seen to be attacked twice by enemy aircraft and was eventually shot down by an M109, crashing into the sea. Two more enemy aircraft were seen over the mainland so Sqn Ldr Colenso decided that his three aircraft would not attack alone. They turned and brought their bombs back.' It was a wise move because, of the 99 bombers that attacked Brest that day, 11 were shot down by fighters and flak. 'Subsequently reported that Sergeants Smith and Hesmondhalgh (Craig's air gunners) are prisoners of war.'

Thus the AOC 3 Group, Air Vice-Marshal J. E. A. Baldwin, echoed the opinion of his subordinates when he declared that the

'Very different, but equally important, qualities are required of a bomber pilot. He must be capable of considerable physical and mental endurance, for it may be necessary for him to remain nine, ten, eleven, or even twelve hours in the air, and to fly for the most part of that time over hostile territory or across the unfriendly sea. During much of the flight he may find his aircraft the object of an attack by enemy fighters far faster and more heavily armed. By reason of their greater speed his assailants can break off and renew their assault at any moment. Surprise, that weapon which more than any other wins a fight, is theirs to wield at will. The bomber pilot must fly doggedly on, defending himself with the aid of darkness and cloud outside and with the skill of his crew and their machine guns inside. The bomber pilot must not forget that he is one of a team and that that team is not flying separated from him in another Hurricane or Spitfire, but in the same aircraft, crouched over the navigator's table or hunched up in the gun turrets. He must be imaginative, yet not dismayed by his own imagination, brave yet cautious, cool yet daring.'

Nevertheless, in spite of these stirring words, the author of the propaganda pamphlet was in no doubt that 'the key man in the bomber aircraft is the navigator. His task is threefold. He must give his pilot the directions necessary to enable the bomber to reach the target at the right time; he must aim and release the bombs, and he must bring the aircraft and its crew safely back to base. Under ideal conditons his task is not difficult, but conditions are rarely ideal. Darkness, clouds, air currents, all singly or together, are his foes. His main pre-occupation is with air currents for he finds himself, unless the wind is directly ahead or astern, in much the same predicament as a man trying to swim straight across a river disregarding the force of the current. It cannot be done. The speed and direction of the wind have to be calculated and taken into constant consideration throughout the flight.

'The navigator has certain aids to help him in his calculations and enable him to check his position. These are: radio position finding, usually known as "radio fix", map reading and astro navigation. The first is limited by distance; the second is useless unless landmarks can be seen; the third can be used only when the stars are visible. The skilful navigator makes judicious use of all three. He is usually working in conditions opposed to accurate calculations, for he carries out his duties in a cramped space, wearing bulky clothes and an oxygen mask. Yet the proportion of bombers that reach their objectives, always very high, is growing higher. "The wind and waves are always on the side of the ablest navigator," runs a quotation from Gibbon upon the wall of the briefing-room of one bomber squadron. In the past many of the greatest sea navigators were British. Today our air navigators are showing themselves to be worthy of their forbears.'

Somewhat surprisingly, there was no eulogy in similar vein on behalf of the air gunners. The poor old gunners always regarded themselves as 'tail-end Charlies' in every sense, probably because most were still only of airman rank at the start of the war. Then on 12 December 1939, the familiar air gunners' brevet was introduced and on 27 May 1940 all air gunners were suddenly promoted to the rank of sergeant and their pay increased accordingly to 7s 9d a day — shortly afterwards, commissioned air gunners started to appear. It was not before time. Gerry Hingley was waiting to undergo pilot training at the beginning of 1940, and it 'made a deep impression on me that the wireless operator/air gunners were still not sergeants. It seemed tough on these men that they should join the long food queues still wearing their flying boots and straight back from gruelling ops'.

Aircrew candidates — those destined to be trained as pilots, navigators, WOp/AGs or just air gunners — were carefully selected by a board of specialist officers. These selection boards sat regularly at many different centres throughout the Empire, and civilian candidates were considered according to their mental, educational and physical suitability. One aircrew selection board president, Grp Capt C. H. Keith, recalled in *I Hold My Aim* (Allen & Unwin, 1946) that 'there was never a shortage of volunteers, as nearly every youngster who comes into the RAF is consumed by a desire to fly . . . They came from every walk of life, from every trade and profession, and represented some of the finest manhood in the country — and a few who were "not so good". Most of them wanted to become pilots, although the educational standard necessary for the training of an observer had to be higher. They could volunteer for any one or two or more of the various crew categories. The type we welcomed was the lad who said: "I'd like to be a pilot, but if you can't take me for that, I'll go for observer or air gunner or anything you like, so long as I can become a member of an aircrew and have a crack at the Hun."'

'Gallantry and keenness are not sufficient alone to make a successful air-gunner; he must have a certain minimum of education or he could never stay the course during training. It was heart-breaking to have to explain this to some of those we had to turn down . . .

'Cold, bitter vengeance by those who had been bombed was the motive that brought

52
Battle order for the first Squadron attack on Berlin.

53
250lb bombs being loaded on to a 101 Squadron Wellington at Oakington. Like the defensive guns, the bombs carried by British bombers in the early years of World War 2 were little different from their World War 1 counterparts, and as such were largely unsuited to the demands made on them. The standard 250lb and 500lb GP (General Purpose) bombs were an unsatisfactory compromise between strength of casing and weight of explosive, and their charge/weight ratio was only about 27% compared with 50% for their German equivalents. To add insult to injury, British explosive fillings were also less efficient and all too frequently they failed to detonate. No serious attempt was made to remedy the situation before the end of 1940 (by which time 1,000lb GP bombs were in use), and although bigger and better high explosive (HE) bombs were developed, notably in two main types — the medium capacity (MC) and high capacity (HC) — their arrival into service was slow.

No. 101 Squadron. BATTLE ORDER. 7th September 1941. SECRET. Serial No. 52.

Flight	Aircraft	Letter	Captain of A/C	2nd Pilot	Crew
B.	Z.8842	T.	P/O. Robertson.	Sgt. Dil	Sgts. Mason, Treece, Dennis, Little.
B.	T.2840	S.	P/O. Polmore.	Sgt. Chandar.	Sgts. Pearson, Johnson, Williams, Edmond.
B.	R.1219	R.	P/O. Imeson.	Sgt. Denning	Sgts. Fowler, Parkinson, Louden, Highfield.
A.	R.1781	B.	F/L. Todd.	Sgt. MacKenzie. P/O. Carroll, Sgts. Midgeon, Hogg, Weston.	
A.	R.1599	D.	P/O. Allen.	Sgt. Christensen.	Sgts. Saxton, Campbell, Spooner, Highton.
A.	R.1780	B.	P/O. Millson.	Sgt. Page.	Sgts. Morrison, Redford, Appleby, Mackay.
A.	R.1778	G.	Sgt. Fooks.	Sgt. Dowling.	Sgts Ryan, Davies, Pollos, McBaw.
A.	X.9822	K.	P/O. Hardie.	Sgt. Moran.	P/O. Millor, Sgts. Andersten, Berry.
A.	X.9920	F.	Sgt. Luin.	Sgt. Wilson.	Sgts. Fenwick, Brown, Calderhead, Perry.

FITTED WITH CAMERAS.

BOMB LOAD. Aircraft B.D.C. 1 x 1000lbs, 2 x 500lbs, 1 x 250lb G.P. Fused .025.
" K.G.T.S. 6 S.B.C. of 30lbs Incendiary s; 2 x 500lbs, 1 x 250lbs G.M. Fused N.D.T.
" R. 1 x 1000lbs, 4 x 500lbs G.P. Fused .025.
" F. 6 S.B.C. of 30lb Incendiaries, 3 x 500lbs, 1 x 250lbs G.P. Fused N.D.T.
All aircraft fitted with Hex. Flares.

BRIEFING 1820. BRIEFING FOR CREWS NAMED 1800 HOURS.

TRAINING.

B.	L.7869	P.	Sgt. Howe.	Sgt. Newton.	P/O. Pilkington, Sgts. Sullivan, William, Sykes.	Landing 9 first then X on Northampton, Marston, Eleaby, Thrapston-Leas.
B.	T.9819	V.	Sgt. Raybould.	Sgt. Watts.	Sgt. Spencer, Bott, F/S. Woodgate, Tracey.	Cross Country as above, no practice landings.
A.	X.9800	A.	Sgt. Williams.	Sgt. Diemer.	Sgt. Kennea, Hooper, Harwell, Crichton.	

TAKE OFF. 1955.
APPROX. TIME OF RETURN. 2030. BRIEFING 1830 HOURS.

Officer i/c Night Flying W/C. D.W. BIGGS. (Signed) D.W. BIGGS, W/C.

---

many before us. Tragedy came into my office the day one volunteer answered my query by throwing down in front of me a pair of tiny baby's shoes. He swallowed and did not say anything for a moment. Then he pointed to the shoes and exclaimed: "That's why. They got my wife and they got my baby, and now by God I'll get them." He passed, and I do not envy the Hun who met him in the air!'

Each squadron in Bomber Command lost an average of one crew a week on operations and one crew a week from operational fatigue, not counting other factors such as moves on promotion. Replacement crews came from the Operational Training Units and each Wellington OTU pushed out 20 crews plus five spare pilots every fortnight. Some of these came to 101 in proportion to its loss rate, and having gone through the OTU training mill together, crews were kept together on their arrival at Oakington if at all possible.

Pilots arrived on the Squadron with 30-hour OTU flying to their name and they were then required to complete five trips on ops as second pilot with an experienced crew to learn the ropes. They then flew two or three sea-mining sorties and one or two missions to 'easier' targets in occupied Europe with their own crews. After this, a new crew was deemed ready to be let loose on its own for a raid into Germany. This Squadron conversion schedule was regarded as the best compromise in the circumstances, but going into the deep-end against the hot spots of the Reich, like a first solo flight, was a plunge that had to be taken sooner or later.

Once ensconced in their Wellingtons, the Squadron crews could certainly range farther afield than their predecessors on Blenheims.

'7/9/41. Six aircraft successfully attacked Berlin by night.'

'10/9/41. Four aircraft are known to have successfully attacked Turin by night.'

A fifth aircraft, captained by Plt Off Allen, also reached the target but engine trouble on the return leg forced the crew to crash-land in France. The Allen crew (who were 'posted as missing') had been one of the most experienced on the Squadron, but some of them managed to return to Britain with the help of French sympathisers. Afterwards they were fully debriefed on their experiences, and one man who listened in on the grapevine was the author H. E. Bates, then visiting Oakington as a public relations officer from the Air Ministry. He was so impressed and moved by their story that he used it as the basis for one of his most successful novels, *Fair Stood the Wind for France*.

To chronicle every bombing mission that 101 subsequently carried out against the enemy would be to produce a list that would often make dull and repetitive reading, not that the Squadron crews would have minded for the most successful raids from their point of view were those on which no incident occurred. Ironically, the best crews were not necessarily those who won awards and accolades for bravery but were those who took their aircraft 'unseen and deadly to the target, bombed it and flew home again through the silence of the night' (*Bomber Command*, HMSO, 1941). Yet no matter who went where and did what, the essentials of 'ops' on 101 remained the same — 'to bomb the primary target or, failing that, the secondary. In every case the bombs are carried by aircraft manned by crews who act on orders issued in accordance with a prescribed pattern, who follow the same technique learnt after long months of training, who encounter the same obstacles of wind, weather and darkness, whose success or failure is measured by the same standard.'

The main priorities for the air offensive were drawn up by the War Cabinet who passed them down through Air Ministry directives to the AOC-in-C Bomber Command. At 0900hrs in the morning, the C-in-C would hold a conference with his operations, intelligence and meteorological staffs to determine which targets could most profitably be attacked that night and by what proportion of his force. The instructions finally transcribed into the 'C-in-C's Daily Allotment of Targets' were then passed down to the Group Headquarters by teleprinter, where the Group Commander would decide how many of his squadrons he would use and from what stations. At the Oakington Station Headquarters the station commander, a group captain, would then send for the squadron commanders of 7 and 101 Squadrons, plus his operations officer, and they would divide the station commitment between them on the basis of serviceable aircraft and crews available.

'The size of the bomb loads is laid down in the Group Operation Orders, but the load may be reduced by the Station Commander if he thinks it is necessary to do so for local reasons. It must be emphasised that, once the target has been chosen and the aircraft "bombed up", to change it at short notice, although not impossible, is difficult. It means changes in the fuel and bomb load. These cannot be made in a few minutes, and if the decision is left too late, it may mean that an unsuitable bomb load will be delivered at the target.'

'As soon as the preliminary orders for the raid have been received, the work of fuelling and bombing-up is put in hand. To do this in a hurry with bombs weighing a thousand pounds or more is not easy and requires skill,

54
Flight mechanics service one of the 1000hp, Pegasus engines on a Squadron Wellington IC. The more powerful Wellington III, which first arrived on 101 in February 1942, was fitted with the 1,500hp Hercules engine.

55

55
Crew boarding their Wellington for a night 'op'. *IWM*

56
Interior view of a Squadron Wellington rear gun turret as seen through the entrance doors. The reflector sight midway up the centre window provided an illuminated circle through optical lenses directly in line with the gunner's eye. Adjustment of the circle's diameter by means of a range knob gave the gunner automatic deflection angle in proportion to the target's known wing span.

56

practice and team work. An expert "bombing-up" squad of 28 men can load fifteen aircraft in two hours' (from *Bomber Command*).

Back in station headquarters the Squadron crews, who had had a preliminary warning that they would be required that night, have assembled in the briefing room. Facing them were the target and route maps and from the dais the Intelligence Officer would open the proceedings by delivering his brief:

'The target tonight is the synthetic oil plant at Gelsenkirchen. It produces petrol from coal and the output capacity is 325,000 metric tons per annum. The most vital section of this plant, and also the most vulnerable, is the hydrogenation plant itself. It lies in the top half of the target and a direct hit with a large bomb on the compressor house will put the whole plant out of action. The plant lies on the northern bank of the Emscher Kanal, which at this point runs parallel and very close to the Rhein-Herne Kanal.'

Particulars would then be given of the 'opposition' with crews being shown maps of where night fighters operated and where the flak, searchlight belts and barrage balloons were situated. A description of the landmarks by which the target could be found and the suggested lines of approach were then given, but these were only guidelines. Crews were given a great deal of latitude in the choice of routes to the target once the area in which it was located had been entered; after the briefing, captains and navigators would spend some time together working out the course that suited them best. 'This is natural, for it is impossible to foresee the exact circumstances in which they will be called upon to make the attack.'

Back in the briefing room the navigators, who were also the bomb-aimers, would then be issued with target maps. These maps were kept as simple as possible and were printed in various colours to represent woods, built-up areas, water and other easily distinguishable features. Photographs of the target were also shown to the crews and it was a wise bomb-aimer who studied these carefully because his memory and the simple map would be all he had to go on on the bombing run.

The crews were then addressed by the signals officer who informed the wireless operators of the frequencies to be used for identification, 'fixes', and in emergency. The homing and distress procedures were also explained, together with the position of friendly defences and searchlights. The met and armaments officers would then take up the tale and the briefing would be concluded by questions from the crews.

This mass briefing may have lasted as long as 45min but 'the atmosphere in which it is conducted resembles nothing so much as a lecture at a university, though the attention paid by the audience would certainly flatter most lecturing dons. Everything is very matter of fact. There is no straining after effect. The information is imparted clearly, briefly and without embellishment. Questions are answered in the same way. The object, aimed at and achieved, is to leave no member of a crew with the excuse that he did not know that a certain procedure was to be employed or a certain course to be avoided.'

The crews then had a meal, after which they donned their flying clothing over their uniform. The pre-flight meal was somewhat irreverently termed 'the last supper'. Crews had to wear uniform on operations so that if they baled out over enemy territory, they could claim POW status under the Geneva Convention rather than be shot as spies. Crews were then conveyed to their individual aircraft, which were dispersed around the station, in a lorry. The navigator took on board with him a green canvas satchel containing all his gear. In amongst the protractors, dividers, coloured pencils, Very pistol cartridges, forms and astro navigation tables were the 'flimsies' on which were typed the procedures to be adopted if the aircraft got lost and needed emergency wireless assistance. These 'flimsies' were made of rice paper so that they could be destroyed by eating in emergency. It was said that the taste of the ink left much to be desired.

'The aircraft are sent off at short intervals of between two and five minutes by means of a green signal from the air traffic Watch Office. On reaching 1,000ft, course is set for the objective. If the wind is favourable, the captain turns for the coast straight after take-off; if not, he circles the aerodrome to gain height or to make sure that they are right on course from the start. Generally, there would be little chat on the "inter-com" on the way out because the crew members would be too much occupied and they wished to conserve oxygen; the silence would only be broken by staccato changes of heading from the navigator. Lights were kept down as much as possible while the gunners tested their turrets and loaded and cocked their guns. Over the seas the bombs would be made "live".'

'The striking thing about a tail turret,' wrote one rear-gunner, 'is the sense of detachment it gives you. You're out beyond the tail of the plane and you can see nothing at all of the aircraft unless you turn sideways. It has all the effects of being suspended in space. It sounds perhaps a little terrifying but actually it is fascinating. The effect it has on me is to make me feel that I am in a different machine from the others. I hear their voices; I know that they are there at the other end of the aircraft, but I feel remote and alone.'

Time passed and the aircraft would approach the Dutch coast. If the night was clear, the coastline, rivers or bursts of flak would act as signposts; if ground features were obscured by cloud, the navigator would have to shoot the stars to find his position. 'Few bomber men will forget the magnificent spectacles to which we were treated night after night. Arcturus, Vega, Deneb, Polaris were familiar as the fingers of one's hand. Old stuff, some might think, but to the bomber crew they remained sure and certain signposts' (from *The Great Raid — Essen*, J. Searby, Nutshell Press, 1978).

As the crew neared their target zone, the navigator would go forward to lie prone in the bomb-aiming position, and on his command the captain would turn in. By this time the captain would have decided whether to attack direct or make a gliding attack. Either way he would be 'jinking' and flying with engines desynchronised to confuse the anti-aircraft predictors and listening devices on the ground, but on the final bomb-run

57
Examples of propaganda leaflets
dropped by 101 over occupied
Europe and Germany.

where a steady platform was desirable, he might glide down to confuse the sound locators still further. As the bomb doors opened, the navigator would pass last minute refinements to his pilot. 'If he wishes him to turn to the left he will say, "Left, left". If, however, he wishes him to turn right he will say, "Right", once only. The reason for this is that there is often a considerable amount of crackling on the "inter-com" which makes it difficult to distinguish the exact words spoken. If he hears two words, the pilot knows that they must be Left, left; if only one word, it must be Right.'

A bomb-run lasted from four to five minutes and these were probably the longest minutes of most crews' lives because they felt themselves at their most vulnerable. A straight and level course was essential for bombing accuracy as well as for the night camera nestling in the aircraft's belly which could tell the whole Command where the crew had (and had not) been. As the navigator gazed through his bomb-sight, he would shout 'Steady, steady, steady' in ascending pitch until the emphatic 'Bomb gone'. At the moment of release a magnesium flash illuminated for the benefit of the night camera, and then it was time to close the bomb-doors and beat a retreat back home through the flak and searchlight batteries once more.

Wireless silence would be maintained as far as possible throughout the sortie, but approaching Britain the wireless operator would switch on the IFF (Identification Friend or Foe) and transmit the code-letters of the aircraft in morse for a 'fix' if necessary. The IFF allowed friendly aircraft to superimpose a distinctive mark over the radar blip it made in the air defence radar screen to enable Fighter Command controllers to differentiate between the RAF and the Luftwaffe. 'It was always good to hear the welcome station call-sign greeting you on your return,' recalled one pilot, and as soon as a Wellington arrived back over base, the watch office would pass landing instructions depending on such factors as the number of aircraft simultaneously recovering, which were lowest on fuel, and which were in emergency. Each bomber would circle the aerodrome at its designated height before dropping down for the final approach. A brightly illuminated 'T' would mark the beginning of the flare path and on the ground would also shine the Chance light — so-called after its inventor, not as some crews believed because it was only switched on haphazardly.

On landing, the crews would once again be picked up by lorries from their dispersal points and brought back for individual interrogation on route weather, defences and targets by the intelligence officers. Then, as the dawn broke, they would go to breakfast and then to bed — it took 9hr 40min to make the round trip to Berlin, and 10hr 20min to get to Turin and back.

However, at the end of the day, travelling long distances deep inside enemy airspace and surviving to tell the tale counted for little if the bombs were not dropped in the right place. Clear and bright nights were a boon to navigators, for even the blackout could not mask the illuminating effects of the 'bomber's moon'. But there are not many cloudfree days and nights a year in Western Europe, and the winter weather of 1941/42 only served to highlight the problems of navigating and bombing accurately without adequate aids.

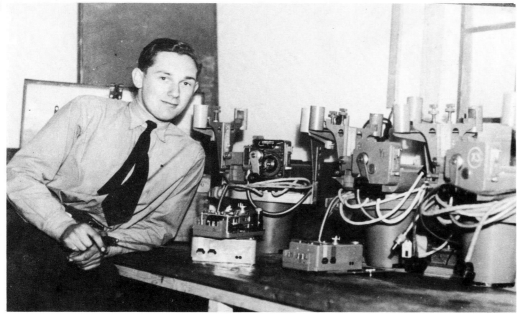

Vic Redfern, an instrument repairer in the Squadron photo section at Bourn in April 1942, with some of the night cameras that now accompanied all 101 aircraft on their raids. 'Once the Squadron had learned to accept the night camera,' said one pilot, 'we became very keen to use it properly such that when Bomber Command started what might be termed a photographic competition by publishing the monthly photo results, 101 always came in the top four.

59
Having loaded and tested his photographic charges, Vic Redfern poses for the ground camera from the pilot's window. The attractive WAAF driver was Eileen 'Bobbie' Clarke who served on 101 for four years.

'12/2/42. Four aircraft did a daylight op against battlecruisers *Scharnhorst*, *Gneisenau* and *Prinz Eugen*. Targets not sighted owing to bad visibility.'

'16/2/42. Sgt Cowley's crew went on a Nickel raid (propaganda leaflet dropping) to Lisle. Eight packages of leaflets dropped on ETA above 10/10ths cloud.'

Cowley's men were reduced to dropping on time because they had no better means of accurately determining where they were. It was an old problem. Before 1939, numbers of aircraft were everything in Bomber Command. Little thought was then given to what was operationally possible, what targets could be reached, how accurately they could be bombed, and the effects of the bombs if they did fall accurately — to have a large number of aircraft that could carry bombs seemed to be sufficient in itself.

The weight of bombs dropped by bomber Command during May 1941 was more than twice that dropped in May 1940, and the weight of bombs dropped in June 1941 was half as much again as the total for the previous month. But like the 'shop window' force of 1939, these figures meant little in themselves because they took no account of whether the bombs were being deposited to good effect or not. After being driven out of the sky by day to all intents and purposes during the first year of the war, Bomber Command continued to think that it could cripple the German war effort by hitting crucial pinpoint targets such as oil refineries by night. Yet this again was far too ambitious — in November 1940 the evidence revealed that no fewer than 65% of the bombers dispatched had failed to find their targets.

After the Luftwaffe attack on Coventry,

60
Sergeant 'Mac' Mackay standing by B-Beer, or Beer the Bitch as she was known affectionately to her crew. B-Beer was a Wellington IC which had the unique distinction of being the only aircraft of her genre to live through service on 101 to be retired back to Vickers.

Bomber Command was allowed to aim for larger targets in the hope that the crews could at least find these. But it was not to be. There were cases in the Command of navigation errors up to 100 miles, yet on these occasions 'the pilots, relying blindly on a met wind forecast and flying above 10/10ths cloud, have been convinced that the area bombed through the gap in the clouds was their target'.

Thus the brave claims that considerable destruction was being heaped upon Germany, and eloquent propaganda such as *Bomber Command* which declared authoritatively that the proportion of bombers reaching their objectives was 'always very high' and was 'growing higher', were simply not borne out by reality. No blame could be attached to the crews for this — at the end of a long and arduous outbound leg, lasting up to 700 miles in darkness and with virtually no navigational aids or accurate meteorological data to help them, Wellington navigators were expected to place their bombs to within 1,000 yards of a target they could not see. It was asking too much of crews, even though they never failed to operate to the best of their ability with the limited equipment they had to hand, and the aerial photographs now being taken during and after raids drove the point home. The Butt Report of August 1941 made a careful study of a large number of these photos, and concluded that only one in ten aircraft was getting through to bomb within an area of even 75 square miles around assigned targets in the Ruhr, and a radius of five miles around any German target other than Berlin consisted very largely of open countryside. 'The

air photographs showed how little damage was being done,' wrote Winston Churchill. 'It also appeared that the crews knew this, and were discouraged by the poor results of such hazard. Unless we could improve on this there did not seem much use in continuing night bombing.'

Added to this was the problem of vulnerability. Throughout 1941, Bomber Command dropped a total of 31,704tons of bombs but at the cost of 333 aircraft crashed and 701 'missing', or nearly 20 aircraft and crews a week. In all, close to 4,000 individual crew members had been taken out of the front line in a single year of not very effective offensive effort; it was only thanks to the superb courage and determination of individual crews that squadrons such as 101 achieved as much as they did with so little. The first two years of the war were basically ones of trial and error as Bomber Command adapted its philosophy from what was theoretically desirable to that which was operationally possible, but the fact that morale in the Command remained as high as it did throughout, and formed the springboard without which future expansion would have been unthinkable, says wonders for the dedication and preseverance of the squadron personnel who bore the brunt of it all.

Fortunately for them, there were bright lights on the horizon. The first was the appointment of Air Marshal Arthur Harris to the post of Air Officer Commanding-in-Chief, Bomber Command, on 20 February 1942. 'What did we think of Harris?' mused Sgt 'Mac' Mackay, a 101 rear-gunner. 'He was *always* known to us as "Butch" or "The Butcher", nothing else, and our opinion of him varied in accordance with our losses. If they were heavy, then his "popularity" — if that is the right word — suffered. You must remember that most aircrew never saw him. I can see him now on the only occasion he visited Oakington — stone faced, severe and even cynical over our efforts — but I disagree with those who dubbed him arrogant. He certainly was not.'

Nevertheless, if his crews did not see enough of Harris to love him, they certainly appreciated what he was doing for them. For a start, he gave his Command a much needed sense of purpose. Up to the end of 1941, many people both inside and outside the RAF tended to regard strategic bombing as little more than a wasteful sideshow. It was Harris who proclaimed loud and long that Bomber Command was vital to the war effort and that his crews should be given the best of everything because their efforts would be decisive in the final outcome. After a particularly successful raid the C-in-C would send a signal to the Squadron saying, 'Good show, keep it up, you are winning the war', and this meant a great deal to men who knew that they stood a less than an even chance of surviving a tour of operations.

Harris was also a great innovator. Before his appointment, poor bombing results were often excused on the grounds that crews were not putting in enough effort. Harris saw differently and he not only campaigned for better bombing and navigation aids but he also tried to solve the problems of bad weather and night flying. To this end he demanded a better instrument panel for blind flying and had car headlights mounted as landing lights which could swivel so that the beam angle could be altered during the approach. He also called for an electrically-lit flare-path to replace the crude paraffin flares of the time. All this reinforced the view at Squadron level that here at last was somebody in high places who *cared* about them.

The nickname 'Butcher' hurt and surprised Harris when he first heard of it, but he soon came to regard it as a term of endearment from his crews. 'One point,' recalled a Squadron pilot, 'which I think shows the respect in which our C-in-C was held, was that the bomber offensive was such an entirely new method of warfare that very senior officers could obviously not have taken part in it. Nonetheless, I never heard anyone suggest that Harris himself would not have gone into battle with us if he could have done so and that he would not have made a first-class operational pilot.'

The second problem to be faced was that of vulnerability, which previously the crews on 101 had only been able to overcome by raw courage. Sgt A. C. Spencer for instance was navigating on the Raybould crew when their aircraft was shot up on the way to Germany. Although the captain avoided further trouble and carried on, Sgt Spencer was badly wounded in the thigh by shrapnel: notwithstanding, he continued his navigational duties until the pain became so intense that he collapsed. On recovering, he noticed that not all the bombs had been dropped so he dragged himself forward to the release gear to jettison them. Then he crawled back to his seat where he succeeded in fighting off unconciousness until he had navigated his crew back to safety. For the exceptional courage and dedication displayed on this sortie, Sgt Spencer was awarded the DFM.

Sgt Ward was also rewarded with an immediate DFM on 9 March 1942 when he brought back his aircraft after it had been riddled with flak: he had to crash-land at Oakington and, although the crew were injured when the Wellington caught fire, they all survived. But such bravery and dedication by itself was not enough. The answer was to replace twin-engined 'medium' Wellingtons with more powerful, longer ranging, four-engined 'heavy' aircraft such as the Lancaster which would be far more capable of taking care of themselves. But this would take time, and in the short term the momentum of the strategic offensive could only be sustained by concentrating the bombers closer together in time and space. A loose gaggle of aircraft stumbling about all over Germany on a raid that could encompass seven hours was not only inefficient but it also meant that individual aircraft could be picked off at will. A concentrated force on the other hand, routeing in with far greater accuracy, dropping their bombs in quick succession, and beating a retreat 'en masse', would provide protective cover for each other and stood a better chance of getting in and out before the enemy had time to do much about it. But this goal could only be achieved if every navigator knew precisely where he was all the time, and this in turn demanded better equipment and techniques.

The first of these devices was 'Gee', which enabled a navigator to plot his position relative to a ground station and the introduction of which, in the words of one navigator, 'turned navigation from an art into a science'. Fortunately Gee came into service just after Air Marshal Harris' arrival at High Wycombe (HQ Bomber Command had moved to High Wycombe, Bucks, in March 1940); at the same time, the Commander-in-Chief received a directive ordering his Command to commence a prolonged and specific offensive against Germany with particular emphasis on '. . . the morale of the enemy civil population and in particular the industrial workers'. In blunt terms, this meant 'area bombing' against German industrial towns and cities because, in all honesty, these were the only targets that Bomber Command stood any chance of hitting at night at the beginning of 1942.

61
B-Beer showing the battering she had taken during her operational life. But why the change to U-Uncle? The original U-Uncle had suffered somewhat on her last raid and was to be out of action for some time, leaving her crew with only five trips to complete to the end of their tour and no aircraft of their own in which to fly them. As the Millson crew were in the process of converting to Wellington IIIs, it was decided to give B-Beer to Uncle's crew. But 'we were all understandably a superstitious lot', and since Uncle's crew refused to fly under any other code letter than 'U', B-Beer became U-Uncle.

61

Selection of many targets was restricted by the range of Gee — up to 400 miles — but this encompassed the urban and industrial complexes of W and NW Germany. It was appreciated that there would be a period when only a proportion of Bomber Command aircraft would be equipped with Gee, so some means had to be found whereby the Gee crews could guide their less fortunate brethren to the target. Consequently, the 'Shaker' technique was devised whereby the attacking force would be divided into three sections — the illuminators, the target markers and the followers. The first of these were the illuminators, consisting of 20 Wellingtons fitted with Gee, which were expected to drop bundles of flares to illuminate the target. The target markers were then briefed to drop incendiary bombs into these flares to produce a concentrated area of fire into which the followers, not yet endowed with Gee, could drop their high explosive bombs.

Throughout the latter half of 1941, 101 Squadron operated Wellington ICs from Oakington in company with the Stirlings of 7 Squadron. Occasionally the Squadron operated from Oakington's satellite landing ground at Bourn, a few miles to the South-West, but as the tempo of Stirling operations increased at Oakington, it was decided to relieve the pressure on the parent station by moving 101 and its newly received and more powerful Wellington IIIs permanently into Bourn on 11 February 1942. Gee was not yet available for operations, but on 3 March Bomber Command decided to test the flare

aspect of its 'Shaker' plan by sending 235 aircraft to attack the Renault motor and armaments factory at Billancourt near Paris. Three 101 crews, captained by Wg Cdr Nicholls, Flt Sgt Raybould, and Sgt Attwood, 'successfully attacked' the factory, and aerial photographs taken the following day revealed that 'very great devastation of the target' had been achieved. It seemed that the force concentration had been excellent and it was estimated that 40% of the Renault machine tools had been destroyed. The Squadron recorded that 'a message of congratulation was received from the AOC on the effect'.

Yet Paris in good weather conditions was a far cry from the Ruhr, which was the primary target given to Air Marshal Harris in the 'area bombing' directive and which was protected by a formidable defence system supported by almost perpetual smoke haze and searchlight dazzle. On the other hand, Bomber Command soon had 150 aircraft equipped with Gee, and one of the first units to be so endowed was 101. Thus within a week of the Renault raid, Bomber Command, with 101 Squadron in the van, was ready to test the 'Shaker' technique against the supreme target — the giant Krupps Konzern at Essen.

'8/3/42. Eight squadron aircraft attacked Essen. Plt Off Luin and crew failed to return.'

'9/3/42. Six aircraft successfully attacked Essen.'

These were the first of eight major attacks which employed the Shaker technique or a variation of it against Essen during March

62
Oakington Ops Board for the raid on the Renault factory at Billancourt on the night of 3 March 1942.

and April. Yet on none was any substantial success achieved. 'I had joined 101 as a navigator on 1 January 1942,' recalled Plt Off A. A. Castle, 'and I did four sorties during that month. My log book shows that I did no operational flying at all during February, but I did 13 cross-country flights and this fits my recollections that we were withdrawn from ops whilst training to use Gee. The last of these training flights was on 26 February and my next flight was the Paris raid'.

The first time Plt Off Castle used Gee operationally was against Essen on 8 March. 'I flew with Sgt Don Attwood as pilot and we were briefed to drop flares over the target not by visual means but simply when the two Gee blips coincided. It was rudimentary pathfinding but we were not really good enough at it. I still have my navigation log and I am not proud of it, but I was only 19 and it was only my sixth operational trip.' In all fairness to Plt Off Castle and his contemporaries, although Gee was an admirable aid to dead-reckoning navigation it was not accurate enough for precise blind-bombing.

Back in the autumn of 1941, the Air Staff had concluded that saturation incendiary attacks were likely to prove far more destructive than attacks with conventional high explosive. This theory was still to be proved so, on the night of 28 March, 234 Bomber Command aircraft were dispatched to Lübeck, an old Hanseatic port on the Baltic beyond Gee range but which, being largely of medieval wooden construction, was built to burn. The moon was nearing full and the weather was excellent as the first wave of Wellingtons dropped their flares. Sgt Attwood's crew, who took-off at 1945hr and landed six and a half hours later, were the first 101 Squadron aircraft to reach the target, and they were to record: 'Incendiaries dropped in centre of town, many fires already started.' The next three Squadron crews (Captains — Sgts Llewelyn, Cowley and Earley) all dropped their incendiaries in the centre of Lübeck too, then Flt Sgt Raybould's crew dropped a stick of bombs — one 1,000lb and six 500lb General Purpose — into the fires. To help the conflagration, the Millson and Callender crews dropped 12 bundles of flares across the town, while the 101 Squadron contribution was completed by Flt Lt Watts' men who dropped another stick of bombs across a factory. This practice of combining a general area attack against a city with a specific assault on a particular target, such as an aircraft factory, within or near that urban centre, was becoming the standard Bomber Command procedure.

Post-strike photo-reconnaissance carried out in daylight on 12 April revealed that 'large areas of total destruction amount to probably 45-50% of the whole city'. It was estimated that some 200 acres of Lübeck had been devastated, mainly by fire, and that additional heavy damage had been caused in the suburbs. Two thousand houses, the central power station, and four factories appeared to have been destroyed or damaged beyond repair. The main railway station and workshops were damaged, as were a number

63
An eventful landing.

A Squadron Wellington III which came to grief on 20 April 1942 as a result of 'finger trouble'. Thankfully no-one was hurt in the accident.

of warehouses, and the cathedral, Reichsbank, and Market Hall were destroyed. Despite the fact that the town was particularly vulnerable to fire, the raid on Lübeck was an outstanding success and far exceeded anything previously attained by Bomber Command. By way of comparison, Coventry had 100 acres destroyed by enemy aircraft between 1939 and 1945.

On 5 April, nine Squadron crews were detailed to form part of a raid on Cologne. Flt Sgt Machin's and Sgt Chuandy's aircraft failed to take off because both had become bogged down on the soggy grass airfield* while taxying. The other seven aircraft got through without incident but cloud over the target prevented accurate identification of the point where the incendaries and high explosives fell. Three nights later, nine crews flew to Hamburg but 10/10th cover ensured that 'no damage was seen by some aircraft or glow of fires seen under clouds'.

However, life was not always so hectic on 101. '23/9/41. Weather — fog and drizzle in morning. Overcast until the afternoon. Vis poor. Squadron stood-down — organised sport in afternoon.'

'24/12/41. The Squadron stood-by at two hours notice for a daylight op throughout the

*Although the RAF laid its first concrete runway in 1937, only three operational bomber stations had concrete runways by March 1941. These soon became essential however, following the introduction of heavy, four-engined aircraft.

day. No aircrew were allowed off camp in the evening.'

Nor was every operational flying hour devoted to bomb-dropping deep inside enemy airspace. '2/4/42. Three aircraft went "gardening" at St Nazaire. Each crew dropped two 1,500lb mines from 650ft.' Minelaying was known as 'gardening' and periodically crews spent a relatively relaxing night planting 'vegetables' in evocatively named enemy waters such as 'forget-me-not' and 'wallflower' areas. A very nice crop was to be harvested from these 'vegetable' missions over the next three years.

But it was back to the hard stuff all too quickly. 'On Friday 8 May 1942,' recalled Plt Off Castle, 'we joined some 300 other aircraft detailed to attack an aircraft factory at Warnemünde. Of these, about 18 of us were briefed to go in at low level (50ft) while the main force attacked from high level as usual. I was flying with Sgt Don Attwood in G for George and we were told that there were almost no defensive guns around the target but this was far from the fact — there was quite heavy fire from the ground, starting on the jetty into the sea which we were to use as an aiming point before turning west on to the target. My only vivid memory as we neared the target was just missing hitting a church spire with the port engine and then immediately after dropping our bombs, the whole aircraft started to vibrate. It quickly became apparent that there was something wrong with the port engine; Don Attwood

tried to feather it but he was unable to do so and we had no alternative but to put up with the vibration. I remember very clearly that I could not write properly. I had to write very slowly to stop my pencil skidding about the paper and all that I did write was composed of wavy letters and figures — it looked quite amusing really! The vibrations continued as we made our way home and as we did not know the cause, we were quite apprehensive that we would finish in the drink. However, we landed back at Bourn and then found that we had lost all three tips off the port propeller and that the propeller boss was crushed. The only explanation was that we had hit a barrage balloon cable and that it had wrapped around the propeller boss before breaking. This explanation was borne out by a photo of the target taken before the raid which showed a single barrage balloon, whereas one taken immediately after showed no balloon.

'I recall that the BBC reported on the raid the following day and stated that "one of our Stirling aircraft had hit a barrage balloon cable but had got back to base". We were quite annoyed that the Wimpy was denied the credit it deserved. The raid itself was quite costly in aircraft, and did little damage to the factory — this was perhaps why we attempted no more low level attacks at night.'

Thus in 1942 long range targets did not succumb easily to Bomber Command, and notwithstanding the introduction of Gee, difficult objectives nearer home such as the Ruhr were no less difficult to bomb. Billancourt and Lübeck had been unrepresentative in that their defences were light and the skies above clear enough to allow crews to come down low and identify their target visually. Over the Ruhr, where the defences forced the crews up high and gave them a nerve-wracking run-in, and where the industrial haze made visual identification of whole towns impossible, the results were nothing like as good — of the 212 aerial photographs showing ground detail taken by bombers during the attacks on Essen, only 22 of them proved to have been within five miles of the target.

The staffs at High Wycombe believed that they would solve some of their problems if they could concentrate even greater numbers of bombers in the target area to swamp the enemy defences thereby giving crews a better chance of an uninterrupted run-up to the aiming point. This proposal also had political advantages. At the very time when he was arguing for even more aircraft and better equipment, Air Marshal Harris was under pressure from many in high places who saw strategic bombing as an expensive waste of valuable manpower and resources while more immediately pressing matters such as the Battle of the Atlantic had still to be resolved. As April passed into May, the Admiralty and War Office presented an urgent demand to the War Cabinet for the immediate transfer of 50% of the bomber force to be divided between the Atlantic, the

65

Wg Cdr Nicholls and his officers at Bourn in May 1942. (L-R) Back row: Plt Off Waterkyn (just off photo), Plt Off Castle, Plt Off Beer (Bombing Leader), Plt Off Tregea, Plt Off Beechey, Plt Off Spencer, Plt Off Osbon, Plt Off Davidson, Plt Off Stratton, Flg Off 'Tubby' Whitbread (Eng Off), Flg Off Ross (Medical Off). Front row: Plt Off Gardner, Flg Off Doig, Flt Lt Pilkington, Flt Lt Harper, Sqn Ldr Watts, Wg Cdr Nicholls, Flg Off Eagleton (Adjutant), Flt Lt Edwards, Plt Off Callander, Plt Off Pidgeon, Plt Off Muggleton.

Middle East, and India. It was Harris' moment of truth. 'If only we could put on something really big,' he mused. 'One spectacular raid, big enough to wipe out a really important target. Something that would capture the imagination of the public.' (From *The Thousand Plan* by Ralph Barker; Chatto & Windus, 1965.) So he decided to gamble everything on a massive 1,000-bomber raid. If it succeeded, or more accurately, if his crews proved his point for him, the war-winning potential of the strategic offensive would be plain to all; if the grandoise scheme failed, and his force suffered unacceptable losses or inflicted insignificant damage, there would be no worthwhile expansion of Bomber Command.

By committing not only the whole of his front-line strength, but also by mobilising as many aircraft as possible from his second-line and Operational Training Units, Harris amassed over 1,000 bombers in preparation for a night attack against either Hamburg or Cologne as soon as possible on or after 27 May. This was a moon period, for Harris insisted that the raid take place in bright moonlight or not at all, but for three frustrating days the operation was postponed until the weather was right. Then at 0920hr on 30 May, the weather forecast became acceptable; there were to be no more delays and that night over 2,000 tons of bombs in 1,046 bombers set course for the fourth largest city in the Reich, Cologne.

'Towards the end of May 1942, I was in the final stages of Bomber Command training with my crew at 23 OTU, Pershore,' wrote Plt Off L. R. Sidwell. 'Suddenly a flap blew up which called for scratch crews to be hurriedly formed from instructors and a few pupils for an unknown purpose. So I (an Air Gunner) came to be in a detachment of five crews to take our old training Wellington ICs to Bourn. All we knew was the official line — a "practice Liaison Scheme for an indefinite period".

'Hopes of enlightenment when we arrived at Bourn were dashed; the blokes of 101 Squadron were equally in the dark but rumours were plentiful. We found that Bourn was one of the wartime aerodromes that had hurriedly come into being — it had the unfinished air of newness about it and lacked many comforts but our welcome helped to make up. The officers' mess was only a small Nissen hut — a bit rough and ready but the friendliness was typical of many such temporary wartime aerodromes.

'Our venerable Pegasus-engined ICs looked down-at-heel and ancient compared with the Squadron's latest Wellington IIIs with higher powered Hercules engines. A bad hold-up for weather meant we were cooped up at Bourn with 101 in great secrecy with rumours running wild. We checked and rechecked our old IC bangers and we filled in many sessions in friendly rivalry with the Squadron blokes on the popular shove-halfpenny board in the little ante-room. The eventual briefing came amidst mounting excitement. Group Captain Adams, Station Commander at Oakington (Bourn's parent station), came over for the briefing — then we knew it was to be the first Thousand Bomber Raid.'

As in every other bomber briefing room, a special signal from the Commander-in-Chief was read out to the 101 Squadron crews:

'The force of which you form part tonight is at least twice the size and has more than four times the carrying capacity of the largest Air Force ever before concentrated on one objective. You have an opportunity therefore to strike a blow at the enemy which will resound, not only throughout Germany, but throughout the world.

'In your hands lie the means of destroying a major part of the resources by which the enemy's war effort is maintained. It depends, however, upon each individual crew whether full concentration is achieved.

'Press home your attack to your precise objective with the utmost determination and resolution in the foreknowledge that if you individually succeed, the most shattering and devastating blow will have been delivered against the very vitals of the enemy. You are a thousand strong. Let him have it — right on the chin.'

Twelve 101 Squadron aircraft took-off for Cologne that night. Their bomb load, as for most of the force, was incendiaries and the whole raid was to be concentrated into the space of 90min. The force ran into dirty weather as it crossed the North Sea, but conditions improved markedly beyond the Dutch coast and there were only small amounts of high level cirrus over Cologne. The moon was above the horizon and 90% full, and the visibility was reported as good both by attackers and defenders.

Most of the first aircraft to bomb came from 3 Group, with selected crews from 101 Squadron in the van. These crews in the leading Gee aircraft had no difficulty identifying the target on arrival, and by the time the main force arrived there were 'considerable' fires to help them identify the aiming point.

'30/5/42. Cologne.

Captain	Time Off	Time Down	Bomb Load	TOT*	Comments
S/L Watts	22.55	03.40	9 SBCs†	01.05	Height 12,000ft. Weather good. Many fires seen.
F/L Harper	23.00	04.10	9 SBCs	00.55	Height 15,500ft. Weather good. Many large fires seen. Started two more fires.
F/L Edwards	23.15	00.00			Returned safely — mag drop.
Sgt Attwood	23.00	03.10	9 SBCs	01.02	Height 18,000ft. Weather good. Many large fires seen.
P/O Callender	23.05	02.55	9 SBCs	00.55	Height 19,000ft.
Sgt Llewelyn	23.05	03.35	9 SBCs	01.03	Height 14,000ft.
P/O Gardner	23.15	MISSING			All killed.
Sgt Earley	23.05	03.15	9 SBCs	00.55	Height 16,000ft. Weather good. Many large fires seen.
Sgt Deimer	23.05	03.00	9 SBCs	00.59	Height 18,000ft.
P/O Read		MISSING			All POWs.
P/O Kennedy	23.10	02.15			Returned early — rear turret U/S.
F/S Williams	23.10	03.05	9 SBCs	00.50	Height 18,000ft.'

*Time on Target.

†Small Bomb Containers, which were long aluminium boxes holding 90 incendiaries each. Thus, each aircraft carried 810 4lb incendiaries.

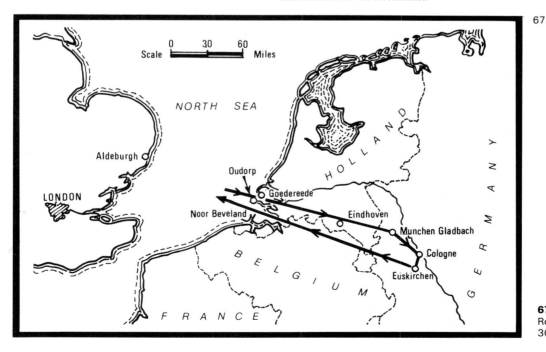

67
Route to and from Cologne on 30 May 1942.

When at last the smoke had cleared, the daylight damage assessment photographs showed that the damage inflicted on the unfortunate Cologne was 'heavy and widespread' and that it was 'on a much larger scale than any previously inflicted on a German city'. Six hundred acres of Cologne, including some 300 acres in the city centre, appeared to have been completely destroyed, and there was no 'considerable' part of the city which appeared to have escaped damage. No less than 45,132 people were rendered homeless and while some of these were only displaced temporarily, there was no denying that the 1,046 bombers dispatched that night inflicted far more damage than the 1,364 aircraft sent against the city over the previous nine months. Harris' crews had unmistakably proved his point for him, and the vindication came in the shape of the following message to the C-in-C from the Prime Minister:

'I congratulate you and the whole of the Bomber Command upon the remarkable feat of organisation which enabled you to dispatch over 1,000 bombers to the Cologne area in a single night, and without confusion to concentrate their action over the target into so short a time as one hour and a half. This proof of the growing power of the British bomber force is also the herald of what Germany will receive, city by city, from now on.'

Moreover, the victory over Cologne had been achieved without unacceptable losses. Two 101 Squadron crews had failed to return but they went down in circumstances that said much about Bomber Command in 1942. The first crew to fall was captained by Pilot Officer Reece Read. Read had always wanted to be a doctor but there was no money in the family during the Depression to send him through university so he eventually went to West Africa to work as a mining engineer. He was still there eight years later when war broke out.

When he joined the RAF, Reece Read was 'short and unremarkable in appearance', but his dogged perseverance and sympathetic handling of people marked him out as a big crew leader rather than a dashing, solitary fighter man. He was posted to bombers and early in 1942, after five trips as a second pilot, he was made a captain on 101 and given a crew. Since then he had been on three missions to French ports and had never operated as a captain over Germany. At the relatively elderly age of 28, Read was to receive his baptism of fire against Cologne.

Soon after take-off Read's engines began to run roughly and he was unable to get full climb power. One by one his crew called him up to pass comment on the matter and it was at this stage that Read learned about the loneliness of captaincy. He knew that it would be a popular decision to turn back but he also knew that if every captain with a small mechanical fault opted out, the mass impact of the Thousand Bomber Raid would be negated. So, although he was unhappy, Read did as most others would have done and 'pressed on'. At first his engines seemed to settle down, but as he neared the Dutch coast the trouble returned. The starboard engine suddenly lost power and the Wellington began to lose height rapidly. Then the port engine went the same way — Read called his gunners out of their turrets and, as the aircraft dived ever more steeply, he gave the order to bale out. Everyone got out safely and the next thing Read knew was that he was on his knees in a muddy field. Like the rest of his crew, he eventually finished up as a prisoner of war where he occupied his mind with what he had always wanted to do — the study of medicine. Perhaps there was a moral there somewhere.

Plt Off Gardner's crew from 101 Squadron was not so lucky. They were in the bulk of the force, rocking in the slipstream of other aircraft, altering course to avoid collision and weaving continually to upset the flak predictors and to give the gunners a view of the blind spots underneath. All this had been foreseen, but what the planners had not been taking into account were the bomber crews' long-standing habits of independence. The anti-collision element of the Thousand Plan hinged on the assumption that all the crews would fly in approximately the same direction, but some crews who found themselves south of the target simply looked for a pinpoint on the Rhine and then flew northwards to drop their bombs, against the stream. Other attacked across the stream, while some crews added to the confusion by orbiting over the target like a moth round a candle, fascinated by the sight of the burning city below.

The illuminated night sky probably lulled some crews into thinking that they could get away with shortcuts if they kept a good lookout, but there were always blind spots. A pilot in a 408 Squadron Hampden was trying to avoid the mêlée when he noticed two aircraft not more than 400yd ahead of him and slightly to starboard settling down into the most dangerous configuration of all — one on top of the other. The top aircraft was a Stirling and the one underneath was a Wellington, and unless someone in the lower was looking straight up from the astrodome, neither crew would spot the other. It was obvious that no one in a Wellington over Cologne would have the time to gaze at the heavens, and in the space of 10 seconds the inevitable occurred. As it weaved, the Wellington rose slightly, while the Stirling sagged and then levelled out. Then the Wellington came up again and, as the two aircraft touched, the Wellington's propellers cut the Stirling's tail completely off. Both aircraft rose together for a moment and then fell to earth — Plt Off Gardner's Wellington blew up and no parachutes were seen to come out. It was the Squadron's second casualty.

After Cologne, Harris was not content to rest on his laurels and while the moon was still up, and his force still in being, he launched it against the Ruhr. This time 101 exacted a measure of revenge for the loss of their comrades over Cologne.

'1/6/42. Wg Cdr Eaton assumed command of 101 Squadron in place of Wg Cdr Nicholls who was posted. Once again over 1,000 aircraft operated, their target being Essen. Ten out of ten Squadron aircraft took-off and bombed Essen successfully. All aircraft returned safely. Sgt Earley's aircraft received superficial damage to its port wing but his rear gunner, Sgt Ferguson, shot down an Me 110 and damaged a Ju88.'

But, as usual, industrial haze was on duty over the Ruhr and the force leaders had to drop their flares on ETA and blind Gee fixes rather than visually. In consequence, although no less than 767 crews claimed to have dropped their bombs on or near Essen, post-strike photographs showed little damage in Essen and none to the Krupps works. Some 30 or 40 houses in the suburbs were hit

but it was clear that most of the bombs had fallen elsewhere.

Immediately after the Essen attack and with the waning of the moon, the Thousand force was disbanded and 101 returned to normal 3 Group attacks on Germany. They returned to Essen twice again in the next seven days and, on 26 July, Wg Cdr Eaton led 14 Squadron aircraft on a raid to Hamburg. 'Thirteen crews attacked the primary target between 0110 and 0155 hours and all of them attempted photography from between 15,000 and 19,000ft. Bombs dropped — 4,050 4lb incendiaries, 30 500lb, five 1,000lb and two 4,000lb GP bombs. Whole town a sea of flames, especially old town. Smoke pall up to 17,000ft. Sgt Raymond's crew failed to return.'

Two nights later, 13 Squadron crews were detailed to attack Hamburg again, but it was an unlucky number for some. 'Three attacked the primary target, three attacked the secondary target (Cuxhaven) and six returned early after experiencing severe icing (three brought bombs back and three jettisoned them over the sea). Sgt Teall collided with a Stirling after take-off and all his crew were killed. Results of raid seen — nil.'

The Squadron lost 35 officer and NCO aircrew in July, and airborne collisions such as befell the Teall crew seemed to be an unavoidable consequence of trying to cram a large number of aircraft into the crowded skies over Britain without a radar system to

68
101 Squadron's partner at Oakington, 7 Squadron, had flown Stirlings since 1940, and on 5 May 1942 a Bomber Command letter announced the intention to convert 101 Squadron to Stirlings also. At that time, each heavy squadron was obliged to set up a conversion flight, and 101 went so far as to establish 101 Stirling Conversion Flight on 1 June 1942 under the command of Squadron Leader Crompton. This photo shows a Stirling of the 101 Conversion Flight at Oakington before they had time to paint 'SR' on it, but a shortage of aircraft prevented the rest of the Squadron, then at Bourn with Wellingtons, from following suit. 101 eventually converted to Lancasters and 101 Stirling Conversion Flight combined with three others to form 1657 Heavy Conversion Unit on 7 October 1942.

69
The King and Queen at Oakington railway station on 12 June 1942 when they came to inspect 7 and 101 Squadrons. They are talking to AVM Baldwin, AOC 3 Group, while on the far left is Grp Capt Adams who was known to all as 'Daddy'.

70
The Duke of Kent and Wg Cdr Eaton leaving the Control Tower at Bourne on 30 July 1942. Wg Cdr Eaton was a great personality and a fearless man who was killed on ops two years later. He was buried in Durnbach War Cemetary in S. Germany alongside several other members of 101. The Duke of Kent was also to die in an air crash in Scotland less than a month after this photograph was taken.

70

exercise effective control over them. These wasteful accidents due to haste, tiredness or misjudgement were just as frustrating to the Squadron as the failure to bomb effectively.

'6/8/42. Accident, in which two aircraft collided on runway, prevented circuits and landings being carried out. War ops over Duisburg. Eight crews carried out attack — all attacked primary target and returned safely. 8/10ths cloud over enemy territory plus ground haze made identification of target difficult. Haze also rendered flares useless.'

At least there was hope around the corner. After a period of musical chairs, when 101 moved to Stradishall on 13 August to make way for 15 Squadron's Stirlings, which had themselves been manoeuvred out of Wyton by the Pathfinder Force, the Squadron received orders on 27 September to prepare to move to Holme-on-Spalding Moor. Holme was north of the Humber between Selby and Hull, and the Squadron was being transferred from 3 Group to 1 Group 'in order to rearm with the Avro Lancaster'.

71
The remains of a Ju88 intruder which tried to sneak into the circuit to shoot down returning bombers. The German aircraft itself however was dispatched by an outer perimeter defence point and crashed in a nearby cornfield. All the airfield lights were then switched off in case there were other intruders in the vicinity and returning Squadron aircraft had to land without visual aids — fortunately there was a full moon that night.

72
The Rhine at night near Dusseldorf. 'The extraordinary beauty of the Rhine,' wrote one pilot eloquently, 'will never be forgotten by anyone who had the privilege of seeing it.'

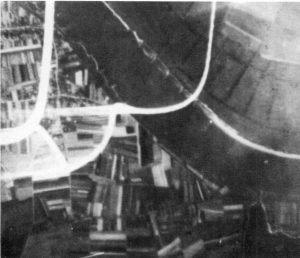

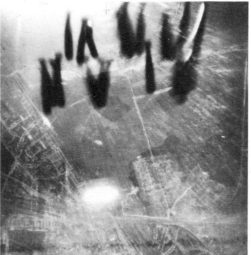

73
The moment of release — incendiaries starting to fall over Nuremburg at the end of August 1942. Pictures like this proved that crews were dropping their bombs in the right place at last.

74
Hamburg from four miles up on 26 July 1942. The wavy lines are flak. 'There was an army officer who studied German flak and who visited 101 on a number of occasions,' wrote a W/Op. 'We called him 'Major Flak' and each time he flew with us he asked to be taken close to the flak wherever it might be so that he could study it a little more closely. I can assure you that we were not too happy whenever we saw him around.'

75
Battle order for the attack on Hamburg on 26 July 1942.

75

No: 101 Squadron
SECRET
Officer i/c Night Flying :— S/Ldr: Watts

BATTLE ORDER
Serial No: 194

SUNDAY, 26th: JULY,1942

Duty Plotter :— P/O: Lhlcoln

Flt	Aircraft	Let	Pilot	Observer	W/T: OP:	Front Gunner	Rear Gunner	E:T:D:	Time Off	Time Down	Capt: u/t
A	X:3654	K	F/S:Brown	Sgt:Baker	Sgt:Justice	Sgt:Oakley	P/S:King-Scott	22:10			Sgt:Waterhouse
A	X:3391	A	P/L:Harper	P/O:Waterboyn	Sgt:Mullin	Sgt:Skinner	P/S:Mullineaux	22:15			Sgt:Spinney
B	BJ:699	T	Sgt:Inhanoy	Sgt:Colhoun	Sgt:Sauve	Sgt:Springer	Sgt:Brtin	22:20			
D	X:3657	Q	S/L:Paterson	P/S:Sibbald	Sgt:Lewis	Sgt:Sandborg	P/O:Seooly	22:25			
B	BJ:698	U	W/O:Ollier	Sgt:Caldwell	Sgt:Lewis	Sgt:Lbore	Sgt:Magrove	22:30			
B	X:3547	P	P/O:Eaton	F/L:Pilkington	P/O:Finucane	Sgt:Otter	Sgt:Ede	22:35			Sgt:Brown
A	X:3650	B	W/O:Vauteur	Sgt:Daniel	Sgt:Ward	Sgt:Sine	Sgt:Skipsey	22:36			
A	Z:1661	F	P/O:Fahnestock	Sgt:Lbride	Sgt:Chadleigh	Sgt:Carter	Sgt:Hill	22:37			
A	BJ:590	H	Sgt:Raymond	Sgt:Liller	Sgt:Lgle	Sgt:LbGregor	Sgt:Jarvis	22:38	Missing		
D	BJ:689	O	P/S:DeBartok	Sgt:Drury	Sgt:Haskins	Sgt:Dyehouse	Sgt:Bailey	22:39			
A	BJ:844	C	Sgt:Poderingham	P/S:Gordan	Sgt:Stewart:A	Sgt:Cobbett	Sgt:LbPadyen	22:40			
A	X:3541	B	Sgt:Paxcraft	Sgt:Clarke	P/S:Cook	Sgt:Coleman	Sgt:Angelo	22:41			
A	Z:1662	D	Sgt:Bemmoe	P/O:Jefferson	Sgt:Buckland	Sgt:Lblenman	P/O:Selover	22:42			
A	X:3668	G	Sgt:Foall	Sgt:Webster	P/O:Stubbings	Sgt:Bridge	Sgt:Corber	22:43			
B	X:3455	V	Sgt:Doale	Sgt:Rowles	Sgt:Swann	Sgt:Roberts	P/O:Butcher	22:44			
B	X:3366	H	Sgt:Fallott	Sgt:Bennett	Sgt:Swann	Sgt:Kearns	Sgt:Armstrong	22:45			

OPERATIONAL LOAD:—
Aircraft K:A:T:Q:U:P: to carry Incendiaries (810 x 4lbs)
Aircraft B:F:H:O:D:G:V:H: to carry 1 x 1000lbs: + 6 x 500lbs:
Aircraft C:E: to carry 1 x 4000lbs:
All aircraft to carry GAMIAS
All aircraft to carry 750 gallons of fuel

Briefing :— 17:00 hrs
Supper :— 19:30 "
Transport leaves Sgts: Lbss :— 20:15 "
Lbt: Briefing :— 20:25 "

Time of Origin:— 16:00 hours:

(signed): D: C: EATCH,
Wing Commander, Commanding,
No: 101 Squadron, R:A:F:

Holme Sweet Holme

On 28 September 1942, 'the Advance Party under WO Beesley, consisting of 18 NCOs and 57 aircraftmen, left for Holme. Wg Cdr Eaton and Flt Lt Ross travelled by road'. They were joined the following day by the main party which 'proceeded to Holme by rail and by Squadron vehicles in convoy. Fifteen officers and 86 airmen aircrew proceeded by air, while two officers and 23 airmen aircrew travelled with the main party under the charge of the Adjutant, Flt Lt E. W. Eagleton'.

These figures give some idea of the size of 101 at the end of the Wellington era, and the Squadron was going to increase once the new bombers arrived. On 30 September, '10 complete aircrews proceeded to No 1654 Heavy Conversion Unit, Wigsley, Notts, for conversion training on to the Lancaster. Some were ferried by air, the others by rail'. The remaining crews continued to fly the Wellington because Bomber Command could not afford to take a complete squadron out of the front-line, and in between carrying on the fight against Germany they helped the ground staffs unpack and settle into Holme. There they were welcomed personally into 1 Group by their new AOC on 1 September. 'He explained the damage being done to Germany both materially and morally, and he enjoined the Squadron to "keep it up".'

The No 1 Group Summary for September 1942 was equally pleased to record that 'No 101 Squadron has arrived at RAF Station, Holme, from No 3 Group. This is an excellent piece of news and we are very pleased to welcome this Squadron with its fine record. We wish it the best of luck in its new surroundings.'

Holme-on-Spalding Moor was a typical purpose-built Bomber Command station with the sleeping accommodation dispersed away from the Messes, which in turn were removed from the work areas and aircraft to minimise the effect of any enemy bombing. Such were the distances involved that '125 bicycles were issued to Squadron personnel, the control of which was a continual headache for the Adjutant'.

The huts in which both officers and men lived were 'poorly heated by a small coke stove with one bag of coke being supplied per week, if the residents were lucky. Water for washing was more often than not cold, but life was lived to as full an extent as possible'.

No 101, 103 and 460 Squadrons were the first units in 1 Group to re-equip with the Lancaster, and there followed a hectic race between them to see who would be quickest to get the new type into operational service. The first two 101 Lancasters arrived at Holme on 11 October 1942, and eight days

76
On 23 October 1942, Wg Cdr Bruce Bintley of 102 Sqn, Pocklington, landed his Halifax at Holme after a raid on Genoa. The airfield was shrouded in fog and before the Wing Commander could leave the runway, a Lancaster also returning from Italy landed on top of the Halifax, killing Bintley and his wireless operator. It was just one of many tragic accidents to result from the strain of ops.

77
WO Oliver AFM and his crew after they finished their tour of ops on the last night that 101 flew Wellingtons in anger. (L-R) Back row: Sgt Franchuk (Rear gunner), Sgt Moore (Bombardier), Sgt Lewis (W/Op). Front row: Sgt Caldwell (Observer), WO Oliver, Grp Capt Blucke (Station Commander, and member of the station hockey team when he could find the time).

77

later 'the first party of aircrews to complete their conversion training returned from Wigsley: they are full of enthusiasm for the Lancasters and are itching to get operational with them to show the world, and Hitler, what 101 can do with them'. By the end of the month, no more Wellington sorties were being flown and 101 was the proud possessor of 14 Lancasters. 'The entire Squadron is keen to get on ops with our new machines,' but there were unavoidable delays while the new aircraft were checked on their receipt from the manufacturers and modifications such as the fitment of flare-chutes were carried out. 'The supply of spares and necessary parts is very difficult,' lamented the engineers, 'but aircraft are being initially checked at the rate of three every 2½ days.'

They need not have worried — 101 dispatched eight Lancasters to attack Turin on 20 November 1942, just winning the race with 103 and 460 Squadrons.

The Avro Lancaster was regarded by many as the ideal bomber. 'There can be no doubt at all that until 1942, the success of Bomber Command was extremely limited,' declared an experienced Squadron navigator. 'The Wellington was not really suited to the type of work being asked of it, and even newer four-engined bombers like the Stirling had their limitations. I rather liked the Stirling but without going into rich mixture, when the enemy could see the cowlings many miles away and the fuel consumption soared to around 300 gallons an hour, the Stirling was incapable of getting anywhere above

78
The photographic beauty of impending destruction over Duisberg. All the lines are tracer shells converging upwards towards a point represented by the light mass at the bottom right. The curved nature of the tracer lines is caused by the bomber taking evasive action. 'Personally, I disliked flak more than fighters,' said Flt Lt Misselbrook. 'Needless to say, flak was most heavily concentrated in the target area. I know this to my cost as I got a direct hit over Munich in December 1942, and it took the side of the aircraft away just where I was sitting plus some of the controls. We had a rough old trip back home.'

'discontinued second pilots and came down to five man crews'. In fact, if all the aircraft concerned had required two pilots, the 1,000-bomber raids of 1942 could not have been launched.

The meeting on 29 March was also innovatory in other ways. For a start, none disagreed with the Chief of Air Staff when he 'considered that the title of 'observer' should be changed to 'navigator', but more importantly the staff officers were not happy with the practice of the navigator leaving his post some 50 miles from the target in order to concentrate on bomb-aiming — in the age of new devices such as Gee, it was felt that he should remain with his black boxes and charts throughout the raid. Consequently it was decided to add a specialised bomb-aimer to the heavy bomber crew, to be known as the 'air bomber', together with a flight engineer to assist the solitary pilot.

A 101 Squadron Lancaster crew henceforward numbered seven highly specialised individuals. Up front were the pilot, who was always captain, and the flight engineer. The navigator was now solely responsible for the navigation, leaving the air bomber to drop the bombs or occupy the front turret whenever he was not dropping bombs. The wireless operator was also released from gunnery duties and mid-upper and rear gunners were no longer required to undergo wireless training. These changes had a considerable effect. Up to now, there had been no clear idea of what a bomber crew did beyond the general rule that the pilot flew the aircraft. The rest of the crew had titles and seats, but the precise nature of their duties on the Wellington, and the extent to which they required pre-operational training, was obscure. Once Bomber Command got its crew specialisations right on the 'heavies', it opened the way for each crew member to specialise to a much greater extent and thereby receive a much more thorough training than had hitherto been possible. It was all part of the growing efficiency and sophistication that was enveloping Bomber Command, and nothing demonstrated this more forceably than the fact that in 1940 an embryo 101 Squadron Blenheim crew could be rushed through training in a matter of months whereas it took around two years to train 101 Squadron Lancaster aircrew in 1944. However, one less satisfactory by product of this extension of the training period was the increase in training casualties: one in seven (8,000 men) of all the Command's casualties occurred during training.

The RAF took no pressed men for its aircrew but relied wholly on volunteers. 'During the war the normal method of providing flying personnel for the RAF is by

20,000ft.' Unlike the Wellington III, which could only carry 4,500lb of bombs over 1,500 miles, the Lancaster I could transport 14,000lb of bombs over 1,660 miles. Moreover, on 101 Squadron trials during January 1943, Lancasters reached heights of between 26,800ft and 28,100ft with full fuel loads and they could cruise at 185mph fully laden. For a large aircraft the Lancaster was also extremely manoeuvrable, and the combined all-round view from front cabin, mid-upper and rear turrets was good. Consequently Sir Arthur Harris spoke for all on 101 when he declared that the Lancaster soon proved immensely superior to all other types in the Command and that, measured in no matter what terms, the Lancaster was incomparably the most efficient and far surpassed all its rivals in range, bombload, ease of handling, freedom from accident and casualty rate.

Until the spring of 1942, 101 Squadron Wellingtons had always carried a first and second pilot, but Bomber Command lost 107 aircraft in the first 18 nights of August 1941 alone and the continual replacement of two pilots for every bomber lost eventually imposed an unacceptable strain on the training organisation and diverted too many men away from other roles. Experienced operational personnel had to be conserved until the Command received more potent aircraft and up-to-date equipment, and so at a meeting held on 29 March 1942 it was decided to dispense with the second pilot altogether. From now on, a 20-aircraft Squadron such as 101 would have its quota of pilots reduced from 40 to between 23 and 26. As a result, from 4 May 101 Squadron

HOPE BROTHERS LTD.
Military & R. A F. Tailors & Outfitters
Established 1874:   Head Office :- 44 & 46, Ludgate Hill, London, E.C.4.
Local Address: 78, BRIGGATE, LEEDS. 1.
Telephone No: LEEDS 26191

R. A. F. Price-list

UNIFORM Ready for Wear					Shirt	R.A.F. Regulation		12	6
Tunic & Slacks from	...	£9	5	3	Collar	,, ,,		1	10
Slacks	... ...	3	1	9	Gloves	Unlined from		8	6
Greatcoat ...	... ...	12	15	11	,,	Lined from		10	3
Raincoat		4	19	0	Socks	from		2	2
					Ties	from		2	9
UNIFORM Tailored to Order									
Tunic and Slacks from		£10	9	0	R.A.A.F. Uniform To Order Only				
Slacks	... .	2	12	0	Tunic & Slacks	...	£12	14	0
Greatcoat	... ...	13	13	0	Greatcoat	...	15	0	0
Peaked Cap with Badge		2	6	5	Raincoat [In stock]		4	19	0
Folder ,, ,, ,,		1	7	11	Cap with Badge	...	2	6	5
R.A.F Regulation Shoes		1	17	6	Folder Cap With Badge	...	1	7	11

All Wings, Shoulder-tabs etc. in stock.

We are well known for Ready-to-Wear Uniforms of which we hold large stocks in a wide range of fittings. You are invited to inspect our store — You can be fitted out in a few hours

establishment in the ranks of the RAF Volunteer Reserve for training as a member of an aircraft crew.' The RAFVR age limits were 18-31 for pilots and 18-33 for navigators, wireless operators and air gunners. Whereas a School Certificate was demanded from prospective regular aircrew, by 1942 no prescribed educational standards were laid down for RAFVR men 'except for elementary mathematics. A short and simple test is given in this, but should the candidate fail and otherwise be suitable he is permitted to remain in his civilian occupation while receiving instruction locally.'

Trainee aircrew received their basic flying training in safety overseas under the auspices of the Empire Air Training Scheme, but the Dominions themselves also contributed large numbers of first-rate aircrews to Bomber Command. Such a large proportion of young volunteers travelled from all corners of the globe — including neutral Americans before 1942 thinly disguised as Canadians — that by 1 June 1943 some 37% of the pilots in Bomber Command were Canadians, Australians, or New Zealanders. Thus, like the majority of Bomber Command squadrons, 101 eventually became a very cosmopolitan unit. 'We had a couple of Yanks and when the USA entered the war, they merely changed uniforms and stayed with us. It was the same with the Canadians — they did not join the separate Canadian Bomber Group when it was established. We were very Commonwealth orientated by 1945.'

With the ending of second pilot posts, bomber pilots entering Squadron service had to be up to full captain standard from the start. Additionally, new types such as the Lancaster were far more sophisticated and demanding than Blenheims or Wellingtons so, at a time when it cost £1,000 to train a pilot, it become economically as well as militarily essential 'that those selected for pilot training should have the highest degree of inherent piloting ability and would consist of those most likely to get the greatest value from their training' (from *Notes on the History of RAF Training 1939-44*; Air Ministry, 1945).

As a result, it was decided to introduce what was to be known as the Pilot, Navigator, Air Bomber, or PNB Scheme. Basically this marked a change of training emphasis from the system of 'survival selection' to 'quality selection'. Under the old scheme, volunteers were arbitrarily classified as pilots or observers merely on the basis of a short interview at the Aircrew Selection Board — many designated pilots then went on to struggle at Elementary Flying Training School because they lacked the required aptitude, but just as importantly many who might have had the necessary pilot aptitude never had a chance to show it because they did not impress at an interview.

This wasteful system was altered by the new scheme in that volunteers accepted by the Selection Boards entered training as an unidentified bunch of aircrew known as PNB. Some 10% volunteered for non-pilot categories, but the remaining 90% who hoped to become pilots were sent to grading schools where they were given 12 hours flying instruction. Their performance in the air was then marked and the prospective pilots were listed in order of merit: depending on the number of training vacancies available at the time, the RAF started at the top of the list and went down as far as necessary. In this way, those who demonstrated the most aptitude went on for full pilot training while the rest were classified as navigators or air bombers.

A typical volunteer was Sgt C. North, information on whose career was gathered from 'RAF Operational Training' in *Aviation Week* by Ray Sturtivant. He was accepted for PNB training in late 1942, but owing to a reduction in pilot and navigator requirements at the time he was re-mustered for air gunner training. After a course at 3 Air Gunnery School, Castle Kennedy, he was posted to 29 OTU, Bruntingthorpe, where 'we gunners were the first to arrive and had to await the remainder of the aircrew. Following this there was a period of about a fortnight when we received ground training mainly according to category. During this period we were expected to sort ourselves into crews.' Sufficient men for the 16 crews who usually comprised a course would be assembled in a hangar or large hall and left to sort themselves into crews of kindred spirits. In this apparently casual manner crews had to band together for the supreme test of their lives, but it was a good system — there would be no place for square pegs in round holes when it came to working as a single entity over the hectic skies of the Ruhr.

Having learned the basics of operational techniques, and how to operate as a crew instead of as individuals on Wellingtons at the OTU, a prospective 101 Squadron crew then had to convert to a four-engined heavy bomber. And as the Wellington for instance did not have a mid-upper turret or carry a flight engineer, these crew members only joined a crew at the end of the OTU course. By October 1942 four-engined conversions were performed by the Heavy Conversion Units within each Group but, because precious Lancasters could not be spared from the front-line, the HCUs had to make do with Stirlings and Halifaxes. Consequently, at the end of the HCU course, crews destined for Lancasters then had to pass through a Lancaster Finishing School (one per heavy bomber Group) before joining the Squadron. It all took time, and because a crew could cost well over £5,000 to train, and because the Lancaster they would fly would be worth around £40,000, Bomber Command had to look after its men for more than humanitarian reasons. Thus when Sqn Ldr St John, a New Zealander on a short service commission, joined 101 in April 1943, he did a 2nd pilot trip with the Squadron Commander to Spezia on 18 April, followed by a cross-country trip over the UK with his own crew the following night, before finally being let loose to bomb Duisberg on 26 April.

More aircrew were lost on their first six operational trips than at any other stage of their career. Until then, they lacked the experience that training could not teach, and it was war itself that acted as the final trade test. These first operational missions were known as 'Freshman' flights, and a keen crew who put them to good use became alert to most of the enemy's tricks. It was reported on the Squadron that 'Butch' Harris had said that a bomber crew had justified their training and the cost of their aircraft if they flew two successful missions and were lost on the third *after* they had bombed.

Similarly, no matter how steel-hearted or hardy he was, no man was officially allowed on operations once he had reached the age of 40 because the RAF Medical Branch had thought long and hard about such matters. 'A man subjected to prolonged or repeated fear due to battle stress,' wrote the experts, 'will usually persist in fighting that fear as long as his supply of courage lasts. When his courage is exhausted he may either refuse to continue the struggle or develop a psychiatric illness if he has not already suffered death or injury at the hands of the enemy.' It was this kind of dilemma that led the wartime bomber crews to jest that the only alternatives open to them were 'coffins or crackers'.

By mid-1943 it had been decided that 30 operational sorties in Bomber Command were as much as the bravest man could tolerate without a significant risk of developing psychiatric illness. This number could be completed in anything from four months to a year, and survival rates varied throughout the war. Only three crews in 10 could expect to survive their first tour in the most dangerous year of 1942, but later on an average man had a 50% chance of living to see the end of 30 operational missions. Very occasionally, all members of a crew who came through this feat of endurance were rewarded with a 'survival gong' — a DFC or DFM depending upon whether they were commissioned or not — but if a crew had not done particularly well they got nothing at all. Generally, if a crew had had a good tour, they got one or two awards — 'It all depended on the Commanding Officer,' recalled one air gunner, 'and some wing commanders only "gonged" the skipper and nobody else.'

A tour-expired crew would then split up to be posted away as individuals for a minimum 'rest' of six months, to recharge the batteries of courage, usually at a training unit within Bomber Command where they could pass on their expertise. After this, aircrew could volunteer or be called back at any time for a second tour of 20 operations on heavies:

given that only one man in four completed two front-line tours in Bomber Command, it says a great deal for the dedication of the personnel involved that many Squadron aircrew volunteered to stay on 'ops' immediately after their first tour rather than move on to safer but less exciting instructional duties. Either way, those who survived their second operational tour could not be ordered to fly on bomber operations again.

It is probably true to say that 101 Squadron was not in particularly good spirits by the middle of 1942. Life on the Wellington had not been very happy and casualties had been heavy, so the arrival of the Lancaster was good for Squadron morale. But it took leaders as well to motivate men. 'Successful leaders,' observed one Squadron navigator, 'were those who got the best out of their men. "Butch" Harris, despite his critics, was a great commander. Below him came the Group commanders, and they were just as important. I would say that 5 Group would never have achieved the success it did achieve without Air Vice-Marshal Cochrane, and I also believe that Air Vice-Marshal Bennett *personally* had a tremendous amount to do with the success of the Pathfinder Group. In similar fashion, I believe that within 1 Group we had a wonderful combination in the Air Officer Commanding, AVM E. A. B. Rice and his senior Air Staff Officer, Air Cdre Constantine. I only appreciated all this after I came from another Group where, although the Air Officer Commanding was a very nice man, his Group was a bit of a giggle.'

The Station Commander at Holme was Grp Capt R. S. 'Bobby' Blucke, 'and I think one would have had to go a very long way before one found a greater gentleman.' Blucke was a World War 1 pilot and an expert in blind flying techniques, but despite his experience and seniority he was known as an extremely easy person to get on with and one who 'always stopped to talk to everyone, regardless of rank. He was a man of tremendous humanity and understanding, who could also be tough when the need arose.' Grp Capt Blucke was very much part of 101 and, although he was 46 years old in 1943, he periodically exercised his 'droit de seigneur' to take a Squadron crew on operations.

Below the Station Commander came OC 101 Squadron who, after 26 January 1943, was Wg Cdr D. A. 'Tony' Reddick. Before the war, if a squadron commander was posted away he was usually replaced by a man from another unit — to promote a man from within a squadron and to ask him to stand apart from comrades who the day before would have been equals and might have been confidential drinking partners often led to difficulties. It did not matter if the man was not conversant with the aircraft on his new unit — so long as his personality and powers of command were adequate there was time in peace for him to learn the ropes.

Although this arrangement continued in war as career officers returned to the front-line from staff appointments, more and more squadron commanders and flight commanders came to be promoted from within. 'The crux of the matter,' wrote the AOC 2 Group in Novmber 1939, 'would appear to be that a squadron commander requires sound knowledge in current tactics and a capacity for leadership established on operational experience to get the best from his command, and that under war conditions administrative ability in a squadron commander, although desirable, is nevertheless of secondary importance.'

This view was endorsed by Air Marshal Portal on 18 June 1940 when he was C-in-C Bomber Command. 'Squadron Commanders *must* be active and experienced pilots. They should be regular pre-war officers nearing the end of their flying careers and aged about 30 to 35 years, or else they should be the cream of the short service and war entry, aged somewhere between 26 and 30. The pilot aged about 40, who does a minimum number of hours flying yearly, is in most cases utterly useless and ought never to be sent to an operational squadron. The flight commanders should be the best of our young officer pilots aged about 23 to 26.

'The above suggestions are idealistic and may present some difficulties in personnel and posting arrangements. Nevertheless, it is felt that if the introduction of such arrangements can be gradually effected we shall be maintaining and increasing the high standard of efficiency which is vital in all operational units.'

Air Marshal Portal was correct when he foresaw difficulties in implementing his suggestions. As the war dragged on, the hard core of career officers and men on short service commissions became too depleted to fill all the vacancies brought about by casualties and wartime expansion. Consequently, 'two tour' men began to fill flight commander posts in growing numbers, and by the end of the war there were 21-year old squadron commanders. It did not matter if a man came from Cranwell or the RAFVR — if he was good enough, he did the job. The only difference came in substantive rank — an officer on a permanent commission would probably be a substantive squadron leader or wing commander, whereas a VR man could be a substantive flying officer with acting wing commander rank.

Wg Cdr Tony Reddick was an old hand though. He had joined the RAF in the 1920s

as an apprentice armourer at Halton, and he appeared on 101 for the first time as a sergeant pilot back in 1932. He was such a good pilot that he was chosen to fly an Overstrand in mock combat with a Hawker Fury at the Hendon Display of 1936, and those who witnessed the event said that Reddick was quite brilliant and outflew the opposition.

Whilst none doubted his flying ability, Tony Reddick was not an outgoing person and so he, like many others, may well have remained an NCO pilot had not the demands of war swept aside the old shibboleths about 'background' and allowed many good non-commissioned men to become officers. He rejoined 101 as a squadron leader in charge of a Flight in 1942, and when 'Ginger' Eaton was posted in January 1943, Reddick was promoted to command 101.

In those days a squadron commander remained in post for only six months, during which time he was supposed to fly two operational missions per month. He had no aircraft or crew of his own, so he usually slotted in when a captain was not available or sick. Scrym Wedderburn converted to Wellingtons at 25 OTU, Finningly, in 1942, and afterwards he was given the choice of a posting to any squadron in 1 Group. For him there was no question but that he would rejoin 101 at Holme. 'It always gave me great pleasure,' he recounted, 'to contemplate the enthusiasm with which Tony Reddick managed to wangle an aircraft to go on ops — he would use a new one, not yet

allocated to a crew, or something like that. By these means Tony managed to get more than twice his appropriate number of operations in his six months as OC 101 Squadron.'

At the beginning of 1943 there were two flight commanders under Tony Reddick, each of whom was responsible for 10 aircraft and their crews. The Squadron complement however was growing all the time and it eventually reached 30 aircraft (plus three initial reserves). These were divided into 10 aircraft per flight, which meant that a 'C' Flight had to be added to 'A' and 'B'. But who was to command it? The selection criteria had certainly been laid down:

'BC/C.23068/P dated 20 Oct 42

Squadron Commander and Flight Commander posts in operational Squadrons are normally to be filled by pilots, but recommendations for the appointment of outstanding Observer officers to these posts may be forwarded as special cases for consideration by the Commander-in-Chief. All submissions are to be passed through Group HQ.'

Wg Cdr Reddick had no pilot in mind to take over 'C' Flight, but he certainly had a navigator readily available. Flt Lt A. B. 'Sandy' Greig had arrived on 101 on 1 October 1942 after serving on Wellingtons and Stirlings, and he soon made a name for himself at Holme as Squadron Navigation Officer. As an experienced hand, Greig appreciated the improvements that were taking place within Bomber Command. 'With Harris and Reddick in command, we

Flt Lt A. B. 'Sandy' Greig on the left of the front row. Behind him are Sgt Howells (flt eng), Sgt Teasdale (mid-upper), Sgt Webb (bomb-aimer), and Sgt Fryer (W/Op). Seated next to Sandy Greig are Grp Capt Blucke and Flt Lt Beechey, the Gunnery Leader who had 94 ops under his belt by the time he eventually left 101. This photo was taken on 13 February 1943, just after Grp Capt Blucke had flown his first mission on a Lancaster to drop five 1,000lb bombs and 600 incendiaries on Lorient from 12,000ft. 'A most successful and enjoyable trip.'

started doing things we had not done before. In the old days we flew a mission and the air test beforehand, and that was that. Now we did formation flying practice and bombing and gunnery exercises (known as "Bulls Eyes") over the UK. Our ground training programme also increased considerably — as Squadron Navigation Officer I tried to improve the standard of navigation by discussing errors made with the crews. By doing other things like dinghy drills, the whole crew discipline on the Squadron improved. It was noticeable that those crews whose discipline on the ground and in the air was good were the ones most inclined to survive.* In fact I would go so far as to say that for those of us who had done a bit of operational flying, it wasn't difficult to pick out the crews who wouldn't survive. Of course, good crews didn't come back if luck was against them, but the most efficient crews were usually the lucky ones, and we used to say that the more crews practised, the luckier they got.'

The enthusiasm and professionalism that Sandy Greig put into improving standards on 101 soon earned its reward.

*The price of sloppy crew discipline could be severe. On 28 August 1943 the air bomber, W/Op, and two air gunners on one crew abandoned their aircraft without orders when they saw that two engines were on fire over Nuremburg. By the time their captain had sorted out the emergency, he found that he had only two crew members left to take him home. The four unfortunates who abandoned their aircraft too quickly spent the rest of the war as POWs.

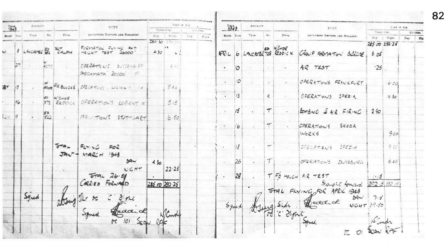

'25 March 1943
Flying Officer (Acting Flight Lieutenant) A. B. Greig DFC — 68753
Navigator — No 101 Squadron — Holme
1. Under the provisions of your letter BC/C. 23068/P dated 20 Oct 42, authority is requested for the above named Navigation Officer to be re-posted to No 101 Squadron to fill the post of a Flight Commander consequent on the formation of a third Flight.
2. This officer has completed one operational tour and six sorties of his present tour. He is an exceptionally able officer and moreover, has an outstanding enthusiasm for flying, particularly operational flying, in which he has shown great ability not only as a navigator but also as an officer. He possesses pronounced organising abilities and has powers of leadership and personality which

82
A page from Sandy Greig's log book.

mark him as fully qualified for the post of Flight Commander.

3. I strongly recommend this appointment as a special case.

> E. A. B. Rice
> Air Vice Marshal
> AOC 1 Group'

This request was approved on 2 April and a few weeks after his 21st birthday Sandy Greig found himself an acting squadron leader in command of 'C' Flight with its preponderence of Australians. Sandy was only the second navigator in the Command to be so favoured, though it was to be a mixed blessing. 'My Australians were absolutely magnificient in the air but on the ground they were just about uncontrollable. They were a law unto themselves — they overstayed their leave, they did as they pleased — and a severe reprimand meant nothing to them while the loss of a day's pay was like water off a duck's back. The Aussies were the most courageous bunch on the Squadron and I was very happy to see them board an aeroplane but on the ground they put years on my life.'

Sandy received an immediate award of a DSO on 20 August 1943 — a far from common occurrence — 'but I did not regard it as an award to me personally, rather I saw it as an award to my crew and as an appreciation of the work of the Squadron.' At the end of his tour on 101 he was posted to instruct at an Empire Training School in South Africa where he married a local girl and settled down to become the father of the future England cricket captain, Tony Greig.

In concert with the flight commanders were the specialist leaders — bombing leader, navigation leader, gunnery leader, etc. They were all experts in their jobs, as befitted veterans of many missions, 'and they formed a sort of permanent Brains Trust to guide and advise the aircrews for which they were responsible as well as the Squadron executive officers'. The leaders also gave directions to their particular charges at the mass briefings, and typical of the breed was Flg Off 'Dagwood' Durringer who was the W/Op on Sqn Ldr St John's crew.

'On the occasion of a visit by Butch Harris to the station, we pulled "Dag's" leg and instructed him to take no nonsense from the C-in-C and to tell him that he favoured 5 Group too much as far as specialised targets were concerned. Of course, it was meant as a joke, but nonetheless "Dag" stood up and said "Would it be possible, Sir, if any specialised targets come up, for 1 Group to have a go instead of 5 Group?"

'The result of this was that 1 Group got the Breda works in Milan while the Main Force was bombing the town itself.'

But the 200 or so aircrew on 101 Squadron would have been the first to admit that they could not have done half the things they did without their magnificent groundcrew. 'As far as I am concerned,' said Sandy Greig, 'the non-flying personnel of 101 were quite outstanding, and that applied to everyone on the station.'

A potential recruit for an RAF technical trade spent 4-5 days at a reception centre where he went through a selection procedure similar to that for aircrew. This consisted of what were known as the GVK tests — General, Verbal and Practical — and they were so successful in fitting the right person to the right job and cutting down subsequent remustering that Sir William Beveridge gave the RAF credit for making the best effort of all the services to avoid misdeployment.

From the reception centre a recruit passed to a training centre where the basics of service discipline were instilled. In the middle of 1943 this course lasted eight weeks for men and three weeks for women, a discrepancy accounted for by the fact that the latter were excused combat training. Then it was off to specialist training in a host of occupations.

'Trade Groups in the Royal Air Force

The RAF trades and the groups in which they are placed for purposes of pay are as follows:

GROUP I

Blacksmith and welder	Fitter MT
Coppersmith and sheet metal worker	Fitter (torpedo)
Draughtsman	Instrument maker
Electrician, grade I	Instrument repairer, grade I
Engine driver (fitter)	Link trainer instructor
Fitter, grade I	Machine tool setter and operator
Fitter, grade II (airframe)	Metal worker
Fitter, grade II (engine)	Radio mechanic
Fitter (armourer)	Wireless mechanic
Fitter (armourer) (bombs)	Wireless operator mechanic
Fitter (armourer) (guns)	
Fitter (marine)	

GROUP II

Acetylene welder	Armourer (bombs)
Armoured car crew	Armourer (guns)
Armourer	Balloon operator
Blacksmith	Miller

Bricklayer	M.T. mechanic
Carpenter	Photographer
Coppersmith	Plumber
Electrician, grade II	Radio operator
Electrician (wireman)	Sheet metal worker
Flight mechanic (engine)	Steel erector
Grinder	Turner
Instrument repairer, grade II	Wireless operator

GROUP III

Balloon rigger	Fabric worker
Balloon fabric worker	Hydrogen worker
Concreter	Motor boat crew
Cook and butcher	PAC operator
Drainlayer	Shoemaker
Driver (winch) (Balloon)	Tailor

GROUP IV

Clerk (accounting)	Clerk (special duties)
Clerk, equipment accounting	Equipment assistant
Clerk, pay accounting	Teleprinter operator
Clerk (general duties)	Radio telephony operator

GROUP V

Aircrafthand	Armament assistant
Aircrafthand (under trade training)	Barber
Batman	Musician
Driver (MT)	Motor cyclist
Ground gunner	Parachute packer
Ground observer	Pigeon keeper
Groundsman	PT instructor
Machine-gun instructor	Service police
Maintenance assistant	Telephone operator
Messing duties	Torpedoman

GROUP M

Dispenser	Radiographer
Laboratory assistant	Sanitary assistant
Masseur	Special treatment orderly
Medical orderly under training	Trained nurse
Mental nursing orderly	Dental clerk orderly
Nursing orderly	Dental mechanic
Operating-room assistant	Dental orderly under training

'The minimum daily rates of pay, ie for Aircraftsmen, 2nd class, to the maximum, ie Warrant Officer, are as follows:

Group I, 3s 9d to 16s 6d
Group II, 3s 6d to 15s
Group III, 3s to 13s 6d
Group IV, 3s to 14s
Group V, 2s to 13s 6d
Group M, 2s to 13s 6d

'War pay of 6d per day is issued to all, in addition to the above. Additional payments are made when good conduct badges, etc are awarded. These badges are awarded for very good conduct after three, eight and 13 years' qualifying service rendered after the age of 18 has been reached. Good conduct pay of 3d per day is awarded for each badge. Airmen are eligible for an allowance of 2s a day while under instruction as pilots. Airmen while under instruction as air observers are eligible for an allowance of 1s 6d a day.

'Age limits may vary from time to time, but, roughly, the minimum age for all Groups or trades is 18 and the maximum for any one is 50.'

It is obvious from this pecking order that, not only were a vast number of specialists needed to keep the RAF airborne in wartime, but also that the highest paid personnel, and thereby those with the most status, were those most closely associated with the aircraft themselves. A flight sergeant was in charge of the groundcrew on each 101 Flight, and each bomber was entrusted to a sergeant 'usually possessing trade qualifications of a Fitter, grade I, the highest grade of any trade in the RAF'. Under his direction came an NCO engine fitter plus a flight mechanic for each engine, and an NCO rigger with three or four riggers. They were assisted by varying numbers of electricians, wireless mechanics, instrument 'bashers', and armourers depending on the daily work load, and although the number of tradesmen grew as more sophisticated aircraft systems arrived, the general technical routine remained the same.

'Aircraft must be constantly examined, for upon these expert examinations depend their success and reliability in the air. Fitters examine the engine and all its details. They run over the cooling system, check magnetos, look for leaks, examine the airscrews, and so on. Riggers examine the airframe. Controls are tested. Fabric and metal are carefully searched. Tyre pressures are made exact etc. The wireless mechanic will examine and test the receiving and transmitting set, re-charge the accumulators, and replace any damaged coils. He will also run over all the wiring and see if there is anything wrong. Electrical installations are also tested. These are many and include the intercommunication system between all the members of the crew, the bomb circuits, signal lamps, batteries and circuit fuses etc.

'The instrument repairer tests all the aircraft's many delicate instruments. The armourer looks over the guns and cleans them; he tests the gun-turrets and the bomb releases.

'To sum up, the ground crew maintain the aeroplane. They are as important as the crew who fly. They must be constantly ready to do an urgent job and they cannot afford to make mistakes, for upon their diligence and skill depend the lives of those who fly'. (From *The Royal Air Force*; E. Sargeant; Sampson Low, Marston & Co, 1942.)

With an establishment of 30 Lancasters, 101 not only needed highly trained tradesmen to cope with the sophisticated aircraft — it took nine months to train a fitter grade II — but the Squadron also needed many more of them. In May 1943 the total complement of airmen and airwomen on 101 numbered 757 and, even allowing for the NCO aircrew element within this number, it still left a Squadron groundcrew of considerable size. In addition, this figure did not include all the other station personnel at Holme who were there purely to keep the bombers operating.

Reg Humphries was an electrician, grade I at Holme, and his routine was typical. 'I was with a set of lads who had come from a strange collection of pre-war jobs — a cardboard box maker, a cigarette packet maker, a grave digger, a shoe salesman, an insurance man, and a lad who professed to have "put the nuts in milk chocolate".

'A normal day started with carrying out routine inspections and repairs in the hangars. These inspections were carried out at 40hr flying time intervals whilst repairs mounted up after operations had taken place. There was always a rush to ensure that the squadron had its full quota of serviceable aircraft. This was often achieved by taking parts off grounded planes to put others into service. Once it was announced that operations were on for that night there would be a rush to do the Daily Inspections on all those aircraft scheduled for the raid. As the kites were spread around the 'drome on dispersal sites it meant a long walk if you did not own or could not borrow a bike. Usually these inspections were done in pairs, one inside the kite while the other did the outside. You can imagine the crush as all the trades were trying to do their own inspection on time and all trying to get in and out of the same small hatch in the front of the aircraft.'

There were two engineering officers, a medical officer, and an administrative officer in charge of the various 101 'erks' in 1943,

83
Tea break on the Squadron line with sustenance provided by the NAAFI van: (L-R), Jock (electrician); Vic and Freddie (photo section): Mary (driver).

83

but the lynch pin of the whole Squadron engineering organisation was the squadron warrant officer. This post was filled by WO Joe Beesley, an ex-Halton man who, in the opinion of one navigator, 'was quite the most magnificent Warrant Officer I have ever come across in the RAF. He was a big man in all respects who commanded respect wherever he went. I remember that two other warrant officers were posted back from the Middle East and they both actually applied to the Air Ministry to be allowed to come back to 101 with the reduced rank of flight sergeant to serve under Beesley. Thus we ended up with a warrant officer and three flight sergeants who I maintain were second to none on any squadron I have been on before or since. As a result, maintenance was magnificent — there was nothing one could ask of the ground staff that they would not try to do. This I believe was where success on 101 started, the spirit and basis was there, and Reddick, as an ex-ranker who had a happy knack of dealing with people, got the very best out of them.'

Despite its size, 101 still had the cohesion of one large family and as such the successes and failures were shared by all. 'Just about the saddest job,' wrote 'Mac' Mackay, 'was to be on the "Committee of Adjustment" which usually fell to an officer who had been on ops the previous night plus two ground NCOs. This entailed collecting all the personal effects of those who did not return. One night we lost several crews and I had the heartbreaking job of going to each bunk of nearly 50 chaps, collecting their photos of wife, kids, parents, etc, and other personal belongings. Of course there was always the usual letter to loved ones that crews left on their beds for posting, and at the end of it all I went to the Mess and stood there until friends dragged me off to bed paralysed with drink.'

Nevertheless, according to most, 'We were a happy Squadron. The vacant chairs around the breakfast table spread gloom for a while, but then new crews came to take their place and we got on with it.' Perhaps this sense of resignation accounted for the black humour that periodically surfaced in official reports: '17/1/43. Five aircraft took off in evening to attack Berlin, one returning early owing to nav, Flt Sgt J. C. Brown, collapsing. Reports that this was due to his bomb-aimer having told him that he was dead on track were untrue.'

Although there was not much to laugh about in Bomber Command at the beginning of 1943, one story had a happy ending. The strategic offensive certainly ranged far afield and, on 14 February 1943, 'Wg Cdr Reddick led five crews from A Flight and seven crews from B Flight to attack Milan. A very

successful attack was made in good visibility at target and photos were obtained. Sgt Miller's and Plt Off Bennee's crews returned early, and Sgt Hazard's Lancaster was attacked by a CR 42 biplane fighter coming back over the Alps. Contrary to popular belief, the Italian was pretty persistent in his attacks, wounding the rear gunner, Sgt L. Airey, and setting fire to the rear fuselage of the Lancaster when "hung-up" incendiary bombs started to explode.' Sgt Airey collapsed over his guns but the mid-upper gunner, Flt Sgt G. Dove, waited for what seemed like 'ages' for the fighter to return whereupon he shot it down. Though burnt about the hands and face he then went back through the flames to drag his friend, Sgt Airey, out of the rear turret. While this was going on, the W/Op, Plt Off F. Gates, together with Sgt W. Williams (navigator) and Sgt J. F. Bain (flight engineer) extinguished the fire. In the meantime, Sgt Hazard had found that his port outer engine was on fire and he was forced to dive to 800ft before he regained full control. Having given the order to 'Prepare to Abandon', he was informed of Sgt Airey's condition and so the captain elected to stay with the aircraft. Unfortunately the bomb-aimer, Plt Off Moffatt, misunderstood the instruction and baled out. With one engine out, Hazard

84
One of the many tasks behind the scenes at Holme — parachute packing.

85
Sgt Williams on a 4,000lb bomb.
Known throughout the Command
as a 'Cookie', the 4,000lb bomb
was no more than a thin-cased
can with over 80% of its weight
being explosive. It was primarily
intended as a blast bomb for use
among compact building
complexes such as factories, and
it was complemented in the
bomber armoury by a variety of
incendiary bombs. The most
common and effective of these
was the hexagonal-shaped 4lb
incendiary, a simple stick of
highly inflammable magnesium
which burned fiercely on contact
and was difficult to extinguish.
Incendiary bombs, unlike high
explosives, did not destroy their
targets but set fire to them so
that they could destroy
themselves. Consequently
incendiaries did not grow greatly
in size during the war as the
overall aim was to produce a
great number of small fires, with
all their cumulative effects, rather
than a small number of large
ones.

86
One of the cartoons drawn to
illustrate the 1 Group Monthly
Summaries, which recorded the
achievements of Group
squadrons and disseminated
specialist advice on operating
procedures.

managed to coax his bomber across the Alps,
'and ably assisted by his crew, with Plt Off
Gates hovering between his post and the
badly injured rear gunner, he made the long
haul back to England, landing at Tangmere'.

'How Hazard got that bomber back, I'll
never know,' said Sandy Greig in wonder,
and for this feat of courage and determination Plt Off Gates was awarded the DSO and
Sgt Ivan Henry Hazard, together with all
other SNCO aircrew, received Conspicuous
Gallantry Medals. Plt Off Moffatt's feelings

as he floated down alone over Italy remain
unrecorded.

Some five months earlier, Hazard's mid-
upper gunner, Flt Sgt George Dove, had met
a Leading Aircraftswoman called Christine
who worked in the battery-charging room at
Holme. They were married a week before
Flt Sgt Dove received the CGM at Buckingham Palace to add to the DFM he had
earned two years earlier. 'Nice work. Congratulations,' said the King, and the subsequent photograph of George and Christine
Dove gained a prominent place in the
Evening Standard. This was one of the good
occasions on 101 that helped to compensate
for the bad.

Nevertheless, Italian targets remained a
sideshow as the Casablanca Conference, held
between Mr Churchill and President
Roosevelt in January 1943, issued the following directive to both British and US bomber
forces: 'Your primary object will be the
progressive destruction and dislocation of the
German military, industrial and economic
system, and the undermining of the morale of
the German people to a point where their
capacity for armed resistance is fatally
weakened.' Yet as these words were being
formulated, the daily average of aircraft with
crews available to Sir Arthur Harris for
operations was still only just over 500, of
which approximately 200 were either
obsolescent or of little long-range value. Thus
the success or otherwise of the Casablanca
directive would continue to rest heavily on
the shoulders of Lancaster squadrons such as
101.

There were some strategists who believed
that 'it is better to cause a high degree of
destruction in a few really essential industries

THAT'S DUSSELDORF, THAT WAS!

than to cause a small degree of destruction in many industries', but 'Butch' Harris was not one of them. He poured scorn on the 'Panacea mongers' and their fixation with selective attacks on oil refineries or ball-bearing factories — to Harris there were no key points in the Axis war economy where destruction could not be countered by dispersal, the use of stockpiles, or the provision of substitute materials. Consequently the Commander-in-Chief became the main proponent of the general area attack — in his opinion, the only effective policy was to hit all the major industrial centres so hard and so often that organised German industrial activity would cease under the weight of material and moral devastation.

Yet even larger targets had to be found before they could be destroyed. Navigational standards in Bomber Command had certainly been much improved by the introduction of Gee, but it had already been proved that this device was not sufficiently accurate to bomb blindly through the murk and overcast which perennially shrouded the Ruhr. Nor did it have the range to support operations much further east, and, as expected, the Germans took to jamming Gee from August 1942. To complicate matters still further, intense anti-aircraft defences were forcing the bombers higher and higher while the growing Luftwaffe night fighter force was driving Bomber Command to operate on darker and darker nights so, if crews were to strike as repeatedly and effectively as their Commander-in-Chief wanted, more blind bombing and target marking aids would have to be provided. They were not long in coming and by early 1943 Bomber Command found itself the proud possessor of two new radar blind bombing aids known as Oboe and H2S, target indicator markers to illuminate the aiming point, and a Pathfinder Force to put them all to good use. With these new devices, Sir Arthur Harris felt confident enough to announce that 'a new era in the technique of night bombing was initiated . . . At long last we were ready and equipped.'

Oboe relied on transmissions from two ground stations and its accuracy could be measured, not in miles like Gee, but in hundreds of yards. However Oboe was limited in range and could only guide one aircraft at a time, so H2S was also needed. This airborne radar was precise enough to differentiate between ground features such as waterways and large buildings, and it was a potent bombing aid in that it relied on no signals from ground stations, was unjammable, and was capable of simultaneous use by an unlimited number of aircraft. However, unlike Oboe, it did not always produce clear-cut answers, for the amount of data gleanable

from a radar screen of varying shades of obscurity depended heavily on the skill of the operator.

In view of the limited availability of such new aids initially, and as they needed good men to get the best out of them, it made sense to give priority in both to the Pathfinder Force — henceforward the main force followed on behind, relieved of the responsibility at last for finding the aiming point.

The strategic air offensive was therefore resumed in earnest in March 1943 against the ultimate target, the Ruhr. To the crews on the bomber squadrons, 'the Ruhr' was a grim phrase that always sent a shudder down the spine: it was known familiarly as 'Happy Valley' but there must have been some on 101 who groaned inwardly when they filed into the briefing room at Holme on 5 March to be told that they were to form part of a force of 442 aircraft to be dispatched that night against Essen. This was to be the first occasion on which the Oboe marking technique would be used to guide the main force in a major attack on a German target, and it would not be an easy test. Essen, with the Krupps Works lying at its very centre, was not only one of the most heavily defended targets in Europe but it was also protected by the close proximity of many other heavily built-up areas which easily confused the inevitably harassed and frequently blinded bomber crews. Moreover the Germans had even gone to the trouble of cleverly camouflaging the only significant geographical feature in the area — a stretch of water known as the Baldeney See. For three years therefore Essen had remained immune from any serious damage — it remained to be seen if Bomber Command could do any better in 1943.

The massed attack on 5 March was to be condensed into a mere 40min during which time over 400 bombers were expected to go over the target. Oboe worked best at height, so the high-flying Pathfinder Mosquitos would go in first. Zero hour, or 'H-hour', was to be 2100hr, and at this time the first of eight Oboe-equipped Mosquitos was to drop a salvo of red target indicator bombs over the aiming point, which belonged to Herr Krupp. The second Mosquito would follow three minutes later, the third seven minutes after that, and so on until H+33, when the last Mosquito would drop its indicators. All these 'reds' were to be aimed blindly on Oboe and, to make sure there were no gaps in the marking, 22 Pathfinder Lancasters were detailed as backers-up. They were spread over the 40min of the attack and their crews were briefed to drop green target indicators on to the red markers. By this means it was hoped that either red or green target indicators would be visible to the main force throughout the whole bombing attack.

The main force consisted of three overlapping waves with the Halifaxes first, then the Stirlings and Wellingtons, and finally 143 Lancasters bringing up the rear from H+20 to H+40. Eleven of these Lancasters came from 101 and all Squadron bomb-loads were to be in the proportion of two-thirds incendiaries to one-third high explosive of which one-third of the latter were to carry long-delay fuses. Crews were briefed to bomb the 'reds' if they saw them, otherwise the 'greens' — the 'reds' were deemed the most accurate and bomb-aimers were told to get a red in their bomb-sight on release if at all possible. 'The method of placing target indicators for this target is a new and very accurate one,' recounted the Intelligence Officer at Holme as he read out the Bomber Command Operations Order. 'It is to be impressed on all crews that they should make every effort to concentrate their bombing on the target indicators. If this is done this most important target will be destroyed. Crews are to be warned of the necessity for carrying on after dropping their bombs before turning off.' These injunctions were repeated to captains before take-off — it was feared that Oboe's life would be short because the enemy would soon jam it, so it had to be employed to maximum effect while the going was good and therefore no bomb should be wasted. The order to carry on across the target after release reflected the high density of the attack and was intended to minimise the risk of collision.

Such was the plan, and it was revolutionary in that at no stage did it depend on visual identification of the target. 'Up to this time,' wrote Flt Lt T. D. Misselbrook, then on his first bomber tour, 'each bomber crew used to fly to the target with little or no aids (certainly not over enemy territory) and had to identify the target by visual map reading. The Germans were pretty clever at setting decoys and we often stooged around for five to ten minutes trying to identify the aiming point.' Much had changed therefore from the old days when there was no such thing as an H-hour — navigators for instance now got together to prepare and compare their charts to lessen the chances of stupid collisions or misunderstandings — and this all convinced the crews that strategic bombing operations were now much better organised and this boosted their confidence accordingly.

Flt Lt Misselbrook's log book records that the raid on Essen was 'quite straightforward' and the Squadron diary reinforces this impression. '5/3/43. Aircraft took-off in evening to attack Essen. Sqn Ldr Fisher's crew had to abandon mission over base (Squadron aircraft and crews would join up together overhead base before setting course to meet up with the rest of the bomber stream) owing to port inner engine running a big end, and Sgt Smitheringale had to return owing to rear turret U/S. A very concentrated and successful attack was made on this raid and Krupps received heaviest battering that Bomber Command has been able to hand to it.'

The aerial photographs bore out this assessment. When the Intelligence Officers examined the pictures taken at the time of release, they estimated that one-third of the crews had dropped their bombs within three miles of the aiming point. Moreover post-strike daylight photo reconnaissance indicated that the heaviest concentration of damage was right in the centre of the town which was 'virtually devastated'. An area of 160 acres had been 'laid waste' and at least three-quarters of the buildings in as many as 450 acres had been demolished or damaged by high explosive or fire. The Krupps works also suffered heavily, losing 13 of its main buildings and suffering damage to at least 53 of its separate workshops. Nearly 1,000 tons of high explosives and incendiaries fell on Essen that night, and for the first time Bomber Command squadrons had been able to concentrate massive destruction in an area crucial to the German war effort. Only a year previously the first Gee raid on Essen had come to nought—5 March 1943 heralded the long awaited 'breakthrough' and it inaugurated the start of the Battle of the Ruhr.

To many, the results at Essen that night gave rise to optimistic expectations of a crushing and immediate 'knock-out blow' to Germany, but wiser heads knew otherwise. Bomber Command lacked the means to fell the Reich at a single stroke, and Harris realised that his strategic offensive would be a war of attrition. Unfortunately, as the trench warfare of World War 1 so amply demonstrated, a war of attrition had the one great drawback that the attrition handed out by the enemy might ultimately exceed that inflicted upon him.

101 Squadron certainly appreciated this point for it had lost 35 aircraft in 1942, but in some ways the Squadron could live with these losses because they appeared remediable. The Wellington for instance had only two engines, so if it lost one it was in a far worse position than a four-engined Lancaster. Similarly, when the Lancaster arrived it could operate at levels above the attention of the flak batteries and its new navigation kit allowed crews to eschew the bombers' moon which also doubled as the anti-aircraft gunners' moon.

Even the stupid accidents that were an unavoidable consequence of war could be borne:

'17/12/42. Sgt Fussell and crew — a new but promising crew — were shot down in N-Nan to the regret of the whole Squadron after completing a "Freshman" trip sowing "Vegetables". Their IFF beacon was out of order, and as they returned in very difficult weather conditions they were shot down by our AA fire over the Yorkshire coast at Redcar — all crew were killed.'

Three days later the crew of Q-Queenie made a 'heavy' landing at Holme in bad weather, and on 23 December another Lancaster swung on landing and was written off. A Squadron crew crashed on the beach at Hornsea on 20 March 1943 whilst the second Q-Queenie went the way of the first and hit a tree at Southcliffe nine days later. Yet in such cases there was hope it was possible to improve procedures and skills to prevent repetition — what was less remediable was the impact of the enemy.

Just as Bomber Command was employing the latest radar technology to strike with increasing accuracy over Germany, so too the Luftwaffe was not slow in adapting these same laws of physics to their defensive advantage. In the early years of the war when individual bombers had meandered around Germany under cover of darkness, they could only be found by an enemy fighter force that stumbled around to the same extent trying to pick the attackers off by night vision alone. Now that the serried bomber ranks had arrived, they became much more conspicuous to a German system that was increasingly served by excellent ground and airborne radars. The Luftwaffe was attracted to the bomber stream like moths to a flame.

Some 101 crews were lucky. '21/12/42. On return from raid on Munich, Sgt Wiltshire's crew encountered an Me110 and port tailplane trailing edge was shot away. The rear and mid-upper turrets were also badly damaged, all the electrical circuits except W/T and Gee were destroyed, and the port tyre riddled. In spite of this, good landing made at base in bad weather conditions and captain reported good attack. 180 bullet holes were later counted in this machine and it is fortunate that crew escaped with only slight injury to mid-upper gunner.'

Nor was it always possible to sneak through gaps in the German defences. On 20 April 1943, 16 101 Sqn crews took-off to take part in a raid on the Baltic port of Stettin with the intention of flying low over the North Sea and Denmark to keep under the German radar screen. Sgt Yates was the mid-upper gunner on Flt Sgt Gray's crew and he remembers that 'the sense of speed over the undulating swell of the North Sea in moonlight was exhilarating. We crossed the coastline in a flash — I wondered how people felt with scores of Lancasters whistling overhead at 50ft, seemingly from nowhere. A muttered exclamation from the pilot notified "off track" and then it happened. Dull thuds, a smell of burning, smoke below my turret which stopped rotating. I felt for my legs, remembering you don't feel anything at first; still there thank God. We climbed frantically to gain height; the barrage ceased and everything seemed strangely quiet and unreal. It was then that I realised we had flown over a defended area and were extremely lucky to be alive. By some miracle we were still airborne and, it appeared, not too badly damaged although my turret had been knocked out. We had been lucky and I thought nothing worse could happen on this trip. Tempting fate? We were now over the Baltic and an urgent voice interrupted my musing — "Ships below!" Even as he spoke, red, orange and white lights came up towards us, slowly at first then gathering speed. A jagged hole appeared in the starboard mainplane, a port engine burst into flames, the aircraft shuddered in protest as we savagely banked and dived back towards the coast. "Jettison bombs" was the next sharp command — this was one target we couldn't reach.

'Out of the bomber stream, an alien place to be, the countryside below was bathed in moonlight as the crippled Lancaster limped painfully back the way it had come. The knots in my stomach tightened: I was painfully aware of our vulnerability and isolation. The aileron controls were damaged and the Lancaster complained at every change in course and height. Thankfully clouds began to obscure the moon but we were approaching a German night fighter station. I wondered how I would react when the inevitable happened. At first it was just a shadow on the port quarter, then a blur registered as an Me110. He came in fast, seemingly impervious to the rear gunner's bursts. Instinctively I reached for the turret controls, then realised I was immobilised. I could only watch helplessly as the tracer gathered speed towards us and blasted cannon shells into the starboard mainplane — our evasive action was too laboured to be effective. He came in again dead astern — it was the moment of truth. This time our evasion was more desperate and he missed, breaking away above us and flying on a parallel course at the same speed. He waggled his wings, banked to starboard and disappeared. To this day, I do not know why — was it my imagination or did he really slide back the canopy and wave. Later, as we approached the English coast, I felt completely detached from reality; had it all happened. It was 0430hrs when Lancaster EO422 made a rather bumpy landing at Holme-on-Spalding Moore.'

It would be wrong to give the impression that the Luftwaffe had it all their own way. On 17 January 1943, Flt Lt Misselbrook's crew were detailed to take part in a raid on Berlin. They had visited the German capital the night before when the moon had been near enough full and the target easily identified, and the overall picture at the briefing on 17 January appeared the same. This time, however, 'We were told that a diversionary raid was being carried out on Kiel in the hope of hoodwinking the enemy into thinking it was the main target. As on the previous night it was clear and moonlit until we got near to Berlin. All over the target area there was a thick layer of cloud and it was impossible to see the ground. After stooging about for a bit hoping to find a gap, and the flak getting more intense, I said to my crew that rather than waste our bombs we could divert to Kiel on our way back, which would be easy to find, so the navigator gave me a course. Needless to say this tended to take us away from the main force and it was not long before someone (the mid-upper, rear gunner or the wireless operator used to take turns to look out of the astro dome) said he thought there was a fighter on the starboard side. Everyone was on the alert, including me, and instinct must have prompted me to look to the right just as he opened fire because I remember seeing the flame from his guns as though I were waiting for it. I gave a slight twitch back and rolled towards him. Both upper and rear turrets opened fire and hit him. I didn't know this at first, and thinking he would make another attack I told the bomb aimer to jettison our bombs, which he did. But almost at once there were excited shouts that he was hit and on fire. However, we had managed to get a few stray bullets into us as the starboard outer engine appeared to be on fire, but I feathered it and the fire went out. The flight engineer said one of the fuel tanks was losing fuel so he ran all three engines off it, but after a short time (we had self-sealing tanks) this eased off. Unfortunately by this time we were picked out by searchlights and a lot of desperate weaving and loss of height got us clear. There was no flak so no doubt there was another fighter trying to find us. This was the end of the excitement until we got back to base which was fogged out and we were diverted up to Middleton St George. The aircraft received some bullet holes in the starboard wing and engines and also perspex in the upper turret was broken slightly but no one was hurt. Needless to say, I couldn't see much of the action except tracer flying in all directions and it was the opinion of mid-upper and wireless operator who considered Pat Harrison (rear gunner) actually dealt the mortal blow. Anyway he received an immediate award of the DFM for his efforts'. Unfortunately Sgt Harrison DFM was shot down on the third or fourth trip on his second tour.

But generally the Lancasters did not possess the armament to seriously challenge the German night fighter force. Browning .303in rifle-calibre machine guns were adopted as standard bomber armament in 1937, mainly because of their rapid rate of fire, but although the Lancaster sported machine guns in the three turrets they were almost invariably outranged and outweighed in fire power by cannon-equipped fighters. The only answer was to try to avoid trouble in the first place. 'If we saw a German fighter before he saw us,' recounted Sandy Greig, 'the chances were that we could get away from him. We didn't want to enter into combat and the only way to avoid it was to keep a good look-out. If we saw a fighter, we would turn inside him and "corkscrew" — you had to keep inside him all the time. Unless you were caught unawares by a German fighter sneaking up underneath — and a good crew constantly rocked the wings up and down to check the blind spots below — and you kept your wits about you, the chances of getting away from a fighter and going on to bomb the target were very good indeed.

'Against flak, you had to get out of the searchlight cone as quickly as possible because that controlled the predictors. There were often flak barrages over the target and other hot spots, and the only way past was to fly straight through the barrage as quickly as possible. The chances against you were lessened if you did that. Of course an unlucky shell could get a good crew, but once again, those crews who had practised their procedures and whose discipline in the air was good — they didn't chatter and only spoke when they had to — these were the crews who survived. You could see that some crews were basically survivors while others were basically losers.'

The Corkscrew Manoeuvre

The 'Corkscrew' Manoeuvre enabled a bomber crew to make good their course while at the same time presenting a difficult target to an attacking fighter and hopefully shaking it off in the process. It must be remembered that this manoeuvre was designed for use at night.

'This form of evasion,' described the RAF Trial Report, 'consists of a steep diving turn of about 30° and 500ft, followed by a steep climbing turn of 30° and 500ft in the opposite direction. The manoeuvre must be as violent as possible, particularly at the top and bottom of the corkscrew, to avoid giving an easy deflection shot. It should begin when the fighter attacking is at 600yds and should be continued throughout the engagement unless the fighter attacking can be clearly seen to be out of position, when normal flight can be resumed. This evasion is tiring for the pilot and must be stopped immediately it is clear that no immediate attacks are developing... This evasion does not affect the air gunners' shooting as much as a tight turn.'

Nevertheless, despite the growing offensive might of Bomber Command during the Battle of the Ruhr up to July 1943, the bomber casualties grew heavier and heavier.

88
Flt Sgt Bowyer and his crew. They were one of the first on 101 to complete an operational Lancaster tour on 30 April 1943 against Spezia, but it had taken them 30 trips and 13 abortives to do it. 'The Squadron now loses the services of another good experienced crew but we are glad to see them safely through a tour.'

88

The Ops Board at Holme for the night of a raid against Essen on 27 May 1943.

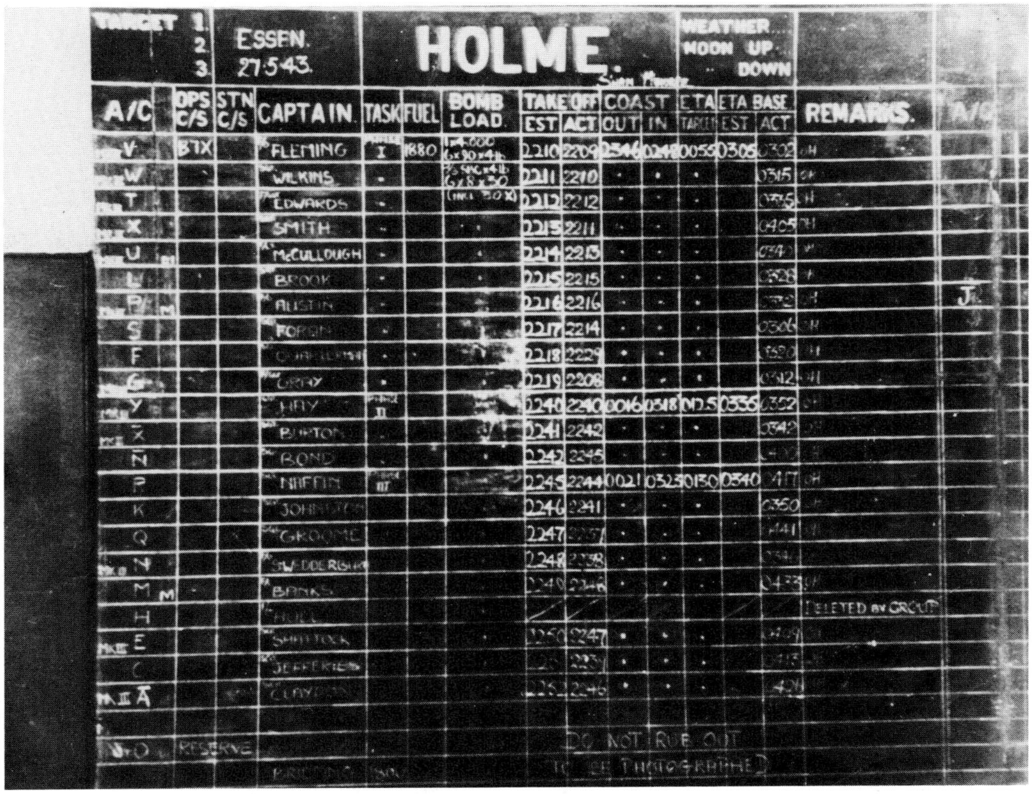

'21/1/43. Five air tests flown by A Flight in the morning and in evening, five aircraft took-off to attack Essen. Misselbrook and Hazard crews forced to return early owing to severe icing.' Flt Sgt R. E. MacFarlane's crew in C-Charlie had a more eventful flight, as the national press vividly described:

' "UNFLYABLE" BOMBER GOT HOME

A Lancaster which was attacked and shot up by three night fighters while returning from a raid on the Ruhr, dropped 10,000ft to escape from searchlights and flak, and finally dived to 80ft above the sea when it sighted five more fighters.

'The captain, a young Canadian, managed to get back to Britain although the plane was almost unflyable.

'Three Ju88s suddenly attacked. The Lancaster was raked with bullets. The rear-gunner was wounded and the mid-upper gunner killed.

'Throughout the pilot was weaving about, trying to shake off the fighters, and at length his evasive action was successful. By then the hydraulic and electrical equipment had been damaged and the gun-turrets were out of action.

'The rudder controls had been hit so badly that the pilot could only turn the aircraft very slowly. One starboard engine caught fire, and although the flames were extinguished, it was out of action for the rest of the trip.

'A few miles over the Channel he sighted five single-engined fighters. One turned to attack.

Defenceless because his gun turrets were out of action, the captain put the Lancaster into a steep dive and did not level out until he was 80ft from the water.

' "He lost the fighters and set course for home," nonchalently comments the Air Ministry News Service.'

Nevertheless, the RAF was grateful, and this engagement, which saw Sgt Singleton killed and Sgt O'Brien wounded, was rewarded by an immediate award of the DFM to Flt Sgt MacFarlane.

There were other losses on that mission to Essen. 'Sgt Wiltshire's crew failed to return and no news heard of them, to the regret of the whole Squadron who lost another first class pilot and crew. The losses of good crews this month has been heavier than the Squadron can afford with intakes from the Conversion Units being so slow.'

'4/5/43. A black day for the Squadron. Operations were ordered against Dortmund and we put up 18 aircraft. Sgt Nicholson and crew, and Flg Off Stanford and crew failed to return. It was Sgt Nicholson's first operational trip as captain but he had been spoken well of by his Flight Commander. Flg Off Stanford and crew had been well tried in previous raids and had achieved a very good reputation indeed — with them, doing his second tour, was Plt Off Lewis (WOp) who had come back to the Squadron to fly again.

'All other aircraft returned to base but some had to be diverted because of weather.

Four of these aircraft crash-landed, killing seven men and injuring seven more.'

At a time when it was calculated that an overall loss rate of 7% would prove lethal to the fighting efficiency of Bomber Command and that a loss rate of over 5% would produce an 'unacceptably low' standard of effectiveness, slightly over 16% of the bombers dispatched on the 43 major attacks during the Battle of the Ruhr became casualties of one sort or another. Although Squadron morale remained good throughout, there was no denying that the tactical and technical developments of the period tended to favour the defenders rather than the attackers. Night fighting techniques were steadily reducing the value of the cover of darkness which had succoured Bomber Command for so long, and it seemed to be only a matter of time before the night fighter mastered the night bomber just as effectively as the day fighter thwarted the day bomber during the Battle of Britain. Consequently it became even more imperative to throw everything into the bomber offensive in an effort to crush the German will to continue before the German defences wore Bomber Command out of the sky.

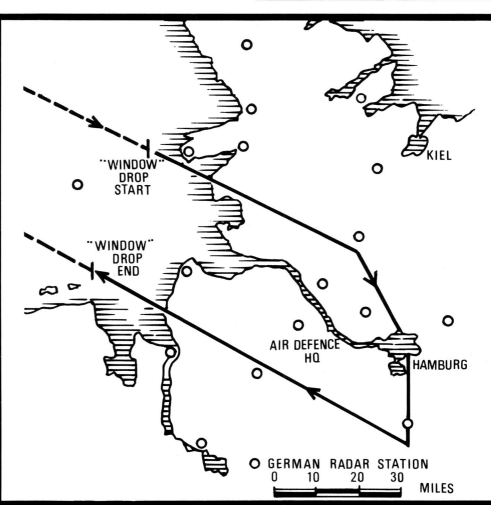

90
Hamburg at night showing the vast docks and waterways which stood out well on H2S radar.

91
The bombers' route to and from Hamburg.

The result was that, in the course of five major operations spread over nine nights between 24 July and 2 August 1943, Bomber Command inflicted catastrophic devastation on Hamburg and struck the heaviest blow yet against Essen. The force of 791 bombers dispatched to Hamburg on the night of 24 July included 24 aircraft and crews from 101, and the whole exercise revolved around the second new bombing and navigation aid, H2S. The massed ranks of Lancaster, Halifaxes, Stirlings, and Wellingtons were routed well to the north so that they could turn on the target from a NW direction and coast-in over the north bank of the Elbe estuary. Water stood out well in H2S radar, and this coast-in point was to be signposted by yellow route markers dropped by six H2S-equipped aircraft and 30 backers-up. Also at this point, the marker aircraft would transmit wind information back to the main force, enabling the latter to cross the enemy coast with far more accurate meteorological information than they were used to. It was all to lead to far greater force concentration and accuracy than before.

The Hamburg raid was also to be the first on which Bomber Command crews were allowed to drop 'Window', those bundles of tinfoil strips which produced echoes equal in magnitude to those of aircraft and which thereby confused the air defence radars. 'Tonight you are going to use a new and simple counter-measure to protect yourselves against the German defence system,' declared the Bomber Command instruction which was read to all crews at briefing. 'The German defences will, therefore, become confused and you should stand a good chance of getting through unscathed while their attention is wasted on the packets of "Window".'

Two points were underlined for the crews. Firstly, the benefit of 'Window' was communal in that the protection afforded to a bomber was not so much from its own foil as from that dropped by aircraft ahead of and above it. Concentration and adherence to the bomber stream was therefore vital both to and from the target area. Secondly, the task of discharging 'Window' would be physically demanding, but it was essential that the correct number of bundles be released at the appropriate times.

As it approached the enemy coast therefore, the whole force prepared to drop 'Window' at the rate of one bundle per minute. The bomb-aimers crawled back to the rear fuselage where the 'Window' bundles were stacked around the flare chute. At the Lancasters' altitude the temperature was −20°C, so it was no fun to stand in the cold darkness, encumbered with parachute, oxygen lead, torch and stopwatch, and heave

out aluminium foil with precise regularity. As the leading aircraft crossed the enemy coast, the flight engineers crawled back to the flare-chute to relieve the bomb-aimers, who would shortly have more pressing duties to perform. Ten minutes later the bombers turned right on to their attack heading, and the large radar echo that was Hamburg, the second city of the Reich and the largest port in Europe, gradually moved into the centre of the H2S screen.

The appointed H-hour was 0100 on 25 July, but the attack opened three minutes before this when 20 H2S-equipped aircraft dropped yellow target markers and flares blindly on Hamburg. These pointed the way for a further eight crews, also with H2S, to try and visually identify the aiming point in the centre of the city which they were to mark with red target indicators. Fifty-three backers-up were then to put down green markers from H+2 to H+48 minutes, during which time the whole main force was ordered to bomb into any reds they could see. If no 'reds' were visible then the bomb-aimers were to aim at the centre of the green concentration, but either way they were to ignore the 'yellows' because these had not been aimed visually. This acceptance of the fact that H2S could not work miracles, and that its role was to guide the Mark 1 eyeball which could not be surpassed when the weather was good, paid ample dividends in that night photography showed that some 306 crews had placed their bombs within three miles of the aiming point.

The unfortunate Hamburg was hit again on the nights of 27 and 29 July, and 2 August, with a total of 66 No 101 Squadron crews playing their part, and the cumulative weight of destruction inflicted on the four nights of Operation 'Gomorrah' was catastrophic. The city was tinder dry, and under the torrent of incendiary bombs the conflagration grew into a fire storm. 'People who thought they had escaped fell down, overcome by the devouring force of the heat, and died in an instant,' reported the distraught local civil defence chief, Major-General Kehrl. Refugees had to make their way over the dead and the dying. The sick and the infirm had to be left behind by the rescuers as they themselves were in danger of burning. Nearly a million people streamed out of the city between dawn and dusk, leaving behind a total of dead alone estimated at 50,000. 'Gentlemen,' observed Goering's deputy, Erhard Milch, to his colleagues, 'we are no longer on the offensive... I am beginning to think that we are sitting out on a limb and the British are sawing that limb off...'

To drive the point home, in between the raids on Hamburg 101 contributed 23 crews to the force which hit Essen on 25 July, and nothing demonstrated Bomber Command's new-found potential more than the Squadron observation that Essen should now be known as 'the Dead City'. Moreover, the Command had achieved all these victories at extremely low cost. 'On our return from Essen on 25 July,' recorded Scrym Wedderburn, 'I went to make my report when I was grabbed by Grp Capt Blucke who was obviously very moved. He said to me, "Come and look at my operations board. It is the first time that you have all come back from Essen".'

Flt Lt Wedderburn was also pleased to note that the defenses around Hamburg, when faced with 'Window' for the first time, 'were feeble in the extreme'. They were still 'disorganised' on the following attacks such that only 86 bombers (or 2.8%) of the 3,095 dispatched to Hamburg on the four nights failed to return, and Flt Sgt D. P. P. Hurst's crew were the only casualties from 101. 'Window' had enabled Harris to concentrate his forces against a single target for long enough to encompass its complete destruction without suffering the usual penalty for such concentration. In vain the German night fighter crews waited impatiently over their radio beacons for instructions from their ground controllers, but in the words of the drinking song that Squadron crews often sang in the Mess, they called for help and no help came. The ether was thick with confusion — as Alfred Price in *Instruments of Darkness* quoted: 'The enemy are reproducing themselves.' 'It is impossible — too many hostiles.' 'Wait a while. There are many more hostiles.' 'I cannot control you.' 'Try without your ground control . . .'

Never again would 'Window' have such an effect because the Germans would not be slow to counter it, but the destruction it helped to inflict on Hamburg staggered the imagination. As his tour as CO of 101 drew to a close, Wg Cdr Reddick could take comfort from the fact that things seemed at last to be going right for his Squadron. When he first arrived at Holme, Bomber Command had finally learned from bitter experience that the bombing results were far from what they were made out to be, and in the depressing winter of 1942 there did not seem to be much point in going on. Then in the spring of 1943 the sun started to shine, the new Lancasters were settled into service, training was seen to be greatly improved, and the revolutionary bombing and navigation equipment was entering service. 'I wouldn't like to say whether a happy squadron becomes an efficient squadron or vice-versa,' said Sandy Greig, 'but the fact remains that 101 then became superbly efficient and tremendously happy and I think these two factors complemented each other. As efficiency grew, so did the happiness, and as the happiness grew, so did the efficiency'. Hamburg put the icing on the cake, and one Squadron member spoke for them all when he proclaimed that 'at last we seem to be winning'.

92

PLEESE! I CHANGE-A DA COAT IF YOU STOP-A DA BOMB!!

92
Further evidence that the men of 1 Group did not hold the Italians in overmuch esteem.

NORTH SEA

Stàvanger

DENMARK

Rheinber
Ha
Hon
D
Huls

München
Glàdbach

Maas

RI

Holme

Bawtry
(HQ I GP)

Ludford Màgna

LINCOLN +

West Raynham

Oakington
Bourn

Stradishall

HQ Bomber Command

High Wycombe

LONDON

100

200 MILES

Cherbourg

Bruneval

Billancourt

Amiens

Abbeville

Albert

Gennevilliers

Poissy

PARIS

Villacoublay

Villeneuve

300

Seine

Lorient

St Nazaire

Loire

400

La Pallice

La Rochelle

500

Ostend

Flushing

Dunkirk
Calais

Bruges

Zeeland

Rotterdam

HOLLAND

Eindhoven

Hingene

Boulogné

St Omer

Lille

BELGIUM

Bethune

Arras

Gembloux

Malmedy

Sedan

Dombasie

Aachen

Rhine

RUHR

Cologne

Wesseling

Neüwied

Koblenz

Lutterade

Limburg

Frankfurt

Wiesbaden

Kreuznach

Mainz

Trier

Oppau

Worms

Mannheim

Saarfels

Karlsruhe

Offenburg

BERNE

SWITZERLAND

Heligoland

Hornum

Flensburg

Kiel

Brunsbüttél

Wilhelmshaven

Bremerhaven

Emden

Bremen

Wenzendorf

Rotenburg

Hemelingen

Diepholz

Hanover

Ibbenburen

Osnabruck

Bielfeld

Paderborn

Kassel

Gottingen

Eschwege

Gotha

Fulda

Wetzlar

Hanau

Aschaffenburg

Darmstadt

Wurzburg

Warnemunde

Rostock

Wismar

Lubeck

Hamburg

Elbe GERMAN

BERL

Brunswick

Magdeburg

Froese

Bernberg

Lutzkendorf

Zeitz

Bohlen

Jena

Coburg

Schweinfurt

Bamberg

Erlangen

Nüremberg

Regensburg

Stuttgart

Munich

AUSTRIA

600

Peene

Leuna

Leipzig

Chemnitz

Schko

Bruex

Bayreuth

Pegnitz

Weiden

Dres

R

THE RUHR

Huls · Hamm
Bottrop · Kamen
· Castrop Rauxel · Soest
· Gelsenkirchen · Dortmund
Oberhausen · Schwerte
Essen
Mulheim
feld
Dusseldörf · Wüppertal
· Remscheid

0   10   20   30   40
MILES

INTERNATIONAL BOUNDARIES AS AT
THE OUTBREAK OF WAR —·—·—·—

DISTANCE CIRCLES MEASURED FROM
LINCOLN (IN MILES)

Danzig
· Marienburg

Vistula
WARSAW
· Posen

POLAND

Oder
Upper   Silesia
700
RAGUE

CZECHOSLOVAKIA

VIENNA

BUDAPEST

HUNGARY

As Easy as ABC

Wg Cdr Reddick was posted to Lindholme on 27 July 1943 and his successor, Wg Cdr G. A. Carey-Foster, took over 101 just after it had moved home yet again. The expansion of 6 Group to the north of York had forced 1 Group to hand over all its stations north of the Humber to 4 Group; personnel from Linton therefore moved into Holme with the result that 101 was ordered south to the Lincolnshire Wolds and its final wartime base, Ludford Magna.

'15/6/43. We moved to Ludford Magna with A Flight sending nine aircraft, B Flight 10 aircraft, and C Flight 12 aircraft. The movement of the whole Squadron as well as the Station Headquarters was accomplished without a hitch, and it was noticed that all sections buckled down in a whole-hearted attempt to make the best of what will no doubt prove a long job.

'The incorrigible Squadron members of course operated on the first night. A very low level attack was staged on Louth, the "Mason's Arms" being the target.'

Situated between Louth and Market Rasen, Ludford airfield had been built by the firm of George Wimpey in the space of only 90 days, and in the beginning it was as bleak as the countryside on which it lay. Every bit of equipment that could be carried from Holme was loaded into the aircraft — 'We must have been hopelessly overweight,' observed Sergeant Schofield, 'because we flew like a Mark I Wellington. The new station was, if anything, worse than the last. There were no perimeter or runway lights, so we had to taxy with the aid of our landing lights and an Aldis out of the bomb-aimer's window which was not a good idea'. At first the aircrews and groundcrews had to set up the Squadron among the shovels and cement mixers, but 'if you couldn't take a joke you shouldn't have joined' and 101 was soon back in business against Mulheim on 22 June.

After the Battle of Hamburg the whole of Bomber Command was not to be concentrated against another single target until November 1943. However there was one famous raid in between against the rocket

93
101 Squadron bases and principal enemy targets during World War 2.

weapon research establishment at Peenemünde. This attack, on 17 August, demanded precision because the usual heavy-handed area bombing tactics were inappropriate against a number of specific buildings, so this was to be the first major raid to employ the 'Master Bomber' technique. In addition, it also illustrated some of the advances that Bomber Command had made in the science of bombing over the previous year.

Peenemünde was beyond the range of Oboe but, being a coastal target, it promised to stand out well on H2S. The bombing force, to which 101 contributed 20 aircraft, was ordered to attack in three waves against three different targets; all three aiming points were in line with a tiny island three miles north of Peenemünde, and it was felt that timed runs from this island would be accurate enough for the Pathfinders to lay down target markers with a considerable degree of accuracy. Radar-placed yellow parachute flares were to illuminate the area around the target, whereupon Visual Marker crews would drop red target indicators supported by Pathfinder 'backers-up' who would drop green markers and bombs. The main force following on behind would consolidate the attack until the time allotted for the first target had expired, when a new marker — known as the 'aiming point shifter' — would appear on the scene and switch the weight of the onslaught on to the next objective. It would be precise and concentrated mass bombing as never before, and the whole force of 597 aircraft was to be through in 45 minutes.

The crews assembled in the Ludford briefing room were hushed by the news that the night's target was a mystery 'research station' which was engaged upon the production of a 'new form of radiolocation equipment' which promised to work wonders for the German night fighter organisation. Such information was doubtless calculated to inspire the bomber crews to maximum efforts and the station Intelligence Officer drove the point home by saying that, 'in order to retard the production of this equipment and thereby help maintain the effectiveness of Bomber Command's offensive, it is necessary to destroy both the Experimental Station and to kill or incapacitate the scientific and technical experts working there.'

There were other signs that this raid was out of the ordinary. Up to now, 'security had not been rigidly adhered to on pre-flight briefings, but prior to this attack police were on duty at the briefing room door recording the names of those who entered and locking the doors after they all went in. Such strict security became the norm at Ludford thereafter and, once a raid was announced, not only were crews not allowed to leave the camp but also they were denied all telephone links with the outside world'.

Such was the plan, but unfortunately as the first Pathfinder crews ran in towards Pennemünde, they found that the H2S picture was not as clear as had been predicted: some of the first flares went down two miles to the south, which cost the lives of several hundred foreign workers trapped in the Karlshagen labour camp. But the correct aiming point — the scientists' housing estate — had been

94

94
Sandy Greig's citation for his DSO (see p76).
95
Praise from the highest quarters followed the award.

95

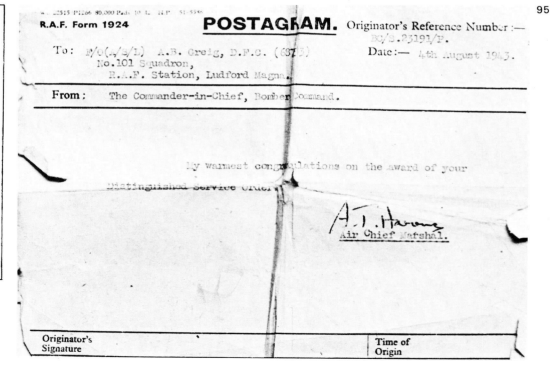

R.A.F. Form 1924   **POSTAGRAM.**   Originator's Reference Number :—
BC/S.25191/P.

To: F/O(A/S/L) A.B. Greig, D.F.C. (68753)
       No.101 Squadron,
       R.A.F. Station, Ludford Magna.   Date:— 4th August 1943.

From: The Commander-in-Chief, Bomber Command.

My warmest congratulations on the award of your Distinguished Service Order.

A.T. Harris
Air Chief Marshal.

Originator's Signature		Time of Origin

accurately marked by a single yellow flare dropped by Wg Cdr John White of 156 Pathfinder Squadron, and four or five of the following Marker crews placed other yellows close by to reinforce the glow. Grp Capt John Searby, the master bomber, or 'master of ceremonies' as he was known to the main force crews, was content with this marking, and when he saw three backers-up correctly reinforce the aiming point yellows with greens he ordered the main force to 'Bomb into the greens'. As a result, over two-thirds of the 231 attacking aircraft on the initial wave succeeded in bombing the correct aiming point or its immediate vicinity. WO Johnson's crew was the first in from 101 Squadron and they attacked from 20,500ft and at 140kts. 'Target identified and bombed on Green TI markers. HC and incendiary bursts very concentrated in target area and large fires seen on leaving target. One of the most concentrated attacks I have seen and Pathfinders were very accurate.'

The last aircraft of the first wave withdrew at 12min after zero hour, but only one out of the five 'Shifters' managed to place his red target indicator on the rocket factory which was the second aiming point. The backers-up naturally ignored the single red and went for the larger, but inaccurate concentration. This was where the master bomber, down at 8,000ft, earned his money, and Grp Capt Searby broadcast a warning that the first backers-up had overshot and that the remainder should not compound the error. He was just in time, and as 113 main force Lancasters thundered in he twice ordered them to ignore the green markers to the south and bomb only those to the north. It was advice well taken by many as witnessed by Sgt Jean-Jaques Minguy, a French-Canadian mid-upper gunner on 101:

'Peenemünde was growing very "lively". On the ground, everything was going up and burning as it isn't possible. This was a mixture of flashes from the ground defences, which seemed to increase their firing in the same measure as we were raining them with bombs, and of explosions which were all more spectacular one from the other. It looked like coal burning — an inferno! Flames were of every colour possible — red, orange, green, blue and what not! Explosions succeeded one another at a rate that surpasses imagination.' (Quoted from *The Peenemünde Raid* by Martin Middlebrook.)

The third and last attack was carried out by Halifaxes of 6 Group and Lancasters of 5 Group, and while they were bearing the brunt of the late attentions of the Luftwaffe fighter force, the 18 101 Squadron aircraft and crews that had successfully attacked were making their way home. Before the raid crews had been assured that if they did not

make a good job of destroying the 'research station', they would be sent back night after night until the task was completed. This worried some returning aircrew like Sgt Geoffrey Whittle, the navigator on WO Walker's crew, because 'we did not think the raid had been very successful. The master bomber was not very encouraging'. But others had seen the damage inflicted on Peenemünde for themselves — 'Buildings seen to disintegrate' reported Flt Sgt Rays' crew on their return. It was a job well done, even if crews at the time did not appreciate the implications for Britain of delaying the arrival of German V-weapons. With hindsight, a 1 Group report in May 1945 was to describe this as 'the most telling single raid of the war'.

Nevertheless, if Bomber Command was becoming more proficient at precision as well as area bombing, the Luftwaffe air defences were also not backward in coming forward to defend their airspace. 'Since the disorganisation of the German night fighters caused by the introduction of Window in July,' wrote Bomber Command's Operational Research Section in the *Monthly Review of Losses and Interceptions of Bomber Command Aircraft in Night Operations — August 1943*, 'a considerable readjustment has apparently been made'. Previously, responsibility for the defence of Germany from air attack had rested with five fighter divisions which controlled a system of fighter 'boxes' running down from Denmark to the Swiss frontier. This was the Kammhüber Line, and any bomber approaching from Britain had to pass

96

96
Sgt Geoffrey Whittle DFM. *IWM*

through one of its 'boxes'. The underground operations room for each division was so well endowed with sophisticated communications and control systems fed from a bevy of advanced early warning and fighter control radars that it was known as a 'Battle Opera House', and from here many controllers could direct small groups of fighters or individual interceptors. This superb German ground-controlled interception system enabled a controller to talk a fighter round its appropriate 'box' until it was precisely into position behind the bomber such that the kill could be completed by reference to the fighter's own airborne radar and pilot's eyesight. Each division could fight its own air battle, and therefore German night fighter crews nearly always operated within a few miles of their own airfields and always under the control of the same ground station.

The drawback to the Kammhüber Line was that it depended for its success entirely on ground and airborne radar systems and once these were 'blinded' by 'Window', close control became impossible. Consequently a former bomber pilot, Major Hajo Herrmann, suggested to Goering that single-seater day fighters be brought into what had previously been a two-seater night fighter preserve. It had been noticed that when a city was being attacked a high flying German pilot could see

bombers below silhouetted against the glow of burning buildings or searchlights, so Herrmann advocated that the Luftwaffe set about the enemy over the targets themselves. All available fighters were to be assembled over radio beacons at the approach of bomber formations, and when the object of their attentions became clear, the fighter pack would be hurled en masse into the bomber stream over the target. They would then pursue and harry the intruders visually to the limit of their endurance and then refuel at the nearest airfield. This new tactic was code-named 'Wild Boar' and it was revolutionary in that it neutralised the effect of 'Window' at a stroke. One fighter control officer could now scramble the whole air defence force and assemble it over the radio beacons thought to be in the bombers' path. 'Enemy night fighters have been identified in groups en route to and over target areas at least 300 miles from their bases,' continued the *Bomber Command Monthly Review* with surprise, 'and during all operations subsequent to 9/10 August a part of the fighter force has been given general directions by a running commentary ... This running commentary gives the height and direction of the bomber stream and the areas over which it is passing. The probable target is frequently given as soon as the target is marked and bombs have

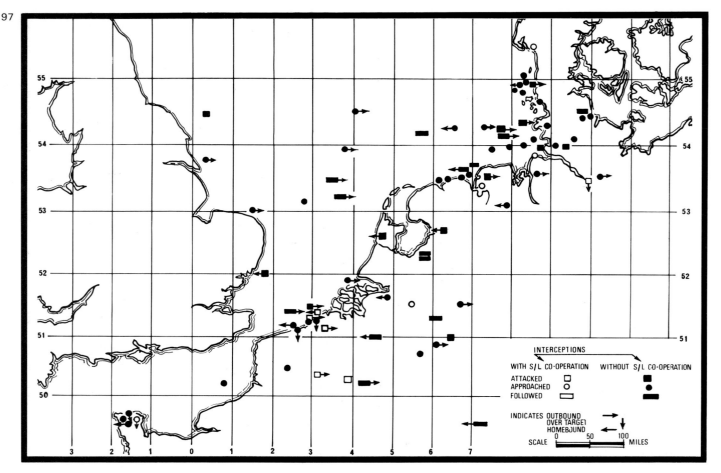

fallen, and the main object of this direction appears to get the fighters to the target rather than into the bomber stream'.

Herein lay the key to the success of Major Herrmann's 'Wild Boar' scheme. Ideally, the Luftwaffe hierarchy would have preferred to confront British bombers over the less politically sensitive approaches to the Reich, but if 'Window' rendered such hopes impossible, then the attacking force had to be hit where it was most vulnerable. Concentrating bombers in time and space, like concentrating merchantmen in convoys, made mutual protection much easier but it also gave the opposition much more to aim at. Over the target itself therefore, all means were employed to enable the fighter crews to find their opposite numbers by visual means. High flying German aircraft would drop flares to illuminate the incoming bombers while the masses of search lights would play evenly on the bottom of the cloud layer so that the bombers could be made out in silhouette, an effect that was further enhanced once the fires started below. Moreover, the bomber crews were at their most vulnerable on their bombing runs, and no amount of tin foil could protect them at such a time.

After overcoming much opposition, Major Herrmann was allowed to try out his theory

for the first time against Bomber Command on 3 July. He and nine other 'Wild Boars' claimed 12 'kills' that night, and Herrmann further proved his point on 27 July over Hamburg, as described in Martin Middlebrook's *The Battle of Hamburg* (Allen Lane, 1980):

'The clouds of smoke over Hamburg were so dense that it made you shudder. I flew over the target several times, and then I saw this bomber in the searchlights. He had nearly reached the top of the smoke cloud at the time.

'The attack was very simple. I went into the searchlights. I was not very experienced; another pilot would have kept in the dark. I was almost level with him, probably just above the turbulence of his propellers. It was like daylight in those searchlights. I could see the rear gunner; he was only looking downwards, probably at the inferno below. There was no movement of his guns. You must remember that, at this time, the British were not generally warned to watch out for us over the target. I had seen other bombers over the target with the gunners looking down.

'I fired and he burned. He banked to the left and then through 180° to the right. As he fell, he turned and dropped away from the smoke cloud. I followed him a little but, as he

97, 98
The growth of the German night fighter threat was represented by the number of interceptions of Bomber Command aircraft plotted for November 1941 (**97**) and September 1942 (**98**).

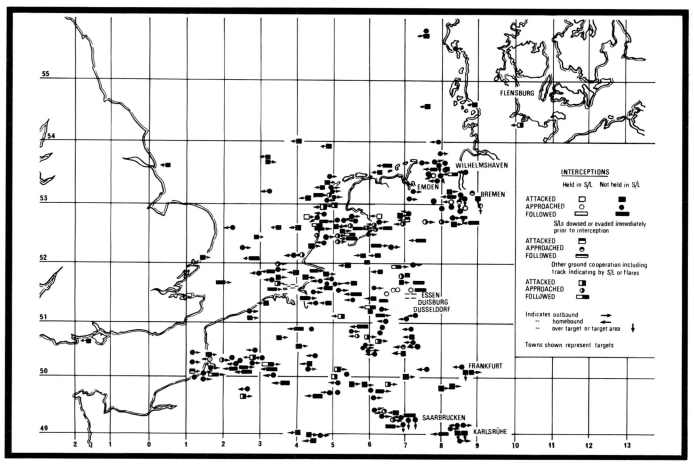

got lower and lower, I left him. I watched him burst on the ground. By the light of his explosion, I could see the "Knicks" — the small walls with bushes built on them against which the cattle found shelter from the sun and wind. That was my homeland — Schleswig-Holstein — as I knew it.'

Major Herrmann's victim crashed into Wellingsbüttel, a northern suburb of Hamburg. It is almost certain that it was Flt Sgt Hurst's crew from 101 Squadron who were then on their sixth mission — there were no survivors.

The Germans were not slow to allocate resources to 'Wild Boar' and the initial British reaction was to mount diversionary raids to protect the main force. 'The reversion to free-lance methods, which commenced at the end of July,' commented Bomber Command's *Monthly Review of Losses for September*, 'has continued on an intensified scale with large groups of fighters (probably as many as 200 on individual nights) being directed by running commentary alone . . . The policy followed has been to hold back the fighter force, orbiting beacons, until the target is known with certainty, the fear of attack on Berlin appearing to be the governing factor and foremost in the minds of the running commentary controllers'. Thus a purely diversionary raid by eight Mosquitos on Berlin coincidental with the attack on Peenemünde led to much confusion and the concentration of over 200 fighters near the German capital so that when the first target markers went down at Peenemünde, the night fighter crews had to transit 100 miles to the north and only got there in time to catch the final wave of attackers. Nevertheless, they still managed to dispose of 41 aircraft or 7% of the bomber force that night, which was a higher loss rate than that being inflicted before the introduction of 'Window'.

Diversionary raids therefore had their limitations, and the clear summer nights of 1943 compounded Bomber Command's problems. The only restriction on 'Wild Boar' missions, besides fuel, was weather conditions at the fighter landing grounds, as at the end of an attack on Berlin on 23/24 August when the fighters were forced down by fog. Not that this did Bomber Command and 101 Squadron much good. 101 lost Flg Off Mahoney's and Flt Sgt Naffir's crews that night, 'and it is estimated that roughly 10% of the force dispatched was attacked'. Moreover, Bomber Command noted with alarm that 'the proportion of total sorties returning damaged by fighter action is more than 50% greater than in the preceding seven months', and the situation was going to get worse. During the Peenemünde raid, Gefreiter Holker shot down two bombers

using two cannons pointing obliquely upwards from his Bf110. This was *Schrage Musik* ('Slanting music' or jazz) and it was to enable many German crews to creep in below and into the Lancaster's blind spot. Here the fighter remained invisible unless the Lancaster pilot happened to be weaving at the time, and as *Schrage Musik* used non-tracer ammunition, in most cases the doomed bomber crews never knew what hit them.

To make life even more uncomfortable and nerve-wracking for the attackers, another night-fighter expert, Oberst von Lossberg, proposed that twin-seater night fighters infiltrate into the bomber stream on the approaches to Germany. Each fighter division retained the responsibility to launch its fighters when it saw a force coming — and a radar screen full of 'Window' was as good an indication as any — but once they were in the air, the best placed operations room would broadcast to all fighters. The subsequent running commentary would not give detailed orders but would rather provide a continuous broadcast of the bomber stream's progress and specifically any changes in its course. The night fighter crews would use this flow of information to find the stream and then use their airborne radars or eyes to strike down individual bombers. If a fighter crew lost the stream, they would return to the running commentary in an attempt to re-locate their quarry.

This technique was christened 'Tame Boar' and it used the RAF's own 'Window' to confirm the position and track of the bomber stream. Von Lossberg was in fact proposing a freelance running battle that might last for over 100 miles and, together

99

99
'Oor Wullie' as painted on Lancaster LL757 by Cpl Jock Steadman. Most 101 Squadron aircraft had gaily coloured mascots emblazoned on their flanks.

100
A hive of activity at 'Oor Wullie's' dispersal at Ludford. 'Wullie's' captain, Plt Off 'Rusty' Waughman, is looking out of the cockpit window and Cpl Jock Steadman is on the wing. The ABC aerials are clearly in evidence and the anonymous photographer must have known that it was forbidden to take pictures of such secret equipment because the photo was taken from inside a ground crew hut. *via Waughman*

with 'Wild Boar', it marked the virtual demise of totally controlled interceptions in neat little 'boxes'. Between them, the 'Boar' packs accounted for 123 RAF bombers and crews in three raids against Berlin at the end of August 1943, and brought an end to any peace of mind that Squadrons such as 101 might have enjoyed following Hamburg and the introduction of 'Window'.

In an effort to regain the initiative, Bomber Command looked for the means to exploit any loopholes that might be inherent in the Luftwaffe's new freelance tactics. Compressing the bomber force still further — and no raid in October 1943 lasted for more than 26min — gave diversionary raids a chance to throw German controllers off the scent until it was too late, but it was not always possible to fool the opposition in this fashion, especially as Bomber Command was increasingly attacking targets deep inside enemy airspace. So it was decided to concentrate on the major weakness of the freelance system, namely that 'while commentaries are still transmitted from several stations, they are now coordinated, authority frequently being delegated to one controller who deploys the whole available force to cover possible targets.' The German fighter crews relied completely on getting timely and accurate information on the position of the bomber stream otherwise they would stumble about all night, and if it had not been possible to stop 200 controllers talking to 200 fighters, it was surely not beyond British ingenuity to prevent the night fighter force from hearing a single controller's running commentary and thereby thwarting the whole freelance endeavour.

The VHF radios fitted to German night fighters covered the frequencies from 38 to 42 MHz, and the first British response was to erect 15 ground transmitters in England to put a barrage of noise over the whole band. This was known as 'Ground Cigar', but as it only had a range of about 140 miles, a similar jamming device had to be taken into the air on raids beyond the Low Countries. Fortunately the Telecommunications Research Establishment at Malvern had a suitable device in the pipeline which was originally named 'Jostle'. 'Jostle' was conceived in early 1943 to counter the fighter control frequencies in the Kammhüber boxes, and a letter from Air Cdre S. O. Bufton, Director of Bomber Operations, laid down the requirements for the 'Jostle' carrier on 23 April 1943:

'The aircraft required must be capable of proceeding with the main bomber force to the target in order to provide protection.

'As enemy aircraft may home on to the jammer, the aircraft must have the performance to give a sufficient degree of immunity from interception.

'It has to be a heavy aircraft to accommodate the equipment.'

The Lancaster was the obvious choice to carry 'Jostle' and by 30 May it had been agreed that 100 Squadron at Waltham would fit the bill. But then a complication arose. 100 Squadron aircraft were then earmarked for H2S installation, and as the Lancaster's power supplies could not cope with the demands of H2S and 'Jostle' together, 'it will be necessary to alter the H2S programme or alternatively fit "Jostle" into a different squadron'. The former was too difficult, so

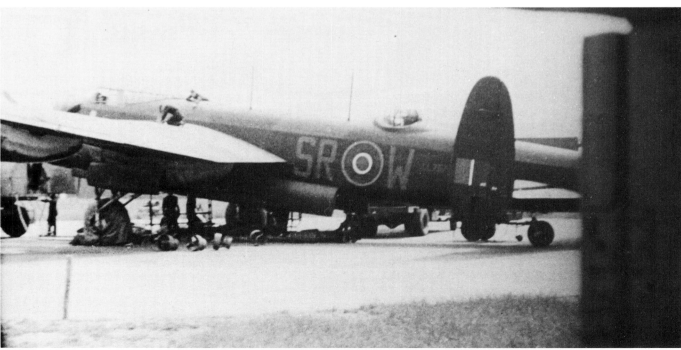

101
Squadron Lancaster SR-B
dropping a stream of incendiaries
over Duisberg on 14 October
1944. The most interesting
features of this photograph
however are the two ABC aerials
on top of the fuselage. Such secret
sights were normally hidden from
the photographer's eye, and
whenever a crew landed away
from base the tell-tale masts were
covered and an armed guard
placed on the aircraft. Thereafter
only groundcrew from Ludford
were allowed to carry out aircraft
repairs. *IWM*

someone must have looked at the next squadron on the list, for on 10 June 1943 it was decided that 101 Squadron would carry 'Jostle' as it 'will not be fitted with H2S in the initial programme'.

Having changed the Squadron, the RAF then decided to change the name. The first 'Ground Cigar' station became operational on 30/31 July 1943, and as 'Jostle' was only an airborne version of 'Ground Cigar', it came as no surprise when 'Jostle' was rechristened 'Airborne Cigar'. However, this was a bit of a mouthful, and 1 Group only legalised common practice when it sent the following telegram to Bomber Command soon afterwards:

'In view of the brevity and simplicity of the term, it is requested that you refer to "Airborne Cigar" aircraft as "A.B.C." aircraft in all future communications.'

ABC equipment trials took place in a 101 Squadron Lancaster on 4-6 September 1943 under the guidance of Flt Lt F. Collins, a radar specialist seconded from Bomber Command. On 8 September a test flight was made over the North Sea to within 10 miles of the enemy coast, and this was so successful that the Squadron was ready to try out the new jamming equipment operationally against Hanover on 22 September. Eight operators listened out that night, and the first words they heard over the ABC were 'Achtung, English bastards coming!'. The new, and highly secret, equipment had a most successful baptism of fire on that occasion, but ironically the only aircraft shot down out of a Squadron complement of 18 dispatched to Mannheim on 23 September was the sole Lancaster to carry ABC.

ABC had a range of approximately 50 miles, and the equipment, which was soon to be fitted into every 101 Squadron aircraft, was officialy described in the following terms: 'ABC is designed for use on bombing raids over enemy territory to interrupt enemy communications by jamming particular frequencies on which radio messages are being sent to night fighters from ground control stations. It comprises three 50-watt transmitters each capable of sending out frequency-modulated jamming signals covering narrow frequency bands selected within the 38.3 to 42.5 MHz range by means of manual tuning controls. A "panoramic" receiver provides means of locating enemy transmissions in this range of frequencies, and setting jamming signals accurately upon them.

'The total weight of the equipment is $604\frac{3}{4}$ lb. When the equipment is switched on, all three transmitters are suppressed simultaneously while the panoramic receiver sweeps over the 38.3 to 42.5 MHz band 25 times each second. Any signals picked up are

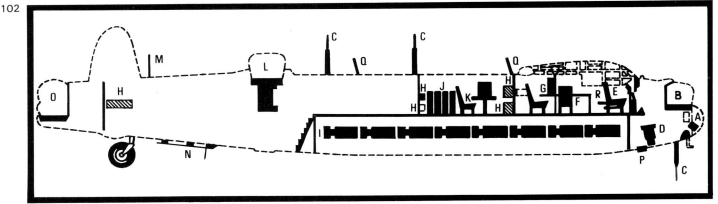

102
Interior view of a 101 Squadron
Lancaster.
 Key:
A: Bomb aimer's position,
B: Nose turret,
C: ABC transmission masts,
D: Camera,
E: Pilot's position,
F: Navigator's position,
G: Radio operator's position,
H: Wing and tail spars,
I: Bomb bay
J: ABC transmitters and receiver
 (mounted on the port side of the
 fuselage),
K: Spec Ops position,
L: Dorsal turret,
M: ABC reception aerial,
N: Beam approach aerial,
O: Rose Rice tail turret,
P: Window chute,
Q: Standard radio fit aerials,
R: Flight engineer's position.

103
View from the rear of a Lancaster
looking forward over the main
spar at the Spec Op's position.
via Waughman

104
Kassel cartoon.

displayed on a three-inch diameter cathode ray tube. Here the frequencies are represented as a horizontal line, and any signals picked up are shown as vertical "blips" which grow out of the base

'When a "blip" appears, the operator sets a bright strobe spot to mark it, and "throws" a switch which stops the panoramic sweep of the receiver; he tunes it to the single frequency marked by the strobe and brings his earphones into the receiver circuit so that he can listen to the incoming signal. Having identified this as an enemy ground transmission, he may then switch on a transmitter and turn the tuning control until the jamming signal, as displayed on the cathode ray tube, covers the marker spot. The enemy signal is then completely obliterated in his earphones by the output of the jamming transmitter. Whenever desirable, the operator may suppress the transmitter in order to determine whether the enemy has changed to a new frequency, and if so, readjust the jamming signal. Three transmitters are provided so that three communication channels

in the enemy Ground Control Intercept band may be simultaneously jammed.'

Such then was the theory, but what did it mean in practice? For a start, 101 Squadron Lancasters suddenly sprouted three 7ft-long aerials, 'giving the appearance of three telegraph poles which looked far from safe'. Two were on the upper fuselage and the third stuck out under the nose until it nearly reached the ground — surprisingly, they had very little effect on the Lancaster's performance.

Then there was the question of the ABC operator, and for this purpose an eighth member was added to the 101 Squadron crews to be known as the 'Special Operator' (one of the reasons for the abbreviation to ABC was that Spec Ops naturally objected to being called 'Cigar Operators'). 'Spec Ops' were selected from all aircrew categories with every man being a German-speaking volunteer for unknown special duties. 'All that was really necessary,' recalled Sgt H. van Geffen, 'was the ability to recognise an R/T transmission as definitely German rather than Russian, Czech, or Polish, but obviously some Spec Ops were more fluent in German than others. (Spec Ops were also taught some of the codewords that the German controllers used, such as 'Kapelle' for target altitude and 'Karussel' for fly an orbit.) After a short course on set manipulation, we were posted to Ludford where we were given further training in searching on our receiver for enemy R/T and back-tuning three transmitters to that signal in order to jam it. Once we were able to do this in 30sec we were ready for business . . .'

101 crews were still expected to carry on with their normal bombing duties while the Spec Op jammed, but the weight of ABC and the extra crew member reduced bomb loads by about 1,000lb. Before flight, each Spec Op was allocated his own section of the VHF waveband that he was required to search and jam. 'We were given a position, usually 6° East,' explained a Spec Op quoted in *Instruments of Darkness* by Alfred Price (Macdonald and Jane's, 1977), 'at which

point we would switch our receiver to "On" and commence to search the waveband for any German R/T. When we saw a signal on the cathode ray tube, we would tune our receiver in to it and listen. If we heard Jerry vectoring his fighters, we would turn on one of our jammers which showed as a blip on the screen base line. We then moved this blip along the line until it was on top of the German blip, and when they coincided, we started the jammer. We would then watch to see if he changed frequency and then carry out the same procedure with the second jammer (leaving the first still jamming), and so on with the third jammer if the German changed frequency again. Thus we could not only hear him but also see which frequency he had changed to so that we could jam him before he had a chance to send his instructions. I could also tune two or three of my jammers to a single frequency depending on the strength of signal I received.' Hopefully, the German fighter crews would then find that the reassuring voice of their running commentator had been replaced by what can best be described as a 'wig-wog' noise produced by a constantly varying audio note running up and down the scale. From then on it was just a matter of following the blips around the screen. 'If the jamming got too bad, the German controller would go off the air altogether. Later he would appear on a different frequency, but it only took a matter of seconds to cover the new blip. Often the German controller would get rather angry and I sometimes felt a little sorry for him, trying to get through while I was stopping him.'

All in all, ABC was a very ingenious piece of equipment. The ABC Spec Op and his black boxes were situated just aft of the main spar on the port side of the Lancaster fuselage, cut off from the rest of the crew except for the intercom. 'We sat in darkness and the nearest other crewman was the mid-upper gunner — his boots were at my level, about 4ft further down the aircraft. We were even more isolated when we operated our sets because we had to cut out the intercom circuit to prevent distraction. Thus we had no idea of what was going on around us, and the only link with reality was a little call light which the pilot could operate to attract our attention in a crisis.'

Over half the Squadron aircraft were fitted with ABC by 6 October 1943 — a modification which took about 3,000 man hours for each Lancaster — and the 101 personnel complement increased accordingly as one corporal and six aircraftmen wireless mechanics were posted in to 'maintain special duties signal equipment' together with an eventual total of 33 Spec Ops to use it. Many of the latter were Britons with a gift for languages, but others such as Sgts Shultz, Liersch, Engelhardt, and Herman probably had a head start in the business. But on a serious note, some of the Spec Ops were German-born, and they not only took a double risk whenever they flew over enemy territory but also those who were German Jews took a treble risk. They were very brave men.

On 4 October it was decreed that 'never less than eight ABC aircraft should operate on a raid, spaced at distances of not more than 10 miles apart'. Besides jamming, Spec Ops 'were required to record any German transmissions received in their logs, together with the times of transmission, and this information was handed in at the post-flight debriefing'. However it has to be emphasised that the ABC operators did not send spoof messages to confuse the German fighter force — they had to know enough German to recognise the language when they heard it, but thereafter their only task was to jam the control frequencies with noise. 'Most of our school German accents,' said one Spec Op, 'would not have fooled a deaf German in a thunderstorm'. Jamming the control frequencies was more than sufficient according to Bomber Command's *Monthly Review of Losses for November 1943*. 'Enemy freelance night fighters had an unsuccessful month, as reflected in the low casualty and attack rates. This was due in part to the weather, which was mainly unfavourable, and also to the continued use of the tactics developed with such success in October. Radio countermeasures, particularly Airborne Cigar, have also played a great part in interfering with the running commentary control.

'Airborne Cigar has fully justified expectations. Frequently the whole VHF band used by the night fighters has been obliterated and, on occasions when operation channels have been found clear of jaming, the ABC operators have found the frequencies concerned and effective jamming has followed

104

ANOTHER PATIENT SUCCESSFULLY TREATED

WO Jack Laurens stands in front
of Lancaster K-King with his crew
at Ludford in January 1944.
Laurens, a South African,
captained what was known on
the Squadron as the 'League of
Nations' crew because of the
many and varied backgrounds of
its members. L-R: WO Laurens
(Pilot), Sgt Davies (Spec Op), Sgt
'Cass' Waight (W/Op) — note the
new body armour being worn on
test — Flt Sgt Les Burton (Nav),
Sgt 'Wag' Kibble (Flt Eng), Sgt
Don Bolt (Mid-Upper), Sgt Ted
Royston (Rear Gunner), Sgt Chris
Aitkin (Bomb-aimer).

106

Post-flight debriefing for those
who returned from Berlin. 'The
intelligence officers had to glean
from us every last bit of
information such as had we hit
the target, had we been engaged
by fighters, had we seen any
aircraft hit, and were any
parachutes seen to open
afterwards? There were lots and
lots of questions until they were
satisfied that we could tell them
no more.' L-R: Flt Lt Henderson
(Int O), Plt Off R. A. Nightingale
(Pilot), Sgt K. F. Scott (Nav), Sgt
J. Muldowney (Rear Gunner),
Plt Off A. McCartney (Bomb-
aimer), Sgt L. Ley (Flt Eng). The
Nightingale crew had just
completed their 11th op to Berlin
and their 27th mission.

immediately. The enemy has been forced to attempt the use of morse and of the higher-pitched female voice in order to minimise the effects of interference.'

The first raid on which all 101 Squadron Lancasters carried ABC was mounted against Kassel on 22 October, and the Spec Ops had a great time picturing the consternation they were causing on the ground. But the real aim of radio countermeasures was to afford a measure of protection for the main force during the forthcoming Battle of Berlin. 'We can wreck Berlin from end to end if the USAAF will come in on it,' wrote Sir Arthur Harris to the Prime Minster on 3 November 1943. 'It will cost between us 400-500 aircraft. It will cost Germany the war.' Such confidence, with its attendant promise of decisive results, impressed Churchill sufficiently to gain his approval, and although the Americans decided not to 'Come in on it' following a period of severe daylight losses, Harris was content to go it alone.

The Battle of Berlin was launched on 18 November by 444 heavy bombers, and although the round trip of over 1,100 miles necessitated a vulnerable 60min flying time over enemy territory, only nine bombers failed to return. It augured well, but unfortunately Flg Off McManus' aircraft from 101 was one of the nine shot down and its ABC equipment fell into German hands. It was sent to Telefunken for examination, and on 30 November Engineer-Colonel Schwenke (the Intelligence Officer in charge of the Luftwaffe sections dealing with captured enemy equipment) submitted the following report to Field-Marshal Milch quoted from *Instruments of Darkness*:

'I have some interesting foreign Intelligence concerning a number of new things that have come to light. Three transmitters have been found in the Lancaster aircraft — in fact it was flying not with the normal seven-man but with an eight-man crew, one of whom was an additional radio operator. This set is called T.3160 (the official RAF designation for the ABC transmitters) and is apparently there for the jamming of our VHF radio-telephone traffic. At present I cannot say how far this jamming can be defeated by appropriate counter-measures or frequency alteration.'

Nevertheless the Germans took an increasing toll of the British bomber force as the winter of 1943/44 progressed. Moreover, 101 Squadron suffered more than its fair share of these losses. It lost three crews on 26 November 1943 against Stuttgart and Berlin, 10 more crews over Berlin between 2 December 1943 and 2 January 1944, and eight more crews against Brunswick, Berlin, and Leipzig before the end of February. In all

the bomber squadron which was supposed to help protect everyone else lost no fewer than 176 aircrew killed or taken prisoner in the first three months of the Battle of Berlin.

What were the reasons for this apparent contradiction? The most obvious answer, and the one which most crews feared to be true, was that 101 Squadron Lancasters made themselves more vulnerable whenever they jammed. Any transmission from an aircraft could be homed on to once its frequency had been established, and the Luftwaffe certainly equipped their night fighters with the means to home on the H2S transmissions from the heavy bombers. But although the Germans considered using ABC transmissions to their own advantage, they dismissed the idea because 101 had foreseen the danger. 'Spec Ops are never to jam for more than a few seconds at a time,' wrote the Squadron orders, and as crews stuck scrupulously to this injunction in the beginning, Colonel Schwenke declared to higher authority that ABC jamming transmissions were of such a short duration that it was impracticable to think of homing on to them.

However, as time went on, and bomber losses grew, what if a frightened Spec Op kept his ABC jammers on for longer and longer? Homing on to the transmissions of another night fighter acting as *Fühlungshalter* (observer of the route of bomber streams) was common in the Luftwaffe, and it would not have taken a German genius to deduce that it was just as easy to home on to an airborne jammer. Certainly the equipment was available in the shape of the FuG 16ZY, a direction finding device which conveniently operated in the 38.5 to 42.3MHz band. FuG 16ZY gave no distance but it could display right or left, and up or down directions to an emitting source, and it is hard to believe that no German night fighter crew thought of using this equipment against ABC.

Nevertheless, there is no evidence that the Luftwaffe ever homed on to ABC in large numbers and therefore the reasons for 101's relatively high losses must be found elsewhere. Partly they may have been due to simple bad luck, for the Squadron's Lancasters were always distributed throughout the bomber stream at the same height and conforming in all respects to the main force attack plan so that they should never have been more vulnerable than anyone else. But the Squadron did have special circumstances of its own. Firstly, 'because of the cover 101's ABC was providing for other squadrons, we were called upon to fly on all major operations when other units in 1 Group might be resting'. From October 1943 onwards, 101 Squadron accompanied *all* main force attacks on German targets by night, the number of air-

craft operating varying from six to 27. Secondly, when 101 flew it sent a lot of men into the air. Some bomber squadrons only had an establishment of 20 aircraft and crews, whereas 101 was established for 30 and had an average of 33 aircraft on charge. It was merely routine to launch 26 aircraft and crews to attack Berlin on 22 November, and 21 eight-men crews were detailed to revisit the German capital on 2 December when Sqn Ldr Robertson's, Flt Lt Frazer-Hollins', and Sgt Murrell's crews failed to return. Yet whatever the reasons, such was the measure of the Squadron's apparent vulnerability that when Bomber Command requested more effective twin 0.5in Browning machine guns for the 'heavy' rear gunners in place of the standard quadruple 0.303s to improve 'under defence', 101 was placed at the top of the Lancaster squadron priority list. 101 Squadron were to win the hamper of 'grog' offered by the firm of Rose-Rice of Gainsborough, manufacturers of the new turret, for being the first unit to shoot down a night fighter with their improved armament.

By the beginning of 1944, Bomber Command possessed the ability to embark on a battle of wits with the enemy. The steady improvement of navigation equipment and techniques* allowed the planners to select routes with the greatest care to

*To overcome the difficulties attendant on one man navigating safely, each bomber now had a 'Navigation Team' consisting of the navigator and two assistants, ie the air bomber was responsible for astro and drift observations, and the W/Op was responsible for Gee fixes and DF assistance.

hoodwink enemy fighters and prevent them finding the bomber stream. 'Dog-legs' were introduced to weave 500 bombers around the sky, and thrusts were made this way and that so that the ground controllers could never be sure where to concentrate their waiting fighters. ABC was further updated in January 1944 by fitting plug-in coils to allow unmonitored jammers to operate on 31.2MHz and thereby thwart the German Benito system of homing fighters on to British bombers. Yet despite such refine-

107

After the Intelligence officer came the other specialists. In this picture Flt Lt Knute Brydon, the Canadian Bomber Leading (seated with greatcoat), is debriefing Flt Sgt Ross (far left, seated). At far left in the background is the Met Officer, Flg Off Stan Horrocks, who was interested in all the route weather information he could gain. At the extreme right, holding a cigarette, is Flg Off Arthur, the deputy Squadron Engineering Officer, who needed to know how the crew's aircraft had behaved and any damage it had sustained. The remaining aircrew members are from the Laurens crew.

108

Route of the Nuremburg raid.

109

Refuelling and bombing up. The standard 101 Squadron operational load on 31 March 1944 was either one 4,000lb bomb, 270 4lb incendiaries, and 168 30lb incendiaries, or one 2,000lb bomb, 1,650 4lb incendiaries, and 36 30lb incendiaries. The fuel bowser is in the process of filling the Lancaster with up to 2,154 gallons of 100-octane fuel at the rate of 30gal/min.

110

Members of the Adamson crew enjoy a 'cuppa' in their billet at Ludford before their fateful raid on Nuremburg. (L–R): R. Luffman (W/Op), Kippen (Nav), J. Goodall (RG), N. Bowyer (Flt Eng), W. Adamson (pilot). Don Brinkhurst was at the Sick Quarters when his photo was taken. He had been wounded in the right arm on the way back from Berlin on 2 December 1943, and Luffman had been awarded the DFM after taking over his turret. Jimmy Goodall shot down an Me110 that night.

ments and electronic wizardry, Bomber Command continued to have a rough passage during the Battle of Berlin. With hindsight, it is not surprising that the average German fighter pilot should defend his homeland and capital with the same degree of dedication and bravery as his opposite number displayed during the Battle of Britain. In addition, after years of fighting an offensive war, the Germans were only now getting to grips with a defensive strategy and this they did with their customary efficiency. For example, the Germans used a captured ABC transmitter to jam their own fighter control frequency, except that periodically they faded it out when orders had to be passed. This was undertaken in the mistaken notion that Spec Ops would not tune into another jammer when they heard it, whereas in fact they had instructions that if there were no signals on their screens, they were to reinforce any other jammer they could hear.

Another German ruse was greatly to speed-up their R/T, in the hope that they could pass their instructions before ABC could be brought to bear. Then again, the ground controllers would broadcast a continuous stream of music, break off to snap out an instruction, and then bring the music back on again. Such devices had their limitations — R/T instructions that were rattled out before the Spec Op could jam them were often too fast for a fighter pilot to catch — but there were always other loopholes to exploit in the electronic battle of wits. For instance the Germans discovered that the ABC operators stopped jamming for a short period every half hour so as not to interfere with the regular wind forecasts from

England. The running commentators used this respite to alter all their frequencies, so that when the Spec Ops switched on again they had to hunt afresh for the new frequencies to jam. It all took time, and gave the Germans several minutes of uninterrupted commentary every half hour. Subterfuges such as this, combined with increasing the power of German transmissions, ensured that although British radio countermeasures caused massive disruption of the enemy aerial defence system, they never succeeded in stopping all ground-to-air communications throughout a raid.

The limitations of the British strategic bomber offensive at the beginning of 1944 were vividly underlined by 101 Squadron's experiences on the night of 30 March. The target this time was Nuremberg, a city deep in southern Germany which housed one of the MAN heavy engineering works and played host to the great Nazi rallies. A force of 795 bombers was dispatched to attack it, of which the largest individual squadron effort came from 101 with 26 aircraft and crews.

Unfortunately the outbound leg not only took place in moonlight without protective cloud cover, but also the crews were briefed to fly in an almost dead straight line for 220 miles across enemy territory before the final turn towards Nuremberg. This prevented any changes of course to cause confusion, and even while the leading bombers were crossing the English coast the German listening service had determiend the stream's path very accurately from H2S transmissions.

The 101 Spec Ops warmed up their receivers before crossing the Belgian coast, and as they approached the first turning

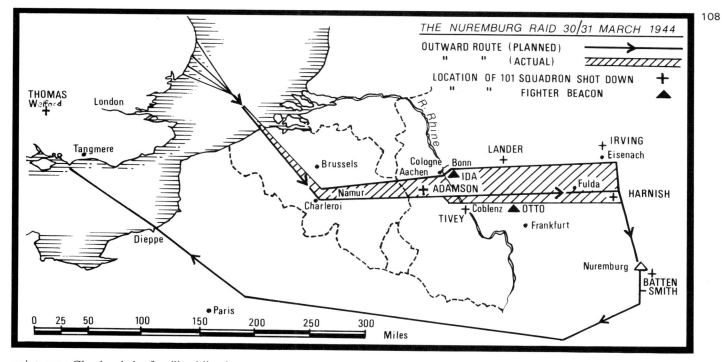

THE NUREMBURG RAID 30/31 MARCH 1944

OUTWARD ROUTE (PLANNED) →
       "   "   (ACTUAL) ///////
LOCATION OF 101 SQUADRON SHOT DOWN ✛
       "   "   FIGHTER BEACON ▲

point near Charleroi the familiar blips began to appear on the cathode ray tubes indicating that the running commentary had started to the night fighter force which had already taken-off. It was the Third Fighter Division's controller ordering all Tame Boar crews to assemble over radio beacon 'Ida' SE of Cologne, and despite the attentions of 26 Spec Ops the running commentary continued to break through. This was crucial, for at Charleroi the bomber stream was to turn straight towards Ida.

The bomber crews had been nervous for some time that they might be caught in the bright moonlight, and these nerves took their toll. 'A Halifax came right over the top of us, about 300ft up,' recorded Sergeant Don Brinkhurst,* the mid-upper gunner on Plt Off Adamson's crew. 'He was roughly 10 o'clock from us when I last saw him and, just as he disappeared, I saw one long burst of tracer come down at us from that direction. German tracer was bluish but this was the pink and red that we used. It caught us down our port side and we were soon on fire. At the time we were weaving and I expect that to a gunner who was on edge and jumpy we could have looked like a fighter making an attack.

'I tried to contact the skipper on the intercom but got no joy. I got out of my turret, got my parachute on and managed to reach the door by pulling myself upwards for we were going down steeply. I could feel the "Special" holding on to the back of my

*This quote, and some of the others, are taken from Martin Middlebrook's excellent book, *The Nuremburg Raid*, Allen Lane, 1980.

"ERRORS DUE TO ... WIND."

111
Wind cartoon.

ABC jamming was spread too thinly and the running commentary came through clearly on most occasions.

It was bad enough that the force had been routed just past 'Ida' and that it was now heading just to the north of 'Otto', the fates had conspired against the bombers in other ways as well. For a start the winds were much higher than had been forecast, so that the stream soon lost its protective cohesion. Then, on top of the moonlight, the night was so cold that long, white condensation trails issued out from behind the bombers, pointing them out for all to see. Finally, a Luftwaffe bomber unit deposited strings of parachute flares high over the bomber stream to unmask what-ever protective cover of darkness still remained.

The German night fighters were therefore able to harry and hunt the British bombers all the way from the Rhine to Nuremberg. Plt Off Lander's crew were the third from 101 to go down, this time at Dillenburg, followed by Plt Off Irving's crew 10 miles north of Eisenach. In all, 59 Bomber Command crews were lost on the long leg and the turn towards Nuremberg did little to halt the onslaught. Even though they twisted and turned and jammed, there was little that a 101 Squadron crew could do to shake off an interceptor that had them in his sights, especially if that interceptor carried Schräge Musik. Leutnant Wilhelm Suess had already dispatched two Lancasters with this lethal device when he came across a third. Once more he crept in underneath his prey and fired, only to see the bomber immediately go into a violent corkscrew. The German had to wait for three minutes while his radar operator changed the 'Schräge Musik' ammunition drum during which time Suess formated underneath the weaving Lancaster to remain unseen. When the cannons had been reloaded he fired again, setting the bomber's wings on fire and igniting the incendiaries in the bomb bay. The Lancaster pilot, Flt Sgt Clyde Harnish, a Canadian serving with 101 Squadron, made a last desperate attempt to extinguish the flames by diving down 7,000ft, but to no avail. Four of his crew got out but Flt Sgt Harnish was to perish as the fifth 101 aircraft and the 67th casualty of the bomber stream went down. Harnish's Lancaster crashed on the village of Simmershausen, some 12 miles east of Fulda. Its 4,000lb bomb exploded on impact causing considerable damage, and one of the crew was unfortunate enough to land by parachute immediately afterwards, whereupon he was attacked by irate German villagers. The mid-upper gunner, Sgt Mike Greer from Canada, had the presence of mind to hide in a nearby chicken house until the fury subsided.

harness and I felt sure he would follow me out.' The Spec Op did so, but he was found two days later hanging dead by his partially open parachute harness from a tree. Five men died on the first 101 Squadron aircraft to go down, and it was tragic that Plt Off Adamson DFC and his crew were on the penultimate mission of their tour that night.

Another Squadron crew, captained by Flt Sgt Tivey, strayed south and was promptly shot down by the flak batteries at Koblenz, so 101 had lost two Lancasters by the time the force reached the Rhine. But this was nothing to the welcome that the Luftwaffe was waiting to hand out at Ida. Not that they had any real idea of the rich pickings coming their way — the element of surprise, as loitering fighters suddenly found themselves inside a bomber stream, was mutual. But once they collected their wits the 'Tame Boar' fighters could make their final kills easily in the moonlight on the straight leg past 'Ida', and the Germans saught to throw every available fighter into the fray by means of the running commentary. The Second Fighter Division came down from northern Germany, Hajo Hermann's First came across from the Berlin area, while the Seventh Division hurried up from the south to wait for the stream by radio beacon 'Otto'. In the process the Germans rapidly switched between nine different speech channels and two Morse channels, and during the main air battle itself the running commentary was broadcast on five separate channels. The Spec Ops found and jammed all of these but the enemy transmissions were so powerful, and so many frequencies were used, that the

To crown it all, few bombs fell on Nuremberg that night. The first target markers were to fall at 0105hrs, five minutes ahead of the main force, but although the bombers were in clear skies themselves, the target was shrouded by ground haze. It was bad enough that the Pathfinders had to mark blindly when they had come prepared to bomb visually, but a sudden increase in wind strength blew some of the Pathfinders off course and they marked in the wrong place. Most main force bomb aimers were content to bomb into whatever markers they could see, but Sgt Alderson, the bomb aimer on Flt Sgt Davidson's crew from 101, refused to bomb on his first run because he was doubtful about the position of the target indiactors. Davidson hauled his Lancaster, together with its mainly Geordie crew, round in a wide orbit to try again, only to find on the second run that their heavy 2,000lb MC bomb had stuck and had to be taken back to Ludford.

The fact that the Germans did not definitely appreciate that Nuremberg was the target until 0113hrs was of little consequence. 'Nach Nürnberg, Nach Nürnberg' came the invocation from the running commentator over the earphones of those Spec Ops still remaining, though for Plt Off Beer — one of the rare breed of pilot Spec Ops — on Plt Off Batten-Smith's crew, it was probably the last thing he did hear. 'Think of me at one o'clock, will you,' said Jimmy Batten-Smith to his WAAF girl friend as he went through his usual pre-flight routine of handing over his writing case containing farewell letters for his parents, who lived in India, which were to be sent if he went missing. Assistant Section Officer Patricia Bourne, an equipment officer at Ludford, dutifully set her alarm for that time, and approximately half an hour later Plt Off Batten-Smith's Lancaster was caught by a German fighter as it flew out of the target area. The wreckage of the Lancaster fell beside an autobahn junction six miles east of Nuremberg and all the crew died — theirs was the 86th bomber lost that night.

The only good thing about the Nuremberg raid from Bomber Command's point of view was that the single-seat 'Wild Boar' units were all too far away to see action, and that the bomber force was so dispersed by the time it left the target that the 'Tame Boar' crews lost is completely. Not that an unmolested return eased the strain on Flt Sgt Thomas' crew — at 0530hrs their Lancaster flew into the ground at Welford, Berkshire, as they tried to land at Newbury.

Back at Ludford, the impact of Nuremberg — 101 suffered the heaviest loss of any squadron taking part with seven of its aircraft and 56 of its aircrew missing — only came with the dawn. 'We waited and waited

and waited,' said E. T. 'Dutch' Holland, an Australian pilot on 101. 'We were accustomed to losing the odd one or two aircraft... but with nearly one-third of our Squadron missing, this was a big kick in the guts for us all. We waited up until nearly mid-day before going to our huts — stunned, shocked and silent, each crew member wrapped in his own mental anguish.'

112
Sgt Don Brinkhurst with members of the Resistance at Herstall near Liege. The man on the right is Robert Oliver who at their first meeting took Brinkhurst into a back room where his mother-in-law was frying mushrooms. 'What is she frying?' he asked Brinkhurst in perfect English. Brinkhurst gave an immediate answer whereupon Oliver uncocked the revolver he had in his hand and said that if Brinkhurst had stopped to think or hesitated, he would have been shot as a German imposter. The girl is Jenny Dubair. She got Brinkhurst across a guarded bridge over the Meuse by pretending to be his girl-friend. Such photographs are extremely uncommon because of the obvious risks to the brave people involved (see p108).

113
Safe at last — a relieved Don Brinkhurst in friendly Swiss company.

113

Ludford Magna

Although 101 made the greatest contribution to the 96 Bomber Command aircraft which failed to return from Nuremberg, one man did eventually get back to Ludford and he was Sgt Don Brinkhurst. His crew had always agreed that if they were shot down the survivors would do their best to get home and contact the relatives of those who died or were prisoners of war. So when Sgt Brinkhurst found himself on solid ground some 10 miles inside Germany he started walking towards Belgium through the heavily wooded Eifel countryside. He travelled 40 miles over the next four days, skirting enemy patrols and living off raw potatoes when his survival rations ran out. The raw potatoes were a mistake and, wracked with stomach cramps, he eventually approached 'a very fat lady at an isolated farmhouse who was putting out her washing'. From then on he was given shelter by the Resistance at Visé just north of Liege, and during the next three weeks he was even given a grand 21st birthday party. Then his presence was betrayed by a young woman and Sgt Brinkhurst only just managed to evade the subsequent German search party. He eventually reached Switzerland, but he soon became bored with internment and recrossed the border to meet up with Allied troops who had just landed in the south of France. On his return to England, Don Brinkhurst was commissioned and sent back to 101 where, on 2 January 1945, he took-off at the start of another tour — ironically the target for that night was Nuremberg!

All Bomber Command aircrew carried survival aids such as compasses cleverly hidden in collar studs or tunic buttons to help them return home after baling out. There was even a pigeon loft, manned by one corporal and two aircraftmen pigeon keepers, at Binbrook to provide homing pigeons for crews at Ludford to carry on ops to bring messages back after a ditching at sea. (The RAF Pigeon Service was disbanded in January 1944.) But if most crews eschewed the company of feathered friends in the air, that

114

114
Ludford Magna at eventide.

did not stop one Squadron crew from carrying a rabbit mascot on all operations, complete with its own oxygen tube fed into its box, in an effort to bring them enough luck to avoid being shot down in the first place.

Perhaps it was due to lucky rabbit's feet, alive or otherwise, but other members of 101 besides Sgt Brinkhurst did live to tell the tale after being shot down. The unfortunate ones ended up behind barbed wire as 'Kriegies' where most survived to be repatriated after the war, unless they were unlucky like Flt Sgt Cook who was 'shot attempting to escape and died of wounds', or could not take the strain like a flying officer who was 'wounded on baling out over Berlin and committed suicide in PoW camp hospital'. Those with luck on their side came back with the help of the Resistance, to carry on the fight, but even then the ordeal was not over as Sgt Jack Worsfold discovered. On 3 May 1944, Sgt Worsfold was a 19-year old tail gunner who was the only member of his crew to survive when their Lancaster was shot up over France. On his return to England he visited some of the relations of his dead colleagues, 'But only once, it was awful. They tried to talk to me, but there was no communication really. I felt antagonism, as if they were saying, "Why him, and not our boy . . .?" '

Yet there was always 'home' at Ludford Magna to come back to, for although 101 Squadron lost 163 aircrew in the first three months of 1944 alone, in the midst of death there was always life. As 1 Group expanded in 1943, the Air Officer Commanding had found it increasingly difficult to exercise realistic operational control unaided over all his stations, so the Base Organisation was introduced. This sub-divided 1 Group airfields into geographical cells or Bases, each of which was commanded by an Air Commodore, and on 20 November 1943 approval was sought to create No 14 Base at Ludford with Grp Capt R. S. Blucke DSO, AFC as Base Commander. This request was passed by Bomber Command to the Under Secretary of State, Bush House, on 24 November, and the proposal was officially approved on Christmas Eve, 1943.

The newly promoted Air Cdre Blucke therefore found himself in control of a Base with its HQ and 101 Squadron at Ludford Magna, 12 and 626 Squadrons at Wickenby, and 1667 Heavy Conversion Unit at Faldingworth. Ludford itself was a standard heavy bomber station which had cost around £800,000 to build. Its runways were laid out in a triangular pattern, the main one being 5,850ft long and the intersecting ones 4,290ft and 3,600ft respectively. The usual perimeter track, 50ft wide, encircled the airfield, and branching off from this were the dispersal points for the aircraft. Dispersal was all important to minimise losses from air attack, with aircraft only being taken into hangars for major servicing; consequently, the completed airfield covered upwards of a thousand acres, the runways being built on Magna and the dispersal sites on Parva, adjacent to the village of 210 souls after which the airfield was named.

Like every other Bomber Command station was that thrown up in a hurry, Ludford was purpose-built, and that purpose was to fight a war rather than to live in

115
Ludford Operations Room. 2nd left, Grp Capt King (Station Commander); 3rd right, Air Cdre Blucke (Base Commander); Standing right, Sqn Ldr Thompson (Intelligence Officer).

116
'Right, let's get this lot loaded.'
Station armourers plus 4,000lb
'cookies', incendiary containers,
bomb trolleys, and tractors at
Ludford.

comfort. For a start it had none of the brick-built living quarters complete with central heating that characterised the 'permanent' stations — the only brick buildings at Ludford were the gymnasium, education block, and parachute store. 'We lived a life typical of many others in wartime airfields,' wrote a mid-upper gunner. 'Officers and men lived in the same Nissen huts dumped down on "communal" sites often with no such thing as water laid on, and with a mile or more of unmade roads separating us from our messes and working quarters which were just another patch of Nissen huts. The only solid features were the concrete runways, taxiways and dispersals. Everything else was either hard mud or soft mud depending on the weather conditions — no wonder gum boots were an essential item of equipment at Mudford Magna!'

But the bleakness of the Lincolnshire countryside and the periodic heavy rains did not dampen spirits. 'Here the simple necessities of life are catered for,' wrote Cecil Beaton in *Winged Squadrons* (Hutchinson & Co, 1942) — Cecil Beaton was only one of many artists who visited RAF stations during the war to capture the atmosphere for posterity — 'no concessions are made to sensuous comfort. Such a community creates, by its own fervour, the warmth and cosiness in which it lives.'

Another observer was Carl Olsson who visited the airfield for the benefit of *Illustrated* magazine, and his article which appeared on 25 March 1944 began by underlining the fact that Ludford was far from small and that it took a lot more than the aircrew to keep 101 Squadron operational. 'This is one of the war-built stations. Its Lancasters cost £40,000 each and they were delivered, slick and new from the factories. Its personnel strength is about 2,500 officers and men and WAAF. About one-tenth of that are aircrew.

'It costs £3,000 a week to feed the station, and to clothe the groundstaff and aircrew costs £40,000 or the cost of one Lancaster. The maintenance stores is a vast array of spare parts, enough to refit completely about half the aircraft on the station strength.

'The stock includes such items as spare engines (£2,500 each), tail planes (£300), parachutes (£35), turrets (£500), tyres (£50), wireless sets (£250) and countless other items down to rivets, screws, and aluminium sheet for patching flak damage.

'The station is equipped to defend itself with such items as searchlights, (£1,250 each), AA guns (£2,000), Bren guns (£35), ammunition (£7.10s for 1,000 rounds), grenades (4s each), etc, etc.

'It is a township, a factory, a battle head-quarters and a front-line assault point from which men sally forth to attack the enemy. It is never at complete rest — throughout the 24 hours of the day someone is working. Set down among the fields of home its 2,500 men and women can lead an entirely independent existence from the rest of the country for weeks on end.'

Cecil Beaton noticed the same thing. 'There is a timeless quality, exaggerated by the fact that the inhabitants of the station are constantly changing. The men know the date of the month from completing their forms and log books, but seldom are they conscious of the day of the week, for Sunday differs in no way from the other days. Their work is continuous ... Former existence, with its ties and interests, is intentionally forgotten; family or fiancée must remain outside the

117
The Ludford Engineering Officers in 1944. The Senior Engineering Officer, Sqn Ldr Buckingham, is in the centre of the front row.

118
Squadron groundcrew on suitably inscribed 1,000lb bombs.

barbed wires until the big job is over. The aerodrome is the orbit of these men.'

However, Carl Olsson was not there just to look at the station hospital or messes, and he went on to describe a typical day at Ludford as the station prepared to launch every 101 Squadron aircraft to take part in a 2,000-ton long-distance trip into Southern Germany. 'Take-off will be before dusk, say 5pm, so that the long journey out and home is completed before the moon rises or early morning fog settles down on the aerodrome.

'By eight am the handling crews will be hard at work down in the bomb dump at the far end of the aerodrome. Scores of men will be slithering about in the mud bringing 100lb cases of incendiaries to a central section where they will be packed into the special containers carried on the aircraft.

'The men advance from the bomb dump in lines of 10; with the exception of the two end men, each man holds in either hand one handle of the incendiary case. Thus at each journey the men are carrying 900lb of bombs to the packing section.

'In another part of the dump other men are rolling out the great 4,000lb high explosive "cookies" and mounting them on to low engine-driven bomb trolleys. Others are loading flares. All this work goes on without a pause or break till the early afternoon when the trolleys are driven out to the aircraft. Lunch is a hastily eaten sandwich and a cup of tea.

'Meanwhile in another section armament crews are working against time feeding tens of thousands of cartridges into the ammunition belts which will go to the gunners. Over the airfield at the tanks other men are filling the great 2,500 gallon capacity petrol

bowsers and the oil bowsers, each of which holds 450 gallons.

'One petrol bowser holds just enough petrol for filling one Lancaster if it is a long raiding journey. So many journeys must be made back and forth from the storage tanks to the aircraft waiting at the dispersal points. Again it is mid-afternoon before they are all filled.

'At the dispersal points ground crews are swarming over the bombers in their charge. Every point in the bomber is being checked and re-checked, engines, plugs, instruments, guns, turrets, undercarriages, tyre pressures, bomb door mechanism and the host of other things. Some "snag" to one part or another of the bomber is nearly always found, and it has to be set right, with the toiling men always working against time.

'If it is a fault connected with the flying ability of the aircraft it has to be set right in time for a test flight which must be made to make sure that the fault has been rectified long before take-off on the raid.

'It sometimes happens that two or three test flights are made before the sweating ground crews have completed the job to the satisfaction of the captain of the aircraft.

119
Mass briefing at a typical Bomber Command Station. *IWM*

120
Flt Sgt C. T. Akers, an Australian then on his first tour with 101, gets a helping hand to zip up his heated suit from his gunnery leader, Flt Lt Bill Hill. The gun turrets were the coldest place on the Lancaster, and when the centre panels were removed the temperature could fall as low as -40°C. 'In spite of our electrically heated suits,' wrote one gunner, 'which were made of kapok and had their own built-in Mae Wests, it tended to be a mite chilly at times. I recall one occasion when the boiling hot coffee I had poured froze in the cup while I was replacing the cork in the Thermos flask.' Other gunners, such as 'Mac' Mackay, refused to wear the electrical suit 'because I found it too bulky and restrictive even though the cold was paralysing and I once broke off a six inch icicle from below my oxygen mask. Even on warm nights, which were few and far between, I padded myself up as much as possible starting with ladies' silk stockings — they were popular among crews! — and finished with the ordinary Sidcot flying suit.'

121
Wrapping up the in-flight rations.

'Over at the sheds there are almost certain to be two or three bombers getting a special overhaul to put them into full serviceability at the hands of skilled maintenance crews and fitters. Perhaps whole engines may be changed, as a result of damage, patches fitted over flak holes, new instruments put in or pipe line and cables refitted.

'Test flights are made in these cases, of course, and not infrequently the maintenance crews are working on the aircraft right up to a few minutes before take-off. Skilled crews have been known to refit a new engine within less than an hour before take-off, which is certainly running it close.

'While all this sweat and toil is going on in many different parts of the airfield other special staffs are also working against time.

'The intelligence officers are sweating on their filing systems getting out data about the target, getting out target maps and photographs, collecting information from Group Headquarters and from the path-finder force engaged — all to be ready for the briefing of the crews which will take place by 2pm.

'The meteorological officers are collecting and revising up-to-the-minute weather information from their own central channels.

'In the locker rooms another staff is sorting out the items of clothing and equipment which will be issued to each member of the air crews as soon as the briefing is over. About 15 articles for each man ranging from life-saving waistcoats to socks.

'In the kitchens WAAFs are cutting sandwiches for nearly 200 aircrews and parcelling rations of chocolate, fruit, chewing gum and other items of refreshment.

'In the station offices the commander and other officers are selecting the crews and working out technical data for the journey. Sometimes new information comes through from Group Headquarters making a change of plan necessary.

'It may happen that this change has to be made and most of the morning's work altered within half an hour of the briefing.

'The only people who have no part in the unceasing labour are the flying crews who will go on the raid.

'Theirs, perhaps, is the worst part — the waiting from the time they are "warned" for a raid that night until the final take-off. A long wait which is broken only by the briefing and then by the dressing up in the crew room.

'But everybody else on the station goes unceasingly and doggedly on until the moment comes when the last aircraft is signalled down the runway and off on its journey.

'Then, and only then, do the tired ground crews, the bomb crews and the others stretch their aching limbs and take their ease in canteen or mess huts. But not for long; in an hour or so it is time for bed, to be ready for an early morning start and another long exhausting day . . .'

But even Olsson's descriptive powers did not do full justice to every link in the

122
Some couldn't wait to get at their rationed chocolate.

123
Groundcrew of one Lancaster with their mascot.

strategic bomber chain. Take something as small as a Lancaster spark plug for example. There were 96 of these in each bomber, and if they became oiled-up at the wrong moment it could prove catastrophic. So WAAF Group II Sparking Plug Testers had to undertake the filthy job of cleaning hundreds of the things in petrol at regular intervals.

Then there were the wireless mechanics. Marjorie Philips was a WAAF wireless mechanic on 101 in 1944 and her job was to test flying helmets after they had been used on several missions. One day a young aircrew member came to her to say that he couldn't hear the intercom properly in the air, and that he was afraid that he might miss an instruction to bale out. She could tell that he was frightened so she stripped the helmet again and again until she discovered different stores reference numbers on the respective earphones which meant that they were incompatible. 'After his next trip he was so pleased that he gave me his month's ration of sweets.'

It is possible to go and on in similar vein. 'Has it ever occurred to you,' wrote LACW A. M. Douglas in *Slipstream, A Royal Air*

125

Force Anthology (Eyre and Spottiswood, 1946), 'that aircrews would never win their battles had their nerves and sinews, their brains and muscles, their minds and hearts not owed their power to the backstairs service of the cooks'. Before the Battle of Berlin came the Battle for Breakfast, 'and he who has not frizzled 500 slices of bread, or turned out 500 fried eggs before 0700hrs, has yet to know the fullest content, that deepest satisfaction, which can only spring from great achievement!'

The efforts of the 2,250 on the ground at Ludford* were therefore much appreciated by the 250 who flew.

*Up to 1943 the Squadron was a self-contained unit and the Squadron Commander was in complete command of all 101 activities including maintenance. Then, for a variety of reasons it was decided that control of technical personnel should pass to technical officers. This resulted in the formation of separate servicing echelons for all Bomber Command units, and although the ties between aircrews and ground-crews remained as close as ever and the latter still regarded themselves as part of 101, in theory the Squadron's aircraft were maintained by No 9101 Servicing Echelon.

124
A last cigarette to calm the nerves while waiting to leave for Berlin on 20 January 1944.

125
Still more interminable waiting. Approximately one hour before take off, crews would proceed to their aircraft to carry out final checks while waiting for start-up time.

126
'Not a Flanders field but an aerodrome somewhere in England.' An evocative press description as crews paddle across 'Mudford Magna' to the transport which would ferry them to their Lancasters dispersed around the airfield.

127
Forced smiles before boarding the truck. All the crew members are carrying parachutes and escape packs — the latter were small packages containing French money, a map of northern Europe painted on a silk handkerchief, matches, a tiny compass, and other items including malted milk and water purification tablets. In the large canvas bags were Very pistol cartridges for firing the colours of the day in an emergency, together with logs, charts, and code-books.

127

There was certainly a glamorous side to aircrew life on a bomber squadron — discipline tended to be relaxed, there was extra flying pay and much leisure time on non-flying days to spend it, and anyone sporting an aircrew brevet had a head start with the girls at the local dance halls. But on the debit side, the crews lived a life of great stress. 'When at last I found myself in the Mess anteroom,' observed H. E. Bates shrewdly back in late 1941 when 101 was at Oakington (quoted from *The World in Ripeness*, Michael Joseph, 1972), 'it was to be assailed by the impression that I had somehow strayed into a gathering of Sixth Form school boys grown prematurely old. I think it true to say that of all the officers assembled there that evening scarcely more than a dozen were over 25 . . . (However) it was the eyes of these young but prematurely aged officers that made a powerful and everlasting impact on me. Perhaps I can best illustrate it by telling of a young Australian pilot (of whom) I grew very attached before he was finally shot down and killed over Germany. After the war his parents came to see me — they showed me a photograph of him taken when he had first joined the Royal Australian Air Force: a mere boy, starry-eyed, proud too, the new entrant on his way to the big school.

'I did not recognise him. Nor, as I handed them my own photograph of him, the gaunt-faced, glassy-eyed, weary veteran of Heaven knew what Hell had been his lot over Germany, did they recognise him either. In silence, they were more shocked than I, we realised that we were speaking of two different men.'

'Foreigners,' wrote Cecil Beaton, 'often remark on the apparent lack of feeling in the British. They say that we British do not feel anything deeply. A casual visitor to a Royal Air Force station would certainly get this impression from the light-hearted way in which unpleasantness, danger, and the war itself, are banished from talk. Death is mentioned flippantly, if at all. Someone has "gone for a Burton" or has been "bumped off" . . . But the feeling is there, controlled and smothered by a self-preservation instinct. The realisation of their proximity to danger is never far removed from the minds of the men, in spite of their easy grace of heart.'

Sgt Jack Morley, a W/Op, was just one man who appreciated this when he joined 101 with the Harris crew early in June 1944. 'Aboard the bus, which was taking us to our dispersal points, I experienced the feeling of excitement, wonder and apprehension before this first operational sortie. But among the joking and laughter I was amazed somewhat, this first time, at such comments like, "I hope you get yours", or "Can I have your watch if you don't come back?" These remarks seemed cruel but as we were to learn, they were not meant seriously and were only words to hide the seriousness of what was to lay ahead during the next few hours.'

Sgt Brian Hawkins was a Spec Op who flew with Flt Sgt Jenkins' crew until the night they were detailed to bomb Russelsheim. After the standard pre-flight meal of bacon and eggs that was eaten an hour before briefing, Hawkins experienced stomach pains and went to see the Medical Officer who put him straight into hospital in case it was appendicitis. But from that moment on, Hawkins knew that his crew were not coming back. He spent all night in the hospital toilets smoking cigarettes, and in the morning his

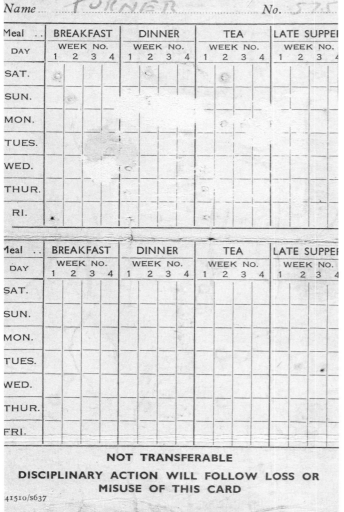

R.A.F., LUDFORD MAGNA
F 1250

Name TURNER   No. 525

Meal ..	BREAKFAST				DINNER				TEA				LATE SUPPER			
DAY	WEEK NO.				WEEK NO.				WEEK NO.				WEEK NO.			
	1	2	3	4	1	2	3	4	1	2	3	4	1	2	3	4
SAT.																
SUN.																
MON.																
TUES.																
WED.																
THUR.																
FRI.																

Meal ..	BREAKFAST				DINNER				TEA				LATE SUPPER			
DAY	WEEK NO.				WEEK NO.				WEEK NO.				WEEK NO.			
	1	2	3	4	1	2	3	4	1	2	3	4	1	2	3	4
SAT.																
SUN.																
MON.																
TUES.																
WED.																
THUR.																
FRI.																

NOT TRANSFERABLE
DISCIPLINARY ACTION WILL FOLLOW LOSS OR MISUSE OF THIS CARD

41510/s637

R.A.F. STATION
LUDFORD MAGNA

*

Sergeants' Mess

*

CHRISTMAS DINNER
1943

SNCOs await this Yuletide fare, 25 December 1943.

fears were confirmed. It was no consolation to find that he only had an upset tummy after all.

Some men also knew themselves when it was their night for the 'chop'. 'After the bacon and eggs, we went by coach to the mass briefing,' continued Brian Hawkins. 'Everyone was always very serious then because we did not know what was in store for us, but once we entered the briefing room and saw the maps with the red lines on, the smiles and the chatter returned. We now knew what we were up against and the uncertainty was replaced by the bustle of planning. But on the coach out to the aircraft I knew exactly who was not coming back and they knew it themselves. I remember one man saying to me: "I wish I was flying in your aircraft."

' "Why?"

' "Because mine isn't coming back."

'And it didn't. Some men were dead even before they took-off.'

Having therefore flown hard, it was not surprising that the crews also played hard. To Carl Olsson, Ludford personnel lived 'a front-line existence almost as completely as if they were operating from newly conquered territory', but this was a little hard on those who tried to make the best of a bad job:

'25/8/43. Weather good. ENSA gave a play this evening, *Dangerous Corner* by J. B. Priestley. About 400 personnel were present. A car park is being constructed and the front of Station Headquarters and gardens are being laid out in front of this building and the Officers' Mess.'

'1/2/44. Weather today is again spring-like. A fifth session of the Discussion Group was held on the subject of "Emigration to and development of the Dominions".'

Nevertheless there were some who soon tired of a station that only possessed a solitary film projector, and who sought their entertainment farther afield.

Aircrew got six days' leave every six weeks, while on non-flying days 'the pubs in the area took a fair share of our pay of 13s 6d per day,' wrote Sgt Whittle, a mid-upper gunner. The 'Black Horse' and 'White Hart' at Ludford had a quiet time during a period of concentrated operations, but whenever circumstances allowed, the Senior Flying Control Officer, Sqn Ldr F. Tomlinson, would organise 'liaison visits' with the precision of a bomber raid. Primary 'targets' were the 'Ship' or 'Wheatsheaf' at Grimsby, with the 'King's Head' at Louth being the 'secondary objective', and although the outings provided moments of welcome rest and relaxation, they always had a serious side. 'Sqn Ldr Tomlinson — known to us as "The Squire" — always arranged for the bus to stop on the return journey opposite a wood yard to allow revellers to relieve themselves. This wood yard was guarded by alsatians, but the Squire would not allow anyone back on to the bus unless they brought a piece of wood with them — we were very short of fuel for the Nissen hut heating stoves at Ludford.'

This theme of living off-duty moments to the full was repeated over and over again during 101's wartime history. 'When we were at Holme,' said Sandy Greig, 'we usually flew two nights in a row. Sometimes we would hang around all day waiting for an op before we were told that it was off at the last moment because of weather. If we were stood down early, we went off in the Squadron bus to York. I personally didn't get much further than Betty's Bar — it was a

133
A happy band of aircrew relax
between ops at Ludford.

favourite haunt of bomber crews and you
could hardly get into the place — and then
maybe on to the de Grey Rooms for a dance.
On the way home we would sing the
Squadron Song — '101 Boys are Returning,
101 are Coming Home" — which we sang to
the tune of *Clementine*.

'What did we do off duty?' mused 'Mac'
Mackay. 'Drink — what else was there in
war apart from the ubiquitous snooker? With
nerves always taut like banjo strings, drink
for us was a blessed salve. Strangely enough,
almost all those unfortunates I knew who
were grounded because they lost their nerve
did not drink. We just lived from day to day.'
Those men who lost their nerve and refused
to carry on flying were classified as LMF —
Lack of Moral Fibre. They were posted off
the Squadron and station within 12hr so as
not to demoralise others.

Nevertheless, although there were
certainly some fatalists who drank because
they feared that they would never survive a
tour, it would be wrong to over-emphasise
the negative aspect of the desire to get away
from the war. For every tear there were gales
of laughter and comradeship which forged
links between men who had originally come
from totally different backgrounds but who
now faced the same dangers together. 'When
a crew completed a tour successfully,' wrote
Jack Morley, 'there were great celebrations,
first in the village pubs and then in the
Officers' and Sergeants' Messes. We sang
many songs such as "101 are Operating"
and "The Monk of Great Renown" but a
favourite Squadron song was "The Muffin
Man" during which the first man, with a
chunky beer glass full of ale on his head,
would bob up and down singing, "Do you
know the Muffin Man, do you know his

name, do you know the Muffin Man, that
lives down Drury Lane?" He would then
point towards another man who would
accordingly (he was jeered if he didn't) place
his own glass on top of his head and reply,
while bobbing up and down in similar
fashion, "Yes I know the Muffin Man, yes I
know his name, Yes I know the Muffin Man,
that lives down Drury Lane." At which, the
whole company, with glasses on heads,
would join in with, "Two men know the
Muffin Man, two men know his name, Two
men know the Muffin Man, that lives down
Drury Lane." So the ritual would continue,
with the number of acquaintances of the
Muffin Man increasing and the whole scene
becoming uproarious, especially if someone
declined to join in. Then the whole chorus
would point at the unfortunate subject for
derision and sing, "He don't know the Muffin
Man, he don't know his name, He don't
know the Muffin Man, that lives down Drury

134
Fog — that treacherous foe —
drifts in towards Ludford from the
East Coast. Fog had always been
a problem for returning bomber
crews, and on the night of 16/17
December 1943 alone, Bomber
Command lost 131 aircrew in 29
crashes around fog-covered
airfields. The Prime Minister had
already instructed Geoffrey Lloyd,
Minister in charge of the
Petroleum Warfare Department,
to find a means of dispersing fog
at airfields, and his experts came
up with FIDO (Fog Investigation
Dispersal Operation, or as the
RAF called it, Fog, Intensive,
Dispersal of). As Ludford was the
highest airfield in 1 Group and
Lincolnshire, and therefore
situated where the fog should be
thinnest, it became one of 15
airfields that were eventually
equipped with FIDO.

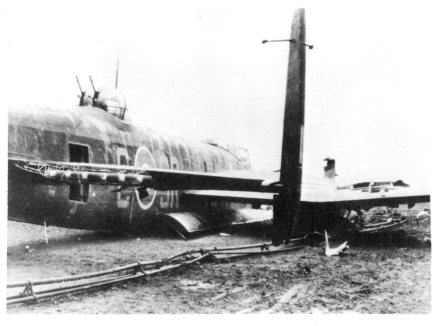

Lane." These, and many other songs and scenes, were our pastimes in the hours between the harrowing flights over enemy territory, contrary to the popular belief that we were always chasing after girls.'

Social life at Ludfrod was not all beer and skittles though. In nearby Tealby, one of the most beautiful villages of Lincolnshire and home of Lord Tennyson, there was an old tea shop full of 'olde Worlde charm' that was run by two dear old ladies. 'It was a regular haven of peace. We cherished those visits with the home-made scones and tea, which served to take us back to a calmer, saner world.'

There was a thriving newspaper called the *Base Bulletin* which was only one of the many examples of productive off-duty ingenuity and enthusiasm at Ludford. Perhaps it reflected the irreverence of the age — '*LOST*. One pair of battledress trousers, belonging to the Senior Intelligence Officer of

a certain Base Station, after a slight Bacchanalian orgy. Finder will be suitably rewarded.' — but the vitality of its contributions and the response to the Editor's plea for 'humorous items of gossip' gave the lie to any outward hint of fatalism or despondency.

'These men therefore create their own circumstances,' concluded Cecil Beaton. Their off duty moments were a time to recharge emotional batteries, but once back at work 'their absorbing enthusiasm towards their duty is like that of a scientist. Everyone is trying to learn more about his particular task. While waiting by their aircraft the pilots are forever exchanging experiences, suggesting new tactics. In the mess they are poring over aeronautic magazines of a highly scientific nature, or still talking the most exciting "shop" in the world. In the face of all difficulties and dangers these men are self-inspired to live up to an ideal. They are ever ready to sacrifice their personal interests and safety in the pursuit of their duty. They believe in the Force and their faith is the motive power behind their judgement and skill.'

101 Squadron's only respite during the Battle of Berlin came in February 1944 when the snows descended on the Lincolnshire Wolds. Nearby Binbrook was completely cut-off and had to rely on supplies dropped from the air, while the snow was 3ft deep with 16ft drifts at Ludford. So hundreds of men, working in shifts throughout the day and night with little more than shovels, set to work with a will to maintain the momentum of the bomber offensive. 'It looks like the Aleutians,' wrote one newspaper reporter visiting Ludford, 'but it is England. Flight mechanics, changing plugs on aircraft required for ops, worked while standing on high platforms in a horizontally driven storm of sleet. As one man turned the plug spanner, his comrade would be restoring circulation to his frozen fingers ready to take over when the first mechanic could no longer hold the spanner.'

The newspaper captions proclaimed that 'even heavy snow did not break their business appointment with Germany,' and if this was not quite true, Ludford was clear enough to launch part of 101 Squadron in just over a week. The Squadron Commander, Wg Cdr R. I. Alexander (who had taken over from Wg Cdr Carey-Foster on 18 January 1944), was very appreciative:

'To: All members of No 101 Squadron.
Date: 5th March 1944.

'During the recent state of emergency, special efforts were called for from all ranks. The response to that call was immediate and the special effort was forthcoming with a spirit which was a subject for admiration.

'We were able, thanks to your loyalty and devotion to duty, to operate six aircraft against Germany on the night of 1st March. That may appear to be a small number, but it was vital that we should operate, and the work required to get those aircraft off called for a maximum effort from all ranks.

'To me, it means more than the fact that six aircraft took off from this airfield. The routine and organisation required to operate under normal conditions calls for effort enough, but the true test of a Squadron is made when they are required to increase that effort to combat emergency conditions. You were tested and did not fail.

'I am indeed proud to serve with you. Thank you.

R. I. Alexander,
Wing Commander, Commanding
No 101 Squadron, RAF'

135
Lancaster C-Charlie after Sgt Dixon had belly-landed at Ludford. Note the buckled FIDO pipelines. These were laid along each side of the main runway with two smaller pipes at each end. Small valves were set at intervals into these two miles of piping, through which jets of petrol were squirted and ignited. FIDO burnt 40,000 gallons of fuel at a time, but the heat generated was so intense that it could burn off the fog in 10 minutes. FIDO's only drawback at Ludford, apart from its cost, was revealed when a Lancaster approached the ring of fire with a fuel leak. After one unfortunate accident, FIDO was modified and the end bars were removed — they only made the approach bumpy anyway.

136
Sgt Sandy Sandford and his crew in Lancaster III G-George await a green from the caravan before taking off on 20 January 1944 from Ludford on their way to Berlin. A spare 'trolley acc' and standby groundcrew wait by the FIDO pipes in case the aircraft stalls and blocks the runway.

Of Valour, and of Victory

In company with many others at the beginning of 1944, Carl Olsson's imagination was fired by the Battle of Berlin. 'It is difficult for ordinary citizens to visualise the effect of concentrated *aerial* bombardment,' he wrote, 'but the following comparison may help. On the Sangro front in Italy, often spoken of as the biggest *land* bombardment of this war, 1,400 tons of shells came down in *eight hours*. Remember that this front was many miles in length and mostly open country, yet they smashed the German defence and prisoners spoke of the astounding paralysing effect of these heavy bombardments.

'And now compare the figures of air assault. To take an instance only, on the night of 20/21 January, 1944, 7,300 tons of bombs went down on Berlin in *thirty minutes*. Remember, too, that the bombs are falling into built-up areas on a shorter front than a land attack. Remember, too, that tonnage for tonnage, a bomb contains a much higher explosive charge than a shell.

'No city, no defence system, can stand up to such attacks, scientifically delivered, as Bomber Command is now making . . .

'Good-bye, Berlin!'

But as the long, protective winter nights drew to a close and the spring of 1944 dawned, it was clear that Berlin was still very much in existence. Moreover, back in November 1943 Sir Arthur Harris had prophesied that the Battle of Berlin would cost him and the Americans 400-500 aircraft — 35 major attacks later, his Command alone has lost 1,047 aircraft with a further 1,682 damaged, culminating in the Nuremburg raid which had accounted for a massive 13.6% of the force dispatched. To the critics of Nuremburg Harris gruffly retorted that if you launch a massive onslaught against an enemy night after night, you must expect a bloody nose once in a while, and certainly the Nuremburg losses were not typical. Nevertheless, the Battle of Berlin neither wrecked Berlin from end to end nor did it cost

137
A Squadron Lancaster sets out to bomb France.

137

138

139

138, 139
During and after the bombing onslaught on the communications systems of France in preparation for D-Day. The Aulnoye marshalling yards after two attacks in March and April 1944 — each of the 32 tracks has been cut in several places and there are signs of scattered damage to sheds and rolling stock. However this damage was minor compared with that inflicted by the concentrated Bomber Command attack on 27/28 April. During the raid the site was completely obliterated. The road at the top of the picture is in use again but it has become a series of curves caused by vehicles and people trying to get to the scene of desolation. *IWM*

140
Wg Cdr Alexander stands before the Ludford Ops Board showing 101's contribution to the D-Day effort on 5/6 June 1944.

140

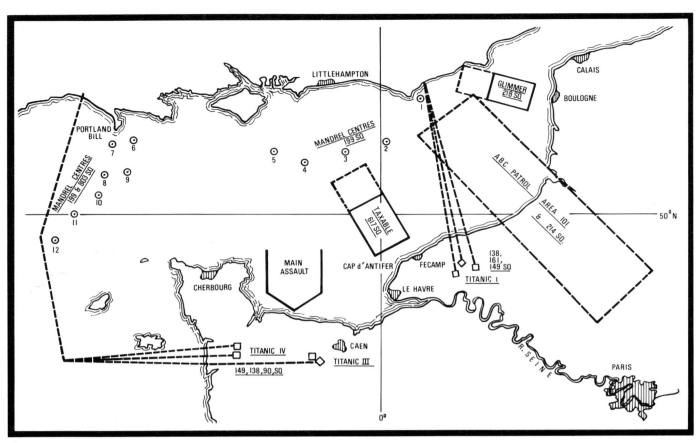

141
How the ABC jammers fitted into the Radio Countermeasures plan for Overlord. 'Taxable' aircraft covered the 'ghost' fleet supposedly aiming for Cap d'Antifer, and 'Glimmer' simulated an invasion force heading towards Boulogne. 'Titanic' consisted of 29 bombers simulating a fake airborne invasion in the Caen and Cap d'Antifer areas, and the 'Mandrel' aircraft jammed the German early warning radars.

Germany the war; it was time for a shift of emphasis.

Up to now Bomber Command had been employed almost exclusively against long-term strategic targets, 'but with the approach of D-Day we switched our attacks to targets of immediate tactical importance'. Anything which could reinforce the German forces of occupation west of the Rhine or hinder the invasion was to be attacked, and even though 101 had suffered terribly against Nuremburg, there could be no time for respite or the licking of wounds. The success of the invasion of Europe was vital, and so seven aircraft from Ludford were back in action against Villeneuve St Georges on 9 April.

Because such 'tactical' targets were relatively close at hand rather than in deepest Germany, Bomber Command decided that all raids on French targets should only count as 1/3 of an operational trip when it came to calculating tour lengths. 'But even on these short, and so-called easy ops,' wrote one W/Op, 'the enemy was not going to let us drop our "eggs" at will'. The proof came on the raid against the military depot at Mailly-le-Camp on 3 May, which 'was one of the most scaring raids that I did', recalled A. A. Castle who by then was a flight lieutenant. 'I can recall seeing more of our aircraft shot down than on any other trip. It started almost as soon as we crossed the French coast and continued until we crossed it again

on the way home.' Forty-two bombers, or 11.3% of the force, failed to return that night, with 101 losing five of them — fortunately the one-third ruling died at the same time.

The pinpoint bombing techniques demonstrated over Pennemünde were refined and put to even more good use in the run-up to D-Day. 1 Group dropped a total of 13,798 tons of bombs during June 1944, with 101 dropping 1,282 tons of them, yet being a radio countermeasures squadron as well, 101 was just as concerned with thwarting the enemy's aerial defences. It combined both functions admirably when it contributed 16 aircraft to the bombing of the Bruneval early warning radar station on 2 June.

Nevertheless the whole invasion plan could still flounder if the Luftwaffe got through to bomb the thousands of landing craft, or if it was let loose among the huge armada of gliders and heavily-laden troop transports that were to lumber across for a dawn drop on Normandy. Allied fighter escorts could not protect them all — the attentions of the Luftwaffe defences had to be totally distracted away from that crucial area.

Two diversion plans were therefore put into effect, aimed at deluding the enemy into thinking that the invasion was to take place on beaches around Cap d'Antifer and Boulogne. To lend realism to these feints, and to protect the Airborne Forces, a 'Special

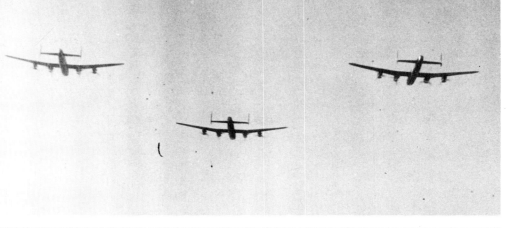

142

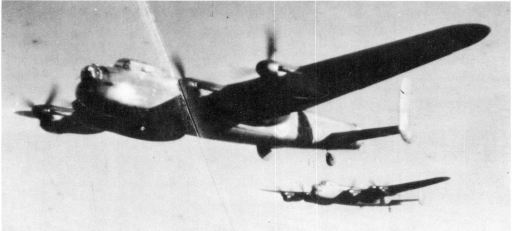

143

142, 143
Squadron Lancasters over France
in formation.

Duties Patrol' was ordered to place a 'curtain of VHF jamming between the area of actual assault and the direction from which the enemy fighter reactions was expected'. This patrol consisted of 24 aircraft from 101 Squadron and five Flying Fortresses from 214 Squadron, and between them they were expected to simulate nothing less than a ghost 'bomber stream' along the line of the River Somme. On board each aircraft crew members tossed out bundles of 'Window' for all they were worth while the Spec Ops monitored the ABC screens, and the combination of 82 ABC transmitters and thousands of bundles of 'Window' were completely successful in their endeavour. 'All the German night fighters that operated were put up against the patrol of ABC aircraft,' wrote the official report, 'which was at first mistaken for "the spearhead of a main bomber force in the neighbourhood of Paris". On their arrival in the area, the fighters found that they were being subjected to serious jamming on the R/T communications channel; then the fighter control plotting became confused due to the presence of German fighters in among the jammers. The fighters returned towards their control points, but appear to have received instructions to go on hunting in the bomber stream as there was sporadic fighter activity in that area between 0105hr and 0355hr. The result of all this confusion was that the Airborne Forces

met no opposition in the air and landed with negligible casualties — a remarkable achievement when it is remembered that a casualty rate of at least 25% was expected.'

Six Squadron crews reported sightings of enemy aircraft and three combats ensued, the crew of Q-Queenie exchanging fire with a Ju88 which broke away emitting smoke. Otherwise it was 'a quiet trip' for all, apart from Plt Off M. J. Steele's crew who were on patrol at 0025hr when an inexplicable vibration began in the constant speed unit of the starboard outer engine. The New Zealander captain feathered this engine, but immediately afterwards both inners also went out in sympathy, forcing Lancaster L-Love and her crew to ditch in the sea at 0050hr some 25 miles south of Beachy Head. After an hour in the Channel they were picked up by HMS *Orwell*.

On 7 June, 101 was back in action against the marshalling yards at Acheres as Bomber Command strove to prevent the German Army from bringing up reinforcements. Other interesting post-invasion targets were the ports of Le Havre and Boulogne, which the Squadron attacked on 14 and 15 June to help sink or damage the entire German E-Boat fleet than threatening the cross-Channel supply lines. The Ludford Lancasters subsequently bombed everything from V-1 flying bomb sites to railway depots,

144
The flying-bomb site at Siracourt being plastered on 29 June 1944.

145
The flying-bomb site at Les Hayons coming in for some attention. Note the camouflaged Lancaster below.

but the most important mission for July was Caen.

For the direct assault on Caen, where the Germans had dug-in in strength, General Montgomery decided to seek the assistance of Bomber Command in a close support role on the battlefield. 'This was the first time that we had attempted a battle of this nature,' he wrote in *Normandy to the Baltic* (Hutchinson & Co Ltd, 1947), 'and it was jointly decided with Bomber Command that the bombline would not be brought nearer than 6,000 yards from our leading troops.' It was a precise objective, but the heavy bombers did not let the Army down — they dropped 2,350 tons of bombs in 40min on the evening of 7 July and, in addition to reducing the defences to rubble, some German defenders were found still stunned many hours after the attack had been carried out. The way was clear for the Army to advance at dawn.

'Having captured Caen,' wrote General Montgomery on 10 July, 'we must now gain depth and space... for manoeuvre, for administrative purposes, and for airfields'.

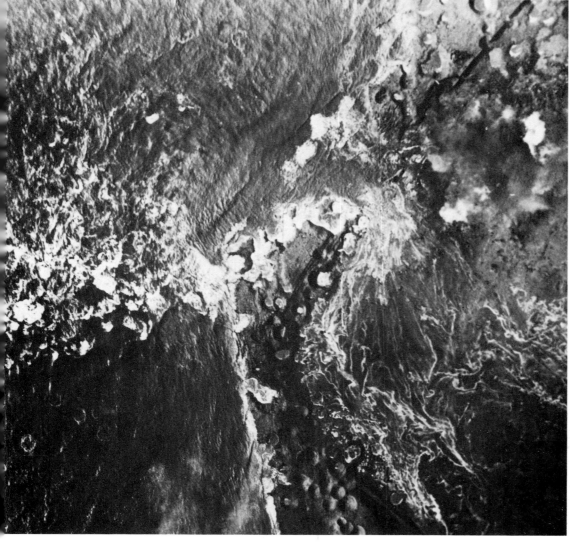

146
Plt Off Piprell's crew attack the oil storage depot at Blaye, just up from Bordeaux on the Gironde, on Saturday 5 August 1944. 'There were prying electronic eyes all along the coast,' said one W/Op, 'so we decided to fly the whole route a few miles off the French coast as low as possible to keep below enemy radar cover. We found out during training that when the Lancaster's trailing aerial was wound out to its full length, it would stream out some 50ft below the aircraft, so we used this aerial to maintain an accurate height of 50ft. I would watch the dials on my transmitter/receiver, and when they dipped I knew that the aerial had hit the water and earthed the set. I would yell out a warning to the pilot who would ease up until the dials indicated that the aerial was clear. This method enabled us to maintain a fairly constant 50ft until we were close enough to climb up and bomb the target.

147
Grp Capt King, Ludford's Station Commander, tries his hand at bombing the dykes at Westkapelle on 3 October 1944 in a 101 aircraft. The aim of this exercise was to flood the German defences and installations on Walcheren and thereby gain access to Antwerp.

147

148
Volkel airfield, Belgium, as seen
by Plt Off Baker's crew on
15 August 1944.

149
The Bowater crew's post-flight
observations on the Volkel raid.

Unfortunately for him, the enemy resolved to deny him this space, and although the Germans had fewer tanks they were dispersed in depth in advantageous positions and fortified by minefields and numerous long-range anti-tank guns and mortars. All these obstacles had to go if the British formations were to break out of Caen, so Montgomery sought the full assistance of the RAF to neutralise this formidable line of defence.

'We were therefore informed,' said Jack Morley, 'that from now on, all aircrew and maintenance personnel were to be on 24-hour standby, ready to be called at short notice for offensive duties to support Monty's forces around the Caen bridgehead. On the fifth day of this standby, we were called from our beds and taken, without a wash, shave or breakfast, to the briefing room; there we were told that a maximum effort was to be made at once on the German gun and mortar emplacements at Mondeville just outside Caen, and we were to reinforce aircraft that were already on their way to attack. As we went to change into flying gear, we received the information that the Lancasters were already "bombed up" with, not the usual load of a 4,000lb "cookie" plus high explosive and incendiary bombs, but just 16 1,000lb HE bombs. We hastily changed and made our way to dispersal, this time to fly in A-Able.

'Once airborne, we set course southwards, and as we climbed and maintained course,

GPA   V LUD LUD36/15 P

FROM LUDFORD MAGNA 151455B
TO HQ NO 1 GROUP
INFO 14 BASE
SECRET QQX BT

RAID REPORT NO 119 15TH AUG 1944

SECTION A
1 GROUP INFO 14 BASE   101/T
15TH AUG 1944   LUDFORD 119
4 X 1000 MC   TD 0.025   LANC III
4 X 1000 USA GP   TD 0.025   LM472
3 X 1000 USA SAP TD 0.025   SGT BOWATER
4 X 500 GP   TD 0.025   NIL
ABC API BOOZER I
VOLKEL A/F FIRST

SECTION C
1   VOLKEL A/F
2   NO CLOUD , GOOD VISIBILITY
3   VISUALLY BY RUNWAYS AND DISPERSAL HUTS
4   1204 HRS , 14,500 FT   086 T   170 MPH
6   DISPERSAL HUT SE OF RUNWAYS IN BOMB SIGHT
8   BOMBING WAS VERY CONCENTRATED AND MAIN WEIGHT OF ATTACK
     APPEARED TO FALL ON A/P
16   M/B HEARD DISTINCTLY SAYING
     " VERY GOOD BOMBING WIZARD SHOW "
     OTHER ATTACKS WHICH APPEARED CONCENTRATED SEEN IN
     VICINITY MUSTANG FIGHTER COVER SEEN EN ROUTE ALSO
     THUNDERBOLT AT LOW LEVEL IN TARGET AREA
17   JER

BT 151455B

HW B K O
           LUD R VIA OPS R.1723B/LHK K

149

we joined up with the greatest force of bombers that I had ever seen — all around, ahead, behind, and on both sides were aircraft, as far as the eye could see. A great column, of which we were part, headed south while at the same time another great column, seemingly never ending, was heading north after leaving the target. We were one continuous stream, to and from France — the scene must have been tremendous from below. Some of the sights we saw as the Lancasters and Halifaxes passed by on their return filled the heart with wonder, and foreboding, as signs that the enemy was grimly prepared to resist us to the best of his ability were plainly evident. There were some aircraft with tremendous damage — gaping holes in fuselage or wings, two in particular flying along minus one tailplane, others flying alone on three, two, or even one engine but still, somehow, managing to keep aloft. But our own effort was still to be made and we went across the Channel, into our bombing run, the flashes from below and the shell bursts around telling their own story. We still had to fight our way to the target — we were not being given a free run. Then "Bombs Gone" from Dai Jones, the bomb-aimer, and with a lurch we were free of our load and increasing speed as we flew out beyond the target area. As we looked back, we could see that the whole of the target area resembled one huge ploughed field and it seemed impossible for anyone to remain alive among that scene of desolation and destruction.

'Back home we heard the news that the effort had been a huge success and that our troops had begun to advance through the gap in the enemy fortifications as we came in to land. This was most heartening news for us all, for the British armies had been having a really hard time of it in the face of very fortified positions and we were glad to have helped in some small way to relieve the situation.' This was certainly confirmed by the AOC, No 83 Group, Tactical Air Force, who subsequently sent a message congratulating 101 Squadron on the part they had played in the Caen attack.

101 lost 12 crews in June and July 1944 because considerable demands were made on them as the Allies consolidated their foothold on the continent.

'*POSTGRAM*

To: Headquarters, No 1 Group
From: Headquarters, Bomber Command

BC/TS/31852/Air/Ops
Date: 1st July 1944
TOP SECRET

ABC, No 101 Squadron

'Whilst this Command is engaged on bombing both tactical and strategic targets, it is becoming increasingly difficult to forecast ABC requirements when the daily preliminary warning is passed. ABC is one of the most valuable radio countermeasures in use at the present time and in order therefore to ensure that ABC aircraft are available, it is

150
Flg Off Harris and his crew. (L-R): Sgt Jock Wood (Flt Eng), Sgt Don Dale (Mid-Upper), Sgt Jack Morley (W/Op), Flg Off John Arthur DFC (Nav), Flg Off George Harris DFC (Pilot), Flg Off Dai Jones DFC (Bomb-aimer), Sgt Vic Congerton (Rear Gunner), Sgt C. York (Spec Op).

150

151
Flg Off Grant's crew photograph
Le Havre burning on
10 September 1944 as the
Germans retreat across France.

152
This picture, taken over Cap Gris
Nez on 28 September 1944 from
Lancaster R-Roger, happened to
capture S-Sugar as well as the
target below. The white marks on
the side of Sugar's nose are her
'Saint' emblem and a host of little
white bomb symbols, for S-Sugar
had then completed some 90
operational missions.

requested that 10 aircraft of 101 Squadron are stood to daily. If these aircraft are not called for by 1600hrs on any day, they may, after checking with this Headquarters, be used for bombing operations which are being undertaken by your Group, provided that a further 10 ABC aircraft from 101 Squadron will be available if required the following day.'

Thus there were even more apprehensive faces in evidence when the Squadron crews found out that they were to combine their tactical duties with a return to the strategic fray. After a few hours of well-earned rest following Caen, it was back to the briefing room again on the afternoon of 18 July to be told that they were returning to the Ruhr Valley, and in particular to attack the giant synthetic oil plant at Scholven.

By now the Harris crew with Jack Morley had learned the operational ropes and had settled into a routine. 'While the skipper signed for the aircraft,' recalled Morley, 'we settled on the grass for a last smoke. I always took the third light as a sign to the gods of fate that I was not superstitious, but as this was to become a ritual of the tour, I suppose I was only underlining the belief that everyone is superstitious in one form or another.

'Then we taxied out to take-off. This was controlled by visual means because radio silence had to be maintained throughout the whole trip except for emergencies. Having been given the all clear by green Aldis lamp or flare, we would start to rev up the engines and there would be a growing sense of excitement amongst the crew. Then brakes were released and the whole aircraft shuddered — slowly, oh so slowly, we began to roll along the runway accompanied by the deafening roar of the engines as the great bird of war struggled to lift the massive load of some 16,000lb. The crew was full of apprehension as the runway in front of us got shorter and shorter, but then beneath us we sensed that the friction of the wheels on the ground had ceased. Struggling still, but gradually gaining height, the skipper called, "Undercarriage up", and we began to turn. As we climbed, the pitch of the engines changed from a might roar to a steady drone. "Rendezvous Beachy Head," said the navigator, a phrase we were to hear many times during the four-month tour, and I peered out of the astro dome. What a wonderful sight it was — Lancasters and Halifaxes arriving from all directions and taking their allotted places, based on time and height, to form a huge stream, some 2,000ft or so in depth and width. If you can imagine a cube of these dimensions, with an aircraft at each point of the cube and one in the centre, and the whole forming into a line, you will get some idea of

the sight. As the stream turned on course for the target area, our position was in the top layer and very near the front end.

'The plan once again consisted of many changes of course, plus our ABC working all out and Window drops, which were all designed to assist our safe passage to the target. But it was not to be on this fateful night. The enemy awaited our every move. At the point where the enemy coast was to be crossed, flares started to light up the sky and fighter attacks commenced immediately. Deadly and swift, no prolonged battles as depicted by films, these fighter pilots were masters of tactics. The attack would come in one swift burst, and the fighter would then disappear back into the darkness from whence he came. The ABC operator was busy doing his little thing while the others kept a special watch to the east, which was the darker side of the sky and the direction from which an attack was most likely to come. We did not open fire if the fighter did not see us — our mission was to deliver a load of high explosives to the target, not to play the hero by engaging in unnecessary fighter combat. Yet even if a fighter came in, the speed of the attacks was usually such that the gunners would scarcely have time to spot him before the attack was over and we were watching for others. Time and time again bombers were seen under attack, and some were seen to go down. Despite our many turns, the flares would also turn as if lighting up a path for us, which in fact they were — they were lighting up a trap to be sprung by the fighters.

'This was the pattern for the whole flight until the time came for the turn on to the final leg to the target area, where the flares died out and the fighter activity ceased. But it was only to be replaced by the expected continual heavy barrage of the fixed defences of this area. The Ruhr Valley in American terms would probably have been known as Hell Fire Valley. The whole sky, as we headed on this final leg towards Scholven, was one mass of exploding shells and coloured tracer, criss-crossing the sky across our path. In a seemingly impenetrable block of fire, our way ahead was made to seem almost impossible. How could anything get safely through this inferno of shellfire?

'Our mid-upper gunner, Don Dale, called out to me to have a look out of the astro dome. All around, as now we were running in towards the target, were the red and green tracers. Smoke from shells bursting in the distance, and red, or white flashes, followed by the ping of shrapnel as it hit us. I clung to the handrail attached to the astro dome mountings, absolutely terrified. I was not to leave this position until we had got out of the target area, and anyway I was so frightened that my legs would not have supported me had I let go of the hand rails. As a consequence, I missed one of the quarter hourly broadcasts, but fortunately, before going in for interrogation, I learned that it was just the normal check broadcast and got it copied down before my log was examined. At the time nothing seemed so important as seeing what was going on. If I was to die, I wanted to see how it happened. I can hear Dai's voice now as he gave his instructions, and the calm words from the skipper, "Steady Chaps", as right into the centre of this hell we went. Then, "Bombs Gone", and our Lancaster was relieved of its load and gave an upward lurch, as if it was a living thing and it too wanted to be away from this storm of destruction. We were suddenly away from it all, and heading for the safety of the dark sky beyond the target. The relief was almost too much for us, as, expecting vengeful fighters to be waiting, we turned on to a different heading for the journey homewards. But fortunately they ignored us and were still hunting the incoming force, in an attempt to prevent at least some of them from reaching the target. Despite all the setbacks we had succeeded in hitting the target, and as we turned we could see the smoke and flames of many fires, accompanied by intermittent explosions, as the giant oil plant was systematically being reduced to mounds of burning and exploding rubble. It was many many miles along our return journey before the glow of these great fires was eventually out of our line of vision.'

The homeward journey was uneventful but the arrival back over Lincolnshire after a night op exposed the Harris' crew to another perennial danger. Ludford lay between Binbrook, Kelstern, and Faldingworth airfields, and as their circuits crossed one another, the scope for collisions in the dark was considerable. The stations tried to solve this problem by flying designated clockwise and anti-clockwise circuits, but even so the Squadron Commander had the trailing aerial whipped away from his Lancaster by another aircraft one night. 'On approaching the airfield, therefore,' continued Jack Morley, 'our skipper transmitted, "Bookworm P for Peter calling Bookshop ('Bookshop' was Ludford's radio callsign and the Harris crew were flying in P-Peter that night), permission to join circuit". We would then be given a height to fly in the stack above Ludford, priority being accorded to badly damaged aircraft. But the close proximity of so many other aircraft meant that there could be no relaxation until we were safely down on the runway and back at dispersal. Yet, in spite of the danger, it was a really wonderful sight to see all the warbirds arriving back at base together'.

'It was always nice to come back from a trip and hear a friendly voice with a friendly joke from Air Traffic,' said one navigator. The flying control officers were a boon as well when it came to getting a host of bombers down — the average landing time for each aircraft in 1 Group was 4¼-min in July 1943, but by the end of 1944 this had been reduced to 1¾min. Nevertheless, it was never safe to trust completely the skies over Ludford — on 27 September 1943, after battling their way to and from Hanover, Plt Off Skipper and his crew were shot down over Wickenby by a German intruder lying in wait.

With pinpoint guidance from the Master Bomber, 101 could now place bombs to within an accuracy that could be measured in yards rather than in the miles of the bad old days. Such precision was greatly appreciated by the men on the ground. 'On 26 September,' wrote Jack Morley in his diary, 'we set off once more on a low-level daylight mission, but this time against the guns at Cap Griz Nez which since 1940 had been hurling daily devastation and death against the inhabitants of the Dover area. It was time to dispose of these guns, but the area around their emplacement was occupied by, amongst others, troops of the Canadian Scottish Regiment, so arrangements were made for them to mark the exact locations of the positions. As we approached the target a semi circle of colour could be seen — the Canadians had laid their kilts all around the perimeter of the coastal area still occupied by the Germans. Plt Off Dai Jones, our bomb aimer, once more did a very technical piece of bombing. We clearly saw our bombs hit the gun emplacements and soon afterwards the national papers published pictures of the huge gun barrels either broken in two or tilted over at the most crazy angles. This gave all of us who had been on the mission a great deal of satisfaction and pride in a job well performed'.

By 23 October the Harris crew had come through it all and were standing by for their 30th and last operational mission. As they trooped into the briefing room it must have seemed that the fates were having one last laugh at their expense. 'The target, in Happy Valley, was to be the giant Krupps works at Essen, still one of the hottest spots in the whole of Germany. It could not have been a more dangerous ending to our tour — they must have picked this one out for us. At least the planned route had many twists and turns, and we hoped to catch the enemy defences napping by coming in towards Essen from the south so that we could bomb from the "wrong" side.

'Then aboard the bus to our aircraft. At the dispersal we found a congolmeration of our comrades from 101 Squadron who were not flying that night and who had come to wish us good luck. To the accompaniment of their

153

153
The Rhine bridges at Cologne well and truly 'pranged'. 'Our own special target on our last mission,' wrote Jack Morley, 'was the bridge leading directly to the great Cathedral, which we had firm orders not to hit!'

132

cheers and waves from our groundcrew who had served us so well, we slowly taxied away from dispersal.

'Once airborne the tensions eased a little, but as we made landfall over Europe our port outer engine began to overheat. George Harris nursed it as much as possible but to no avail as flames started to flicker from this engine with increasing intensity. George hit the extinguisher button and feathered the engine. We were all ears now as the flames died out, and George trimmed the controls to keep us on an even keel. We lost a little height and George put it to the rest of us that, as we were so far along our journey, he thought we should press on to the target, to which we all agreed as this was our last trip, and we wanted to get it over. No distractions for now from enemy fighters, and shortly afterwards we approached the target area, bomb doors open, with Dai in his position in the nose, levelling out for our run in to the target. Then fate took a hand once more as the starboard outer received a hit. This engine provided most of the electrical power for various equipments in the aircraft, including the bomb release system, and consequently it left us with the problem of releasing the bombs manually by means of what was named the dead-man's lever. To achieve this, an implement similar to a car jack handle was inserted into a slot in the floor of the aircraft above the bomb bay, and then

rocked back and forth. By this means the hooks on which the bombs were hung could, in theory, be opened to release the bombs. In fact, on this occasion at least, despite all the frantic pumping back and forth they remained firmly secure on their hanging hooks. Over the target, trying all the time to effect release of our load, but to no avail; doing a circuit of the target, then once more, through the barrage of fire and death, trying to unload our eggs. George threw the aircraft about to try to dislodge them, but still to no avail. With sinking hearts we finally turned for home, full of disappointment now, jinking about for the whole time to try to get rid of our load, even when far out across the sea, but fate was against us, and try as we did, they still hung there.

'Losing more and more height now, and with only two engines serviceable, George tried once more to re-start the port engine, but he could only re-start the flickers of flame. We tried again and again to rid ourselves of our load, to no effect, losing height all the time — we were in dire straits now, but every minute took us nearer and nearer to home. Then, at last within range of Ludford Magna, using battery power, the skipper informed them of our predicament, and after they received confirmation from us that we could make the trip, air traffic control told us to land at the crash land strip at Carnaby, a few miles south of Bridlington.

154
The Ops Room of No 14 Base, Ludford Magna, on 8 October 1944.

This place was a specially built huge concrete strip, used by aircraft in such a predicament as ourselves. With only two serviceable engines and a bomb-load which we could not be sure would say fixed when we bumped on landing, it was a very apprehensive time for us all. Would we get down without crashing, and even if everything went right in this attempt would the bombs drop off and explode? We had done a great deal to make this a distinct possibility by the numerous efforts that we had made to dislodge them.

'The controller below gave us instructions to fly out to sea and approach as low as possible when we attempted to pancake. In giving us these instructions he then added to our misgivings by forgetting to switch off his microphone when he tannoyed to all personnel to clear the immediate surroundings of the airfield because a Lancaster with two engines out, and with a full bombload which was expected to explode on landing, was approaching the landing strip. What a time to let us hear his message, when we were the Lancaster involved.

'With the aid of the trailing aerial technique, George turned, and at a height of 50ft we flew towards the lights. Rising to clear the cliff-tops, the whole crew, except pilot and engineer, braced for crash landing; we waited and hoped, then, after what seemed an eternity, but was in fact only a few seconds, I said to the skipper, "Aren't we down yet?" to which the reply came that we were indeed down, and were just starting to come to a

stop. Engines off in the next minute, and to the scene of a greatly excited crowd of ground crew people, we climbed out, and kissed the earth, one and all.'

So the Harris crew returned to Ludford to receive the expected news that they had not yet finished their tour of ops because, although they had flown over the target at Essen, they had not dropped their bombs and therefore the mission was abortive. It was not until 28 October that they finally completed their tour by bombing the bridges over the Rhine at Cologne. 'As Dai Jones called "Bombs gone", the whole crew gave a great cheer. We then flew around Cologne as first one Squadron aircraft, then another, completed its bombing run and joined up with us to return to Ludford. After we switched off engines in dispersal we all shook hands before climbing down to meet the crowd of well-wishers who had come to congratulate us.

'After a night's hectic celebrations, we spent the next few days collecting our kit before going on leave. Then came the parting of the ways, some of us never to meet again.'

Given such experiences over Cologne, it might be assumed that Bomber Command had the skies of Germany to itself by late 1944. Certainly since D-Day Bomber Command had been operating by day as well as by night, and the ABC Lancasters went along dutifully on all occasions 'until some genius realised that the Germans could see us in daylight and there was little that ABC could do to stop them'. Thereafter 101 flew

155
155
Flt Lt Scrym Wedderburn with his crew in the autumn of 1944 after he had completed his second Lancaster tour and his third tour of ops on 101. Known as 'Wedderburn's Chindits' they were from L-R: Flt Sgt Schofield (Flt Eng), Flg Off Hunter (Bomb Aimer), Flg Off Patrick (W/Op), Scrym, Flg Off Sidwell (Nav), Flg Off Booth (Mid Upper), Flt Sgt Armishaw (Rear Gunner). Scrym was remembered with affection as a 'very colourful character who drove an ancient car, couldn't bear red tape, and who didn't give a damn for anyone. In the air he was superb.'

only by night, and at the Fourth Meeting on Radio Countermeasures Policy and Progress held at High Wycombe on 22 September 1944, it was agreed that '101 Squadron should be relieved of its ABC commitment and become a main force squadron again'. This piece of reorganisation was designed to concentrate all radio countermeasures activities within 100 Group, and an existing Halifax unit was to be transferred to that Group for ABC duties to fill the gap left by 101 so that 1 Group did not lose a Lancaster squadron. However this tidy scheme foundered in the face of German opposition. Although the Allied armies were advancing on the Rhine and capturing many of the German early warning radar sites in the process, the Luftwaffe did not capitulate. In fact the German fighter crews only responded to the enemy at their gates with the sustained and tenacious vigour of men who had nothing to lose. For 101 this meant that although they could now fly a decreased proportion of ABC missions, the Command could not do without their services altogether, especially as the British bomber effort was being divided increasingly between a number of targets separated in time and space. Consequently, when 1 Group broke all previous records by launching a force of 292 aircraft on a most successful attack against Freiburg in October, eight ABC aircraft were also detailed to support another Group in an attack on Neuss. Certainly Bomber Command still needed all the defensive effort it could muster, and 101 was to lose 20 crews between 1 November 1944 and the end of the war in Europe.

Sgt H. van Geffen arrived on 101 as a Spec Op towards the end of the war. Born in Holland in 1917 to a Dutch father and an Irish mother, Van, as he was known to his friends, was brought up in France where he learned to speak both French and German. 'My family returned to England in 1931,' he explained, 'and by the time I found myself at Ludford Magna I was no longer at all fluent in German'. His operational experience makes fascinating reading. (Quoted from *Lincolnshire Life* by Bruce Barrymore Halpenny).

156
Sgt van Geffen outside the Sergeant's Mess while he was a member of the Lloyd crew. (L-R): Back row: Sgt 'Happy' Mummery (Mid-upper), Sgt 'Timber' Woods (Flt Eng), 'Van' (Spec Op), Flg Off 'Skip' Lloyd (Pilot), Sgt Wally Edwards (Nav). Front row: Sgt Phil Axford (W/Op), Sgt Des 'Blimp' Lamb (Bomb-aimer), Sgt 'Shorty' Satherley (Rear gunner), Sergeant Binder (Crew dog).

156

157

157
Sqn Ldr McLeod-Selkirk's crew bomb a snow-covered St Vith on Boxing Day, 1944. St Vith was an important road and rail junction for the Germans who were then counter-attacking and advancing through the Ardennes during the Battle of the Bulge.

135

158
Cartoon.

159
Lancaster SR-H 'How', together with her groundcrew who were known as the 'Naafi Gang'. There was an exciting race between H-How of 'A' Flight and S-Sugar of 'C' Flight to see which would complete 100 ops first. Sugar, with 'The Saint' as her crest, completed her 'ton' against Hanover on 5/6 January 1945, whereas How had to wait until 7/8 January when Plt Off J. A. Kurtzer RAAF and his crew attacked Munich. H-How survived the war to fly 121 operational missions not out, and although S-Sugar reputedly beat her by one op, 'The Saint' was finally shot down by a jet fighter on 23 March 1945 over Bremen Bridge after her crew 'pressed on' with three engines.

160
A load of 1,000lb bombs leave Z-Zebra for Bremen Bridge while S-Sugar was meeting her end. T-Tommy is the 101 Lancaster below which looks extremely vulnerable.

"1 GROUP DESPATCHED 312 SORTIES IN ONE EVENING."

'On my first three ops I flew with Flg Off Lloyd and his crew, who were then posted to a Pathfinder squadron, leaving me to find another crew. I joined up with the A Flight Commander, Sqn Ldr McLeod-Selkirk, and flew regularly with them until they were allotted a brand new aircraft which was not then fitted with ABC. This left me as a "spare bod" again, so I arranged to join up with Flt Lt McClenaghan, with whom I had flown previously on a couple of occasions.

'On the very next day, 23 February 1945, we were briefed to fly in an attack against Pforzheim, a town situated between two major targets of Karlsruhe and Stuttgart. It was now on the list of Bomber Command targets for the first time only because it was an important junction on the main line leading to the American Seven Army front. A force of 300 Lancasters took off in the late afternoon of the 23rd, but at the last moment our aircraft was U/S, so my crew flew without me in another, not fitted with ABC, while I stayed at home. Flt Lt McClenaghan and his crew did not return from this operation.

'7 March 1945 — Target: Dessau, a city situated south-west of Berlin and about halfway between Magdeburg and Leipzig, all former Bomber Command targets. It was a city with 120,000 inhabitants and an important target for it was the home for the Junkers jet-engine and main testing base,

though our main target was to disrupt the rail communications. These had been bombed by a small daylight force of the USAAF on 2 March and we were being sent in to finish the job. The pilot of the crew with whom I was to fly on this occasion was taken ill shortly before briefing. The "stand-by" crew were called upon to take his place and I joined them. Their own Spec Op Sgt Rudy Mahr, had on this occasion already been detailed to fly with Sqn Ldr Gibbons, and Rudy and I applied for permission to switch aircraft, so that he could join his regular crew for the trip. This application was not allowed. Sgt Rudy Mahr and the crew he flew with did not return from this operational mission.

'12 March 1945 — Daylight attack on Dortmund. Not being on the Battle Order for this raid, I arranged to fly as a "passenger", with Flt Lt Harrison, wishing to see for myself what a target under attack looked like. I obtained the necessary unofficial "permission", but being called a "bloody fool" and a "lunatic" in the process. We developed an oil-leak in the port-inner engine on take-off, and were compelled to feather the prop within a few minutes. We flew out over the North Sea, on three engines, in order to jettison our bomb-load, but were unable to climb to a safe height from which we could drop our "Cookie" 4,000lb bomb, without being caught ourselves in its blast when it exploded on hitting the sea, so we had to bring it back with us. However, we were unable to find our base at Ludford Magna, due to ground mist, and we were diverted to the emergency landing ground at Carnaby where we made a safe landing on our three good engines.

'Dressed in full flying-kit, we explored nearby Bridlington to pass the time away while awaiting engine repairs. Eventually, being without ready cash (not usually required over Germany), the skipper explained our situation to a friendly bank manager, and as a result we held an impromptu pay parade on the pavement outside the bank. In funds for one evening at least, we were able to visit the Dance Hall in Bridlington that evening and, in spite of (or was it because of?) our flying-kit, roll-neck sweaters and flying boots, we had no difficulty in finding dancing partners among the Bridlington girls, although we received a lot of black looks from the Bridlington boys! Four days later, our aircraft repaired, we hedge-hopped across Yorkshire and Lincolnshire, back to Ludford Magna.

'On landing there, I learned that Sqn Ldr McLeod-Selkirk, skipper of my former crew, whose new aircraft had eventually been fitted with ABC, had asked for me to re-join his crew. The target, during my absence, had been Gelsenkirchen, and another Spec Op

Sgt Johnny Toy, had volunteered to take my place. One thousand bombers flew to Gelsenkirchen that night — only one was lost, and returning crews reported seeing it blow up in the air above Germany. Sqn Ldr McLeod-Selkirk and his crew (whom I liked to consider as "my crew"), and Sgt Johnny Toy, were in that aircraft.

'I suppose one could truthfully say that I avoided death by "sticking my neck out" and tempting Providence, but after three narrow escapes in as many weeks I found myself wondering how long my luck would last.'

In the end, although bomber squadrons such as 101 never extinguished the Luftwaffe's will to resist — German night intruders had the nerve to shoot up Ludford airfield and village as late as 3 March 1945 with no opposition — Bomber Command eventually wore the German air force down to a state where the will could no longer inspire the deed. Luftwaffe fighter airframes certainly continued to roll off the production lines until the end, for German organisation and native cunning kept factories going in apparently shattered buildings and underground caves, but no amount of subterfuge could overcome bottlenecks inflicted by the bombers elsewhere. Completed engines and airframes often failed to mate as both lay stranded behind canals and railways smashed by the strategic offensive. Even if replacement aircraft did get to the front —

162

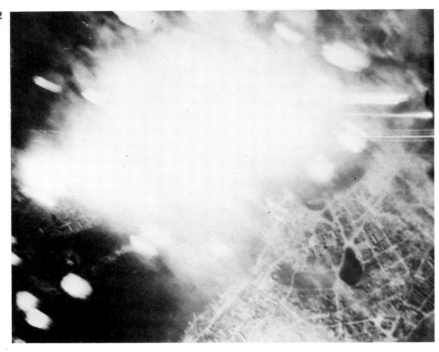

163

and some undoubtedly did as Sgt Ken O'Brien, a 101 rear gunner, discovered when he became one of the first bomber gunners to shoot down an Me262 jet fighter — there were less and less experienced pilots to fly them by early 1945 and minimal fuel to put in their tanks in the wake of the Allied onslaught on the Axis oil refineries. And even if the Luftwaffe did get airborne, the capture or dislocation of more and more of the German air defence system meant that the German controllers and their charges were often 'blind' until it was too late. So it came about that, less than a year after Nuremberg, 101 was able to contribute 21 aircraft and crews to the devastating attack on Dresden, a city much further inside the Reich. 'Adverse headwinds reaching 100mph extended the trip to a lengthy 10hr 25min and we heard the BBC giving out the news of the raid while we were still airborne.' Yet in spite of this increased vulnerability inside enemy airspace, all squadron crews bombed successfully and returned unscathed. Bomber Command had not knocked out the enemy so much as helped to choke him to death.

101 flew a mammoth 920 operational hours by day and 1,215 by night during March 1945 against targets as varied as Cologne, Mannheim, Chemnitz, Dessau, Kassel, Dortmund, and good old faithful Essen. The last Squadron crew to perish on ops was Flg Off Little's — they flew on a daylight raid against Bremen on 23 March and they went down in Lancaster III 'S' Sugar, an old warhorse which was then on its 119th sortie. Thereafter 101 had the German skies to themselves.

Thirty Squadron aircraft and crews attacked Kiel without incident on 9 April to help capsize the pocket battleship *Admiral Scheer*, but nothing underlined Bomber Command's final omnipotence more forceably than 101's last wartime operation on 25 April when it sent 24 crews to bomb

Hitler's redoubt at Berchtesgaden. 'It was a fitting climax to over five years of most strenuous endeavour,' and as the Lancasters streamed over this Bavarian bastion of the Thousand Year Reich in broad daylight, 'we demolished a great portion of that evil encampment in a brilliantly executed attack'. The lion in its turret had come a long way since he first looked out of an Overstrand.

Thereafter, 101 Squadron engaged in more humanitarian pursuits. On 27 April it began evacuating freed prisoners of war — 24 crammed into each Lancaster — back to the UK, and by the end of the month it was dropping up to 5,947 bags of food a day to the starving inhabitants of the Netherlands. It was rewarding work, though the conclusion of hostilities in Europe was greeted with equal enthusiasm:

'8/5/45. No operations are scheduled for today!

'All work on the station with the exception of essential servicing stopped today at midday. The Prime Minister announced the termination of the war in Europe to the whole country and his speech was broadcast over the station Tannoy system at 3pm. The afternoon was then mainly devoted to sports activities, the main feature being a football match between "England" and "The Rest". There were parties in all Messes during the evening.'

There must have been a lot of happy and contented men who rolled into bed that night, for at long last the war for them was over.

By what yardstick should we assess 101's achievements as a bomber squadron? Statistics can give some guide for 101 mounted 2,477 ABC sorties between October 1943 and the final raid on Berchtesgaden, and launched 6,740 Blenheim, Wellington and Lancaster missions during the war. Yet such bald figures mask the human dimension of the bomber offensive. 'Victory inclines to the force which is most thoroughly and efficiently organised,' quoted the AOC 1 Group to his men on 7 June 1945, and it was here that the success story of Bomber Command squadrons begins.

Back in 1940, the number of Blenheims dispatched by 101 on a typical night raid could be counted on one hand. Crews were 'advised' as to their route — it was up to them whether they took the advice or not — and the time on target for the 20 or so bombers which made up the 'mass' raid could be spread over an hour. Even if this less than formidable number reached the target area, which was by no means certain, the 1,000lb bomb load carried by each Blenheim was hardly likely to bring Germany to its knees.

The Wellington era was only superior in terms of numbers, but with the introduction of more suitable aircraft such as the Lancaster, improved aids such as Gee, Oboe, H2S, and ABC, and a Pathfinder Force to lead the way, a whole new era of aerial bombardment came into being. 'In the old days,' observed 'Mac' Mackay, 'we were very amateurish and slap-happy. We took off usually in our own time, flew our own routes, and bombed when we thought we were over the target, or on DR, or where the flak was. However, by the time I came back to do my second tour, it had all changed. Here was aerial marshalling at its most precise. Here was navigation with the minimum of error, and here was military discipline honed to a split second'. Thus aircraft from No 14 Base not only dropped 34,000 tons of bombs in 1944 alone, but they also dropped them with much greater effect. From being a clumsy blunderbuss, Bomber Command had become a surgical instrument capable of striking at the enemy's vitals with clinical precision. Its impact on the outcome of World War 2 was decisive.

Similarly the effect of radio countermeasures such as ABC in protecting the bomber force should never be underestimated. By the beginning of 1944 the German bomber element, lacking effective jamming support, was losing an average of one aircraft and four trained crewmen for every five British civilians it managed to kill. Back over their Reich homeland, it was

161
No 101 Squadron, in all its sizeable glory, in 1945.

162
Kiel docks come in for plastering from 19,000ft on 9/10 April 1945.

163
The final Squadron operational mission of the war — Berchtesgaden on 25 April. This magnificent panorama of the Bavarian Alps was photographed by a flight engineer who had never used a camera before. The target itself is shrouded by the smoke of destruction in the centre.

164
Cartoon.

largely due to the distraction of jamming that the German defences could not deal as severely with their night raiders. As Alfred Price said in *Instruments of Darkness*: 'It is, therefore, no exaggeration to say that the radio countermeasures campaign played a major part in keeping Bomber Command's losses down to a level which the RAF could afford to countenance.'

Nevertheless, all this technological innovation relied for its success on the personnel to put it into effect. 'Instead of the usual game of snooker with some points after a raid,' said a pilot watching the Command improve as 1943 went by, 'I quietly said to the crew, "If we're going to survive this lot, everything has got to be right inside that kite of ours and that means all eight of us working together"'. So the various individuals who had previously filled a bomber were replaced by a *crew* who lived and worked together on a Lancaster. Surprisingly, in view of the strains and survival chances attendant on operations, there were remarkably few cases of 'Lack of Moral Fibre' on bomber squadrons. Perhaps it was because they were all volunteers from the start, and the training system certainly weeded out most weak links, but nevertheless there must have been many men who thought about opting out only to carry on through loyalty to their crew and squadron. 'I can do it alone,' said the injured pilot in *Fair Stood the Wind for France* as he tried to persuade his crew to leave him behind and save themselves. 'If I'd been a fighter boy, there'd have been no question of doing it otherwise.' 'You're not a fighter boy,' replied the WOp/AG firmly. 'You're part of us. We're a unit. We always have been.'

With a spirit such as this, 101 Squadron crews had the faith to move, and destroy, mountains.

The stories of bravery inspired by such dedication are legion, and none is more typical than the occasion at Holme when Sqn Ldr G. W. Fisher ignored the danger of exploding fuel tanks to enter the blazing wreckage of a crashed Lancaster in order to rescue the crew. In 1943, 101 recorded the award of three DSOs, 38 DFCs, seven CGMs, and 33 DFMs, while the following year Squadron personnel received a total of 98 DFCs, 49 DFMs, and one DSO. Yet if this was the profit side of 101's account, the loss side was grievous. Out of the total of 70,253 RAF casualties killed in action during World War 2, some 55,888 officers and other ranks died in action or on active service in Bomber Command. To put it another way, the British strategic air offensive over Western Europe cost 7% of the manpower directly absorbed by the fighting services during the war, but once again, although such statistics may be the only vehicle for conveying the magnitude of the loss, they only tell part of the story. This 7% was largely derived from the best sections of British youth because of the high degree of physical and mental skills needed to operate a heavy bomber. Bomber Command therefore lost over 55,000 men that the nation could ill afford to lose — such was the loss rate of educated men for instance, that by the end of February 1944 it was feared that 101 would soon run out of qualified Spec Ops and Bomber Command considered having to use men who could not even speak German. The bomber offensive therefore has rightly been described as the Passchendaele of World War 2, not simply because it was a war of attrition but also because both destroyed the flower of a whole generation.

These sentiments applied just as much to the groundcrew as to the men who flew, for even in the relatively unsophisticated days of 1941 it was estimated that approximately 35 people were needed on the ground to keep an operational bomber in the air. 'To aircrew is due the highest praise,' wrote Air Vice-Marshal Blucke in June 1945 after he became the last wartime Air Officer Commanding 1 Group, 'but let it not be forgotten that their feats of skill and gallantry were made possible only by the tireless energies and devotion to duty of each man and woman, no matter how great or how small their allotted task, throughout the months that are now past'. Certainly the 'chop rate' among the armourers who loaded the ammunition and armed the bombs was second only to that of aircrew. The maintenance of a squadron of heavy bombers night after night was no easy matter either, and no one needed unserviceable hydraulics or a sick engine to heighten the tension of a sortie, or carelessness by an electrician to cause a hang-up and thereby ruin an attack. 101 Squadron lived and worked as a team, and it only helped to win the war because it was a good team.

Not that the personnel of 101 would have wished to dwell on the dark side of Squadron life. 'I was 19 at the time,' recalled Sgt Geoffrey Whittle, 'and life was for living. We got on with the job — the higher direction of the war was for the older types, 25-year olds and above!! They were enjoyable days and of course we always expected to come back'. Suffice to say, therefore, that at least 277 aircraft went missing from 101 Squadron between 1939 and 1945, and that the Squadron lost a total of 1,094 men killed in action and 178 taken prisoner of war. It was the highest casualty rate of any RAF squadron in World War 2.

What of those left behind? Flt Lt Thomas Rowland was typical of the men who joined Bomber Command in their droves. 'My husband and I were married on 1 June 1938,' recalled his wife, Margaret. 'He was the village postman where I worked as a nanny to the three-year old child of the managing director of ICI, and I left only to marry my one and only love. We rented a small bungalow in the village and were very happy. In those days wages were not very high and my husband did part-time gardening to help-out. He was very well liked and we had our first child in September 1939. My husband volunteered for service in 1940 and did his initial training at Blackpool.

'After various postings he was sent to America to gain his wings. When he returned he was a proud man with his wings in place, and so were we. He looked so smart in his uniform as an officer, and all thought how well he had done even though he had acquired just an ordinary village school education with no scholarship to help him along. He had got on by his own merits.

'In December 1943 he came on what was to be his last leave. Because he had to go back to base for Christmas, we made our Christmas with him then. We had as happy a time as we could.'

On 14 January 1944, Flt Lt Rowland and his crew took-off from Ludford for Brunswick at the height of the Battle of Berlin. They never returned. The first news to arrive at Margaret's house 'was the dreaded telegram'.

'POST OFFICE TELEGRAM

15 Jan 44

Priority CC

Regret to inform you that your husband 127942 F/Lt Rowland T. W. is reported missing from Air Operations on the night of 14/15 Jan 1944 stop Letter follows any further information received will be communicated to you immediately stop Pending receipt of written notification from the Air Ministry no information should be given to the Press

OC Squadron'

'His relatives and I were beside ourselves with shock and grief but we kept on hoping. The waiting continued, interrupted by official letters saying that they would let us know as soon as they heard something.'

'Dear Mrs Rowland,

'I am writing to offer you the sincere sympathy of myself and the entire Squadron in the anxiety you have experienced since hearing that your husband, Flt Lt Thomas Wilson Rowland (127942) is missing from Air Operations on the night of 14/15 - January 1944.

'Your husband and his crew took off on an operational sortie over enemy territory and I am sorry to say failed to return to base. No messages were received from the crew after take off and nothing has so far been heard of it or any member of the crew.

'There is always the possibility that they may have come down by parachute or made a forced landing in enemy territory, in which case news of this would take a considerable time to come through, but you will be immediately advised of any further information that is received.

'This is indeed a great loss to the Squadron for your husband was not only popular with all ranks but was also a most experienced and efficient pilot and captain of aircraft. His splendid record and the many operational sorties in which he has taken part fully testify to the courage and devotion to duty he has always displayed in the execution of his duties.

The personal effects of your husband are now in the custody of the "Committee of Adjustment Officer, RAF Station Ludford Magna", who will be writing to you shortly concerning their disposal.

'I can well appreciate your feelings at this anxious time, and we all join with you in hoping and praying that your husband is safe.

Yours sincerely,
R. I. Alexander,
Wing Commander, Commanding
No 101 Squadron, R.A.F.'

'Then we received notification that he had been awarded the DFC — more tears and heartbreak. My husband's mother and I went to Buckingham Palace to receive the decoration from the late King George. It was a very moving and proud moment. Back home the waiting and hoping recommenced and continued day after day, week after week.' But hope was finally extinguished on 24 July 1944.

AIR MINISTRY
(Casualty Branch)
73-77 OXFORD STREET,
W1.
24th July, 1944

'Madam,

'I am directed to refer to a letter from this department dated 6th March 1944 concerning your husband, Acting Flt Lt Thomas Wilson Rowland, Royal Air Force, and to inform you with regret that a further report has now been received from the International Red Cross Committee, Geneva, which states that Sgt Bateman, Sgt Cornwell, Sgt Clements, and the two unknown members of the crew of the aircraft in which your husband was flying on 14th January 1944, were buried on the 16th January 1944, in the Lower Cemetery, Lautenthal, about 25 miles south of Brunswick.

165
The Control Tower at Ludford in 1945, now brightened up for peacetime use.

166

166
The final reckoning — a devastated Krupps Works in Essen in 1945. *IWM*

'It is regretted that it is still not possible to identify the two referred to as unknown but nevertheless it is considered that you would wish to be notified of this report.

'In conveying this information, I am again to express the sincere sympathy of the department with you in your anxiety, and to assure you that you will be informed of any further news that may come to hand.

I am, Madam,
Your obedient Servant,
for Director of Personal Services.'

'My son is now happily married,' concluded Margaret Rowland, 'and my grandson is very like his grand-dad who never came back to know him.'

'Butch' Harris fought for everyone who had taken part in the strategic offensive to be awarded a special campaign medal after the war, but he was over-ruled. 'This was a sore point with a lot of us,' said 'Mac' Mackay, 'because so many of my good friends who took the damnedest risks and whose middle

names were courage got nothing at all'. So it must be left to an air gunner, R. W. Gilbert, to write the epitaph for them all in his poem, *Requiem for a Rear Gunner*:

'My brief sweet life is over, my eyes no longer see,
No summer walks — no Christmas Trees — no pretty girls for me,
I've got the chop, I've had it, my nightly ops are done,
Yet in another hundred years, I'll still be twenty-one.'

Yet in spite of the horrors and heartache of war, the average man on 101 never lost his human feelings. 'I remember one particular night when the Squadron had been hit very hard,' wrote Jack Morley, 'and while we were resting from our labours we were awakened by the sound of shouting and banging. Coming slowly to our senses we perceived the sight of the other occupants of our hut stamping, banging, and dancing around as though they had gone mad. But we were soon to join in this strange ritual as we realised that we had been invaded by earwigs. The insects were everywhere, covering floors, beds, clothing, kit, walls, and ceiling. After frenziedly shaking clothes and boots we dressed and joined in the war against these invaders. Beaten back by overwhelming numbers, we finally evacuated our hut and retired to the mess, leaving the battle to the ground personnel who moved everything out and painted the whole place with paraffin to clean out the creatures. Here we were, having endured all that the enemy could throw at us on upwards of 30 missions, defeated by a swarm of earwigs.'

'People of the younger generation,' wrote one flight commander, 'can get the impression that Bomber Command was one big happy band of brothers. This was not so. Squadrons were very much individual entities — we didn't mix much with other squadrons — and they assumed the character and charisma of the people who were on the squadron at the time.'

As a result, few outsiders will ever appreciate what it was really like to serve on a bomber squadron. 'Is it any wonder that I avoid memorial services,' said an ex-flight sergeant, 'for I cry very easily and the sound of the Air Force March brings memories flooding back. Men are not supposed to cry but this one does mostly in private, for how many are there who can even begin to understand?'. Without in any way decrying the achievements of the more glamorous fighter squadrons, the classic dog-fight could never do more than prevent defeat. It was the largely unsung heroes on units such as 101 Squadron who took the battle to the enemy night after night for year after year when the other services were in no position to do so, and in so doing sacrificed their youth to sustain civilian morale and bring about eventual victory.

Nearly 40 years later, the scars have largely healed and the ravages inflicted by 101 Squadron have generally been obliterated. 14 Base HQ disbanded on 24 October 1945 and that same month 101 left for Binbrook. Ludford airfield was put on care and maintenance, much to the benefit of the locals. After countless generations of doing without basic amenities, the inhabitants of Ludford village had watched the electricity cables and water pipes being laid past their doorsteps with envious eyes in 1943, but the supplies were limited to the needs of the aerodrome. When it closed the villagers were able to tap the power, heat, water, and drainage for themselves.

The hangars at Ludford Magna were then used for storage, particularly during the ill-fated 'Ground Nuts Scheme', and the runways were removed in the early 1970s, some of the hard core being used in the construction of the Humber Bridge. Only the memories remain, and each year the survivors come back to Ludford where a Book of Remembrance in the village church pays tribute to their colleagues who never returned.

However, memories of 101 are also still vivid in less likely places. Plt Off T. A. Allen joined 101 at the beninning of May 1944, and after flying his 'second dickey' familiarisation trip with Plt Off Waughan against an ammunition factory at Augigne-Racan, he was ready to operate with a crew of his own. The Allen crew was typically cosmopolitan, with the Spec Op coming from as far away as Brisbane, Australia. On 28 May 1944, Bomber Command was briefed to attack a number of targets in Belgium, together with a 'spoof' on Dusseldorf, and 101 was spread among the stream. The Allen crew, in Lancaster K-King, were briefed to drop 18 500lb bombs on Bourg Leopold, a Belgian town in the province of Limburg noted for the manufacture of glass and explosives. Squadron crews were instructed to take-off at intervals from 0005hr on 28 May and the subsequent cryptic Squadron record in respect of the Allen crew was: 'No news after take-off.'

Their Lancaster crashed at Sommelsdijk on the island of Goeree-Overflakee off the Dutch coast in the early hours. The bomb load exploded on impact and there were no survivors; a local Dutchman who fought the flames stated that it was believed that the Lancaster was brought down by a night fighter. This was the only Squadron crew lost that night and they were buried in the civilian cemetery at Sommelsdijk. However the population of the area, who had suffered the traumas of enemy occupation which the British were spared, never forgot. Children at the Middelharnis Technical School made and erected a memorial to the crew in the form of an aircraft wing with the RAF roundel on a camouflaged background, and each year, on the anniversary of the crash, local school children place flowers on the grave in tribute to the men who died so that they might be free.

It is gratifying that the memories of such brave bomber crews will never die, but perhaps the last word should be left to Wg Cdr Tony Reddick who wrote the following message to his Squadron just before he departed in July 1943:

'In taking my leave of the Squadron I want to take this opportunity to express my appreciation and thanks to all ranks for the splendid co-operation and support you have given me.

'Since the Squadron converted to Lancaster aircraft it has gone from strength to strength, and it is now quite definitely the best Squadron in the Group. This is due entirely to the magnificent way in which you have all carried out your duties, under most arduous conditions.

'Very reluctantly I have to say goodbye . . . As some of you may know, my connection with the Squadron dates back to 1932 when I joined it as a very green NCO pilot. You can understand therefore my complete sincerity when I say that wherever I may be, my heart will always be with No 101 Squadron.' This feeling of belonging applied to everyone, no matter how much time they spent on 101, and because this everlasting spirit carried them through the dark times and was never to die, it epitomised everything that was great about a 'Bomber Squadron at War'.

167
The RAF Memorial at
Boxbergheide near Genke in
Belgium. This is just one of the
many memorials to fallen Bomber
Command aircrew in Europe and,
although it is dedicated to all the
airmen who died over the
province of Limburg, it was
erected on the spot were Pilot
Officer Ashton and his crew from
101 Squadron crashed on their
return from Cologne on
31 August 1941.